Screenwriting 101:

Small Steps While Thinking Big

Revised Printing

Jane Bradley
University of Toledo

Kendall Hunt
publishing company

Cover image © Shutterstock.com

www.kendallhunt.com
Send all inquiries to:
4050 Westmark Drive
Dubuque, IA 52004-1840

Copyright © 2009 by Kendall Hunt Publishing Company
Revised Printing 2016

ISBN 978-1-5249-0-6900

Printed in the United States of America

For Elspeth kydd

who got me started on this;

and for my students
who keep me going.

Contents

5. Visual Language and the Image: Think One Frame at a Time   173

6. Dramatic Dialogue   207

7. Setting—It's More Than Just a Place   250

8. Plotting and Scheming   279

Introduction to the Text

Screenwriting 101: Starting Small While Thinking Big is a unique text in that it's designed for practical use by professors preparing a syllabus for a screenwriting class, and it provides students with focused and directed assignments to bring to class each week. This text assumes nothing but that students want to write screenplays, and it will provide the most basic steps for getting started as well as offer directions for completing a script that can made into a short movie. In a final chapter, it gives structural advice for students who want to write a feature-length film. The text is particularly designed for use in an academic framework where weekly assignments and final projects must be considered. Geared toward students who want to be screenwriters, the book asks students first to think of themselves as writers, to sharpen their skills and strategies and writer, and then to apply their talents to the screenplay.

Designed for introductory screenwriting classes at the undergraduate college level, this text meets the needs of film majors who are developing the craft of writing scripts, and it addresses the interests of creative writing majors who would like to expand their writing skills beyond the genres of poetry, fiction and playwriting. The text acknowledges the integration of skills in both visual and verbal elements in the art and craft of screenwriting, and it focuses on offering writing exercises that require students to combine verbal and visual strategies in their work.

The text guides students through various aspects of the writing process. In addition, students are directed toward refining their critical skills by considering how writing strategies work in films they can easily obtain at local libraries, through Netflix, or at video stores. The text provides exercises designed with specific objectives that familiarize students with strategies in using both visual and verbal elements to evoke an emotional and/or intellectual response in the audience. This book introduces the student to the concept of small dramatic "moments" that build into longer scenes and sequences of a completed short film script as well as the feature length screenplay.

Approaching the script from various angles, students will take the steps that will result in a project known as a "spec script," a script meant to be read by potential directors, producers, cast and crew, and of course, professors. Film majors can choose to go on to learn the strategies for writing a "shooting script," which is written for and by directors in the process of actually shooting a film or video. The emphasis of this book is not on how to direct or make a movie, but rather how to write a script that can be made into a successful and powerful movie.

The topics in this work will include an introduction to the concepts of screenwriting and the options for the kinds of script one can write. It also addresses the creative process and offers suggestions for helping students conceive projects unique to their interests, projects that are feasible with a limited budget, and are of interest to an audience.

Students will be given prompts to write assignments specifically designed to help them focus on the particular strategies and elements that contribute to writing a clear and moving script. Designed for easy adaptation to a course syllabus, the exercises encourage students to use tools of the trade from the start of a class. While primarily learning craft by doing, students will develop analytical skills through examples offered in the text and assignments that teach them how to read films and scripts with a critical eye.

The basic pedagogical strategy of the text is to have students start small with exercises. Students can gain confidence and skill with the various elements that contribute to a script, so when they are faced with the task of writing a complete script, they are familiar with writing strategies. Just as an architect needs to know the tools and materials before designing a building, screenwriting students must first learn the tools and elements that go into writing a script. With extensive practice in writing the small bits that contribute to a script, less time, pain and suffering is wasted as students conceive and write the complete script.

Given that this text is a result of lectures and exercises I've written for my screenwriting classes, my teaching voice runs through it. I speak directly to the reader here, much as I would to my students. I also share my own experiences, opinions, and samples of my screenwriting—much as I would in the class. So the tone might be more personal than many texts. I certainly enjoyed the writing, and hope students and teachers enjoy the visit to the classroom that lies in these pages.

Welcome to Screenwriting

If you are reading this book, most likely you are a film or creative writing major in an undergraduate program. Or maybe you are just curious about how movies begin as someone's idea that gets mapped out on paper, then is shot with video or film, and then finally, happily, appears on a screen. Maybe you are passionate about telling stories for the screen, or maybe you are simply looking to meet requirements for your degree. But bear in mind this book is designed for those who love movies in a serious and curious way, for those who like movies on the big screen, who like movies at home, who watch movies with friends, who watch movies alone, who watch some movies again and again, just for the pleasure of re-viewing a character in action or for insight perhaps into just how a scene was shaped, how a plot was mapped, how the whole premise was pulled off.

Many of you were raised on movies, parked in front of the DVD while mom and dad went about their lives. Many of you spend your weekends in front of movies at home—it's cheaper than bars, cheaper than the big screen. But my guess is that most of you so love that opportunity to sit in a darkened theatre, let that big screen overwhelm you with images, action, sound, you love the sensory experience so deeply that you'll rake up, save up that cash to see as many movies as you can right there where movies belong, on that big screen. Movies give us a chance to go somewhere, be someone, live vicariously, and do all sorts of wild, heroic and dangerous things without bearing the consequences. Many of you crave that good ol' escape in movies. Maybe you love movies because they give you a glimpse of who you'd like to be, who you fear to be, and maybe even sometimes you get a chance to discover who you really are.

You're here because you'd like to write a script. You film majors most likely not only want to write a script; you want to make a movie. If you don't know it already, making a movie is quite expensive. A student making a film on 16mm black and white reversal should expect to pay $150 to $200. A roll of film costs between $15 and $20 a roll; each roll provides about two and a half minutes. Processing is also about $15 to $20. At three rolls, plus shipping, and the other little costs, it's easy to spend this amount.

However, when you add sound and color, things get trickier. It's quite common to spend approximately $100.00 per minute for a film. If you want to take your film to a professional level for entering film festivals and competitions, you can spend up to a thousand dollars a minute by the time you cover all costs. No kidding. So if you're planning a movie, you'd be wise to think very carefully about just what you want to shoot, when, where and why. The better your script is, the better and cheaper your movie.

Since digital video is much cheaper, many of you might want to try that format first. Video can be simpler and more forgiving, particularly when you're starting out. Your film professors will consistently remind you that movies are made of film and videos are made with video tape, and will want you to distinguish between the terms film and video when you are talking about your work in progress. But for the purposes of this text, when I use the word "movie" I'm using it loosely to refer to the film or video. In the future, remember that while both film and video use a series of images to tell a story, convey a narrative, or evoke an insight into a situation, the terms film and video refer to different materials, editing, and production processes.

Considering that film is expensive, and that video, while more economical, still requires funds, and lots of planning, labor, more planning, more labor, and love, I would advise all of you to begin screenwriting by starting small. Yes, many of us have the ultimate desire to write for Hollywood, but even those big names in film started with short films, small projects. So plan to write a short script, maybe a few of them. Many of you may not be familiar with "shorts" as they are usually seen at film festivals or in cinema studies classes. But there are many short films out there and available to you.

I recommend a series of short films simply called *The Short Series* produced by Quick-Band Networks. Some of the better libraries contain these, and you can certainly obtain them through amazon.com. The series comes in numerous volumes with each volume containing an anthology of films including narrative films as well as experimental and documentary. Each volume is arranged around a theme such as "Authority," "Trust," "Dreams." I think it's important that you have a look at these, because they demonstrate how big projects—and huge movie careers—start small. You've heard of Vin Diesel. In a short called *Multi-Facial* on the volume, *Diversity*, we meet a young Vin Diesel who wrote, directed and starred in this little film that tells of a young actor—himself—who can't get an acting gig in New York. He auditions for Italian, Spanish, African American roles, and the fact that he is bi-racial continuously raises questions as to whether he's too light, too dark, too something or not enough of anything. In a dramatic monologue at the end of the piece, he explains how he doesn't want to be a black actor but just an actor. He made this movie from his personal struggle, his heart. The short was in time submitted to a film festival; when Steven Spielberg happened to see it, and pick up Vin Diesel for *Saving Private Ryan*, a career was born.

In another short, Some *Folks Call it a Sling Blade* on the volume, *Invention*, a not yet famous, Billy Bob Thorton stars in the little film which was he later reinvented as a feature-length film that won an academy award for best screenplay. There is much discussion of the fine writing in this script in the chapter on dialogue.

Another volume, *Dreams*, contains the classic short *La Jetée*, which inspired Terry Gillam's *12 Monkeys* as well as *Terminator*.

There are many excellent little narratives, as well as experimental and documentary, films in *The Short Series*. I'll often refer to them in the text, and I urge you to order them through amazon.com or find them through your library. These shorts show how a profound and engaging story can be told with a small budget and a very limited amount of time. While many films may not be to your taste, you'll no doubt be surprised at the range of what filmmakers are doing out there. I strongly urge you to educate yourself to the creative possibilities for screenwriters and directors. Study these short films to see what a writer/director can accomplish with a small budget and in a small space of time. While viewing the short films, try to assess what works, and what could use development; also access what sort of films you like, which ones you could do without seeing. In other words, get to know your own taste in short films. Just as I wouldn't advise a student to write a short story without reading as many as possible, I wouldn't advise you to try writing a short script without viewing a few.

Now let's get to the particulars of this class: Screenwriting. You're going to learn to write a screenplay. So what's a screenplay? Think of it as the written blueprint for a movie. A screenplay is the plan, the story, the dialogue, the action, the setting, the sequence of scenes, and the plot. A screenplay involves all those elements that give shape substance, coherence and meaning to the movie you want to shoot, or the movie you'd like someone else—like a big Hollywood producer—to shoot for you. Ah those Hollywood dreams.

When most of you think of movies, you probably think of those feature-length 120-minute, three-act dramas produced by Hollywood or maybe one of the big-money independent production companies who manage to get national distribution. Just about anyone who considers screenwriting has the fantasy now and then of their names rolling up on the credits on that blockbuster film. Nothing wrong with dreams.

But in dreams, as the old saying goes, begin responsibilities. And responsibility in this class means knowing what you're doing, when you're doing it, and why you're doing it as you type out the pages of a script. If you are realistic about achieving success with your work, you need to start small while thinking big.

Be patient. Give yourself time and focus as you learn the tools and materials that go into building a screenplay. You'd never set out to build a house without knowing how to pour foundation, how to plan weight-bearing walls, how to use a saw. And you can't write a solid script without knowing how to make a character talk, how to use a setting to bring a world alive.

With the help of this text you will develop the craft of writing a screenplay by studying the elements that go into the making of a script: character, dialogue, action, scene, and plot. Through writing tightly focused and directed exercises, you will create a premise that can work, and you will develop practical skills in shaping all those elements that come together into a screenplay. In order to learn the craft of screenwriting, you need to start small. Think of the little gesture, the subtext of a word, before thinking of meanings and emotions of epic proportions.

Think character. Consider the inner workings and outward appearances and gestures that render a character, make that character come alive. Once you have a sense of how characters are shaped, you will write small scenes to practice getting your characters talking, moving them around. You will experiment with the use of setting and how it contributes to the tone and theme of a film. You'll work with dialogue exercises and practice writing dialogue that works like action to reveal character and move plot forward.

While most of the exercises are geared toward writing a script that follows narrative conventions, you may want to stretch conventions and push toward more experimental films. But before launching into experiment, you'll need to know the narrative conventions in order to play with how they can be disrupted, ignored. Let's say you're more interested in writing a script that works more like a musical piece or a poem than a story. You're still working with images, and you'll practice manipulating and arranging images to achieve the desired effect. Whether writing a conventional or experimental script, you will benefit from working with exercises that help you understand how image evokes feeling, how the image can work to give an outward, and visible sign of an inner psychological or spiritual state.

Whether writing a narrative film or a more experimental project, bear in mind that both stories and poems are essentially a series of images and events that lead to a discovery of emotion. Which leads us to the issue of audience.

While you are writing for yourself, you are learning, I would hope, to write a script that is particular to you, your passions, interests, questions, concerns, curiosities. However, you are also writing for an audience. Movies aren't made to be shown in a closet; they are made for a screen with a bunch of people sitting there waiting to be entertained, enlightened, engaged. In this class you will practice making that connection between writer and reader or viewer.

Remember viewers only appear to be passive while sitting in front of a screen. Their minds and hearts are open, active, wanting to connect with the characters, wanting to feel the power of a scene. We watch movies to experience something, not just to sit back and watch some guy playing with a camera. We don't go to movies for sermons, for soapbox speeches, or self-indulgent silliness. Sure, we like silly movies, but we want to connect, feel a moment's silliness ourselves, not just have it displayed. By the time you've worked through the exercises in this book, you should be able to avoid that slippery slope of self-indulgence and tell a story that others want to see and feel.

While learning the conventions of storytelling in film, you will also learn and practice using scriptwriting format. You will learn how to arrange scene headings, how to write action, sound, dialogue. There are many screenwriting software programs out there. Final Draft seems to be the most popular. But there are many others. Screenwriting software programs can also be downloaded from the web at www.celtx.com. It would also be a good idea to read as many screenplays as possible. Many scripts can be downloaded from the website: www.script-o-rama.com. The scripts you read won't be exactly in the format I teach in this text—but the scripts will give you a good basic sense of layout and how stories for the screen unfold.

While on the topic of format, I should say this text is written for a screenwriting class, not a production class. There are two kinds of scripts written for screenplays; there is the reading script, which is written to be read by potential producers and directors. Then there are the shooting scripts, which include more technical details such how lighting and camera are to be used. In this class you will practice writing the reading script, or spec script, which later on is easily adaptable to the shooting script format. Start with your story, your characters, your scenes, what you want in front of the camera, and later on you and/or someone else can work with the angles.

Before you set out to write your screenplay, there are a few things to bear in mind. Yes, a screenplay tells a story, but there are fundamental differences between how a story is told on the screen and how a story is told in fiction or on the stage. In fiction, the narrative can go anywhere, digging inside the mind of a character, swinging back to the world of external action, then slipping back inside a character where we might see the world through the character's mind and emotions as we are shown an external world through a character's eyes. While film can certainly use voice over to convey what's going on in the private thoughts of a character, it's a device that goes flat pretty quickly when you are writing in a medium that is primarily visual. In a screenplay you can't so easily think of yourself as an omniscient writer/god who can hover in the minds of characters for long.

With a screenplay you have to think constantly of what is to be in front of the camera, what is on the screen. A screenplay is perhaps more similar to a stage play than fiction, given the primary elements are scene, action, dialogue. But in a screenplay you have many more variables to work with in that you aren't limited to a stage. Your camera can show a city sky line, a boat at the bottom of a lake, chase scenes, cows grazing, shooting stars, setting suns, the world of bugs and burrowing things deep under the earth. A camera can provide a fluidity of narrative that a stage can't—in other words you have many more options to consider.

A camera also has the power to frame selectively. A playwright has limited control over what the audience chooses to focus on with a stage play. The audience might choose to ponder the upholstery of the couch on the set just as the protagonist is giving a pivotal monologue. But in a screenplay you—and the director—have control of just what is be in the frame, what the viewer is to see. There's much responsibility when every line of dialogue, as well as every object, is selected to be in the frame of the camera. Remember that everything you write in a script is seen and heard. You'll have to be deliberate. At every moment you'll need to know what you're doing and why.

My hope is that this text will not only will teach you how to tell a story for the screen, but also will give you a working knowledge of how to read a film. In order to know how to put a movie together, you have to know how to take one apart. Through the viewing and analysis of a variety of films ranging from narrative to documentary and experimental film, you'll develop a new appreciation for all kinds of movies. You'll also discover all the options out there for you as you write.

With the assistance of the reading and exercises here, you will grow not only as a writer, but also as a reader, a reader of movies, a reader of the world around you. You're going to learn how to pay attention to this wild world flying by, learn what you'd like to capture in a frame and why. There will be times you feel lost in the maze of options and restraints. Lost can be a good thing. It's how you find new paths.

So let's get going on developing some ideas for your script. But first let's explore the reasons for daring to write a screenplay. It's a big, risky, and personal adventure. Let's consider the rewards and then some strategies for getting started.

What's the Value of Writing New Screenplays?

If you've chosen to be in this class, most likely you've crossed that line from having a passionate interest in watching movies to feeling a passionate desire to make a movie yourself. Now pause for a moment to ask yourself, why? There are thousands of movies out there, feature lengths, shorts, foreign old classics, movies you've seen many times, movies still waiting on the shelf in some video store or library, waiting to be viewed, waiting to show you something you've never seen before. So you need to ask yourself why, why go through all the strain and effort to write a new movie when there are so many out there, when in fact it is so difficult to expensive to have your movie made? The answer most likely is because you have something to say.

I'm of the opinion that we're all natural storytellers. We do it daily as a way of justifying what we do, as a way of explaining some event around us, and as a way of comprehending the many mysteries that plague and bless our lives. Myths didn't grow in a classroom—I like to think they grew from a few folks sitting around trying to figure things out. Working with the little fragments they did know, they ruminated, speculated, made some guesses, filled in the gaps, and lo and behold, some kind of reality—or fiction—blossomed, made the rounds, started catching on.

Any deconstructionist can explain how living, thinking, believing, being, is a process of constructing reality. And reality, oh dear. I might venture to say here that there are no truths—only operating fictions of the moment. We create fictions when we rationalize bad behavior, when we demand good behavior, when we explain to ourselves why we want what we want, what we abhor. Say a sentence with "because," and you have a narrative in the making. An answer to the question "why" will draw on an operating fiction. When we meet a stranger, watch a politician, negotiate for anything, we interpret words, we look for subtext, we guess at the personality within and behind a gesture. Often we are not aware of the fictions we create to explain and justify our worlds—we simply live them, unaware that we might be acting in someone else's story, that our awareness might be limited by the story we have unknowingly made.

But what's the value of figuring out the relationships between ourselves and the stories we make, those "stories" we believe in—history, religion, psychology, sociology, law? You know the old adage: "an unexamined life isn't a life worth living." I happen to agree with that observation. I like to think that writing is a means to develop awareness, consciousness, a growing sense of what on earth is going on and why.

So why, for heaven's sake, do we need to increase awareness? Why all that strain and trouble to read and, heaven help us, write? Why not just train for a job and get on with the business of getting and spending? Well, because the business of getting and spending isn't as simple as it seems. But then if ignorance is bliss why trouble ourselves with questions? Because, even if we choose to be ignorant, questions will find a way to trouble us. And besides, I can't help but think that ignorant bliss would be boring after awhile. Driving down a long straight uneventful highway can put us to sleep. But if you play a little music, if you see trouble on the side of the road, if you have a close call with an accident, if you get a ticket, your heart changes its rhythm—you feel a little more alive. And most of us like that feeling of feeling more alive.

But then feeling more alive, sweet as it is, often brings its troubles—that song that makes our heart rush often stirs memory, longing, nostalgia, desire. That desire can be as simple as the urge to dance while we're driving in our car, or it can be a hunger for a lost love, a passion to change a less than perfect world.

In Janet Burroway' book *On Writing Fiction*, she says, "You don't have a story without trouble." I might dare to add that you don't have a life without trouble—now I'm not saying there that the human condition is one of angst-ridden despair and conflict. That might be true on bad days, but there are good ones, too. By trouble I mean something as broad and simple as two forces working against each other. Let's get really simple: gravity. We have to get up in the morning and move upright against the pull of gravity. No great art, but consider the beauty of dancers, those leaps and pirouettes—being able to stand on one leg against the pull of earth--that's trouble taken on, a challenge being worked out. Gardening, sewing, driving, physics, mathematics, it's all imposing some kind of order on random fragments, forces hurling and collapsing in space. And when it works, lovely—and when it fails, you've got to admire the risk and effort made.

I only seem to digress. Let me raise a rhetorical question: "Okay, gravity, trouble, it's hard to get out of bed in the mornings—so what does writing have to do with all this?"

As far as I'm concerned, education, reading and writing are all about heightening awareness of both internal and external worlds, worlds that bring their problems, conflicts, conflicting desires. We've got to be able to identify what's in there, what's out there, before we can figure what to do with it, before we can create significant action, meaningful thought. In screenwriting you will have the opportunity to think through the hearts and minds of other characters while also being pushed to think like a camera.

When writing, one is constantly making choices; that's why it's so hard—and so interesting. In writing we have an opportunity to pause, to listen to what's going on inside, and also to explore how variables out there in the world make demands on our attention and define what we do, and often shape who we are. The practice of pausing, deliberating, speculating gives us power. Writing doesn't take us away from the world; it throws us smack in the middle of it. It makes us engage in experience, allows us to invent a few truths as to what and how we are.

Now that all sounds so lovely, but let me destroy any sweet illusions and say that writing, when you're sitting down and messing around, when you're working to discover, to say something that might mean something to someone, well it can be plain awful.

Writing is scary because thinking is scary. We never know what piece of thinking, an idea, concept, problem-solving strategy we may have to sacrifice in order to absorb or discover something new. Structure anything and you will have to draw a line between what works and what doesn't. That demarcation between what stays and what goes requires the sacrifice of some piece of thought once held safe and dear. Be warned. Sure, you can't wait to write your screenplay, but the act of writing, with all its joys and discoveries, can be just painfully difficult. It requires a kind of audacity, discipline and faith. This is hard stuff.

So why do it, why write new screenplays when we can learn so much from all those already on the shelves? What's the use? Why go through all that work to create a little fictive dream for the screen? Because, quite simply, writing requires you to pay attention. In this class you are going to gain a lot of experience in paying attention, to the way people look, the way they move the way they talk, the way light moves on water, the way wind whips through the trees.

Writers might be known as dreamers, but believe me, they are awake and paying attention to this world here and an imaginative world within—they're in the business of knowing what's going on, and they take the risk of recreating some kind of reality discovered on the page. And that process quite simply expands our lives, whether or not anyone else reads our stories, whether or not we get rich and famous for our words. Writing provides a way for us to sneak up on our emotions, thoughts and feelings that otherwise may remain hidden. Writing gives us an opportunity to discover and lay claim to who we are. One of my principle directives for my students is to try to write the story or poem or screenplay only you could write.

Writing just isn't worth the effort unless we do it selfishly, in that we do it solely to discover something about ourselves, unless we write as a way of earning a hard-earned gift for ourselves. But we also have to write selflessly; we have to get that ego out of the way of the stories waiting inside us. Think of writing as kind of like a sacrament. It provides an outward and visible sign of an inner and spiritual—call it grace if you like, or simply call it—state of heart or mind. Writing the piece only you could write gives you quite simply and powerfully an often lost piece of who you'd like to be, maybe who you fear to be, but most definitely in some way who you are. I'm serious about this business of writing, and do hope you are as well.

"To begin is an act of gravity and an act of responsibility, especially if a new world is about to begin. I mean this literally: to begin a world is to ground it, to pull it down—with gravity—from an area of flux onto the firm ground where any subsequent creation can rest on its feet. To begin a world is also to render it responsible—bound to respond and desirous of response—to the worlds that preexist, follow and surround it."

Stanka Radovic, "The Birthplace of Relation"

1. Finding Your Story: Just Get Started

In Flannery O'Connor's essay "Writing Short Stories," she discusses the origins of "Good Country People," a rather bizarre little tale where an arrogant woman with a Ph.D. and a wooden leg happens to have her leg stolen by a Bible Salesman:

> "I wouldn't want you to think that in that story I sat down and said, "I am now going to write a story about a Ph.D. with a wooden leg, using the wooden leg as a symbol for another kind of affliction." I doubt myself if many writers know what they are going to do when they start out. When I started writing that story, I didn't know there was going to be a wooden leg in it. I merely found myself one morning writing a description of two women that I knew something about, and before I realized it, I had equipped one of them with a daughter with a wooden leg. As the story progressed, I brought in the Bible salesman, but I had no idea what I was going to do with him. I didn't know he was going to steal that wooden leg until ten or twelve lines before he did it, but when I realized that this was going to happen, I realized it was inevitable. This is a story that produces a shock for the reader, and I think one reason for this is that it produced a shock for the writer."

Many writers begin with only a vague idea, and with a bit of fear, as to whether the idea is solid enough to sustain a story, or if it is interesting enough to engage a reader's attention. If you have a clear idea of what you want to write, you're lucky. But do be open to the organic process of writing; the imagination is a living thing not a machine. So when your characters start developing things you didn't expect, like having a wooden leg, follow it through and see where things go. Sometimes your characters can write a better story than you. Even if you know what you want to write, you can learn a few things from the exercises in this chapter; they might help you understand why you want to write what you do. They might also stimulate new ideas.

Whether you are here because you have a deep urge to tell stories for the screen or here because you simply need the class to meet a requirement, you need to take the project of writing a script seriously, passionately. Writing is too difficult and challenging, rewarding and yep, frustrating, for you not to be committed to accomplish something that will engage readers/viewers, a work that will make you proud.

No doubt many of you want to emulate movies you love—you want to write a movie, say something like *Fight Club* or *American Beauty*, maybe something like *Stars Wars*, *The Godfather*, *Pulp Fiction*, or maybe *Dumb and Dumber*. Maybe you love the classics, want to write a *Citizen Kane*, or a *Casablanca.* Our writing is certainly influenced by work we love. But beware of imitation that renders your work derivative, predictable clichéd. The kind of movies you love will no doubt influence your work, but tell your own story; aim for your own fresh future, not some celluloid past.

Each one of you should be aiming to write the script only you could write. This doesn't mean you are to aspire to write some wacky thing you hope no one has ever seen before, but rather you should aim to write a script that grows from the particulars of who you are, what you know, what you want to know, maybe even what you fear. In writing, you have a chance to wrestle with your inner demons, and if that seems too dramatic, it's a chance to explore who you are. Each one of us comes to this room from vastly different worlds. Sure there are commonalities. Most of us know, if not all the rules, we know the concept of the Ten Commandments. We know what Wall Street is, even if we have no clue how the stock market works. We all pretty much know what a Big Mac is—even if the ingredients are obscure. We recognize the theme song to *The Godfather*. We know Luke Skywalker. We know in *Titanic*, the ship sank to bubble up big bucks and a number one song with that love story meets disaster premise. We know *Pulp Fiction* is a movie with a great drug overdose scene, and not a cheap, easy-read paperback book you buy off a rack in a drug store.

Popular movies are often popular because they draw on ideas and needs we all share. Everybody wants to be loved—hence so many love stories out there. Most of us want money and power—and so the crime stories. We like to believe the universe doles out justice in the end—which leads to all those too often contrived, Hollywood endings. But each one of you has a unique experience shaped by parents, friends, calculated plans, random events. As you sit down to write, don't forget your unique personal world. You'll also need to explore what is different between us. Writing the story only you can write requires much introspection and honesty and risk. Writing just isn't worth the time and sweat without honesty and risk. I hope you'll take the assignments given in this text as opportunities to learn a little something about yourself and the world around you, an opportunity to grow in some way.

Learning to write the story only you can write, oddly, doesn't seem to come naturally. We tend to imitate what's out there. If the world can't get enough of tenderhearted mobster stories, well, we think, we'll just keep on writing them. Please don't. I've seen too many student efforts at mobster movies where the wise guys are dressed out in trench coats and fedoras; they carry toy guns, and cuss a lot with bad Italian/Brooklyn accents, and do all the standard stalking and shooting with, of course, the close ups on the victims feigning death, with fake blood smeared from a tube.

Other temptations? The graveyard movie. The mad stalker/killer movie. There's nothing like the threat of death to make drama. But there are all kinds of death in this world. In many kinds of deaths, no blood is shed. These are the kinds of deaths that don't make it to headlines, the kinds of deaths we see every day. Other temptations? The old oh-my-god-I'm pregnant premise, the empty booze bottle/syringe on the floor suicide premise. When setting out to write a script, it's easy to fall back on generically dramatic situations. Sure they'll come to mind, but if you've seen it done before, put the idea on the shelf and instead think about why, really why, your imagination becomes drawn to particular clichés or story lines.

Beware of the derivative story. Beware of just copying the movies you like to see. It's hard to know our own stories, our own visions. It's hard to know even our own thoughts when daily we are so bombarded with advertisements, sounds bites, news clips, TV shows, and of course movies, that seem to define our wants, needs, fears, and interests before we even have the chance to make a choice. Given the overload of information out there telling you what to wear, eat, drink, talk, think, it's easy to feel lost when given the chance to declare something about yourself that isn't like donning a cultural uniform.

Telling your own story can so elusive sometimes you may not know even how to try. And a good place to begin is looking at your life. Art grows from the particular struggles and hopes and joys of this life, the life of real muscle and blood and sweat and love and laughter. You want your movies to be recreations of real human experience, not just revamped experiences already shaped for the screen.

Of course you should be watching, reading, studying movies you love. As a screenwriter, it's your business to know what's out there, what's being made. It's your job to know why and how a movie works, and where and how it fails. Certainly you need to know the movies out there, but you also need to know what's inside you. Here's your chance to write about what really matters to you. If you write honestly enough, particularly enough, others will connect with the world you've made, and your experience will take on significance for others. Through your words, your world, and your reader's world, can grow.

You have lots of options, but do keep in mind that most any project you'll want to undertake has some kind of narrative moving it forward. Whether you're writing a drama, a documentary, a public service announcement, a commercial or an experimental piece, usually some sort of narrative structure is involved, and by narrative I mean that there is a defined beginning, middle and end, and a causal connection between the events.

For those of you with a clear idea of what you'd like to write in this class, you'll be tempted to skip the exercises for finding story ideas, but I'd like to push you to play with these exercises. I like to think that for every honest, well-thought-out piece that we write—whether it's fiction, poetry, a journal or a screenplay—for every honest word we write, we lay a little more claim on ourselves. The following exercises allow you to take a personal inventory, to help you recall significant moments, influences from the past that have helped shape who you are today. You'll be invited to reflect on what you like and dislike in this world, what you love, long for, what inspires you, what disgusts you, what contradictions taunt you, puzzle you, amuse you.

Have a look at them all. Do the exercises that intrigue you, but try as many as you can with no worry about the outcome. The idea is to write down whatever comes to mind without censoring, without worrying about what anyone will think. This is your chance to go in, explore, and see what's inside. Then you can determine what pieces of yourself you'd like to share with the class, and perhaps translate to a story for film.

"The true artist is never so lost in his imaginary world that he forgets the real world, where teen-agers have a propensity toward anguish, people between their thirties and forties have a tendency to get divorced, and people in their seventies have a tendency toward loneliness, poverty, self-pity, and sometimes anger. The true artist chooses never to be a bad physician. He gets his sense of worth and honor from his conviction that art is powerful—even bad art."

John Gardner, *The Art of Fiction*

First Loves in Film

You're in this class no doubt because you love movies. Now consider which movies first made you sit up and pay attention. Any genre will do. What we're interested in is helping you know your taste in films and where it comes from and most importantly, why. My first love? No question. *The Wizard of Oz.* Many children—as well as adults—have fallen in love with the fantasy of a child with limited powers being whisked away from a black and white world of mundane chores and rules to obey to a magical world of good battling evil. Most everyone would enjoy the thrill of an outrageous adventure that ends with a once disgruntled heroine now transformed and deeply grateful to wake up back home after a wild ride over the rainbow.

Dorothy's dangerous journey of being whisked off into a brilliant and dangerous world of witches, flying monkeys and unlikely creatures who take on the best of human qualities and befriend her is an unlikely hero's journey which ultimately is a journey toward maturity, a journey toward a new understanding the value the quests, the meaning of home. But some children might be indifferent to the Dorothy story. Some might prefer the myth of *Peter Pan*. The person whose first movie love was *Peter Pan* instead of the *Wizard of Oz* would have different desires, different insecurities, different fears and needs. The things we love onscreen say much about who we are.

Maybe you came late to loving movies. Ask yourself, what movie first moved you to a place beyond being simply entertained? What movie changed the way you saw yourself, human behavior, the world? What movie did you first want to see again and again? Why? What scenes still strike you as particularly memorable or brilliant? Why? With whom did you identify in the movie? Why? What movies made you think about writing a movie yourself? What movie first made you see that the art of screenwriting involves thought, choices in writing, editing? What movie made you want to know more about just how movies are made?

So ask yourself questions about your first loves. Was it the story that hooked you? The protagonist's conflict? Was it the setting? Was it the trick plot? Was it the political context and implications that inspired you? What movie changed you? Is David Lynch land the world you're drawn to? Or do you prefer the Steven King world where horror stirs the quiet town, but all ends well, with family values and the best of human impulses prevailing over evil. Have you had it with American movies? Are you more drawn to international films? There are movies back there in your past, or maybe movies you've seen recently that have inspired you to be here. You owe it to yourself as a writer and as a person to know what movies move you and why.

Your First Loves

List a few movies that you would consider first loves, movies that enchanted, intrigued, and maybe even terrified you.

_____   _____   _____

_____   _____   _____

After you've made that list ask yourself why you loved particular movies. Was it the protagonist's journey? The love story? The fight scenes? The poetic justice? The cool killings? Explosions? Chase scenes? The sex? The humor? The escape? The tale of friends or family riding the tough times out? Or maybe falling apart to move toward change? Write it out here. Jot down what each movie listed did for you.

Other Loves

Consider now other loves, things, places, events, sights, sounds that appeal to you, inspire you, make you feel happy, secure, entertained, amused. Make a list of such things, then ask yourself why the appeal is so strong. Ask yourself what is it precisely about these stories that hold your attention. There are many categories to consider.

You might start with the fairy tales, childhood stories, or maybe even the cartoons that most engaged you as a child; ask yourself why? Or consider songs you love, and why? Do you identify with the lyrics? Does the music engage and release a particular emotion? Are there particular issues and concerns addressed that complement your own concerns?

And television. Most of us were brought up on the stuff. Are there particular shows you go to with that remote? What old sit-coms engage most and why? Some us can't resist reruns of *Friends, Cheers, Sanford and Sons,* or *Home Improvement.* What old sit-coms do you return to and why?

Now places. What are the most engaging places you've been to and what was the special appeal in these places? Maybe it was the first time you saw the ocean. Maybe it was your grandmother's attic. What places, spaces remain vividly in your mind? Why?

Outside of your family who are the people you have loved, and why? Consider romantic partners, dear friends, teachers, coaches. It might even be a stranger you encountered once, who moved you, changed you, opened you in some way, a stranger whose presence is with you still.

Personal Conflicts: Problems, Pet Peeves, Trials, and Tribulations

You don't have a story without trouble, so consider what troubles you consider worth exploring in your scripts. What bothers you? Be as profoundly philosophical or petty as you wish. Is the diminishing ozone layer keeping you up at night? Cruelty to animals? Do you surge with rage when you see a parent hit a child in public. Do you think about the threat of terrorists on a daily basis? How about world hunger? How about social expectations of gender roles? What injustices do you fear prevail in this world?

What ticks you off? Litter? Someone spitting on the sidewalk? Slow drivers in the fast lane? Snobs? Bad fashion sense? The jerk with a full cart in the express check out line? Commercials that try to sell you products by playing on insecurities? There's much potential drama in moments when something out there makes your blood pressure rise.

Maybe something puzzles you. Are there any contradictory events you've heard of, or observed? Are there contradictory realities that puzzle you? Disturb you? Any incongruences you've observed that you still ponder, sometimes struggle to resolve? Do you have trouble figuring how a priest justifies abusing children? Do you puzzle perhaps over a dying relative's last words? Or perhaps you are still trying to figure how light can be both wave and particle? How space bends? Do you struggle to understand why we hurt the ones we love? How some people have an infinite capacity to forgive?

Make a list and be sure to explore why certain things trouble, intrigue, concern you. Do some things offend your general moral sensibility, or do some things in the present disturb you because they remind you of some trouble in your past? In other words, what nags at your brain for a resolution, an answer? You don't have to resolve things. This exercise is all about raising questions, not providing answers.

Make a list of troubles, pet peeves, and consider writing a scene where one of these troubles is confronted by a character. Maybe, imagine a scene where something happens when a character tries to find an answer or changes a circumstance felt to be wrong.

Stories Out There

When teachers ask students to find stories, we usually ask them to start by looking within. Most creative writing students seek writing as a means of expressing themselves, as a means of discovering themselves and putting it out there on the page for others to experience. Many hope that by writing down what's important to them, the cherished thing can become important to someone else. But maybe you want to write about something/someone else. Flannery O'Connor once said that the writer "doesn't write to express himself, he doesn't write simply to render a vision he believes true; rather he renders his vision so that it can be transferred, as nearly whole as possible to the reader." So maybe you don't want to share your vision of thing; maybe you want to show something else. But bear in mind, no matter whose story you choose to tell, as the teller your beliefs, values, feelings will cast a light on any story you tell.

You never know where you'll find a story. My screenplay, *Blood Sisters*, was generated from a conversation I had with a poet while I was participating in a writing conference in my home town in Tennessee. He pointed out that since I seemed to be interested in writing dark, violent, and slightly weird material, I might want to know that about an hour away they once hanged an elephant for killing her trainer. Well, I got right on it. And this was in the days long before internet and Googling for information.

I went to the local library's microfiche room, and scrolled and squinted though the small town papers of Johnson City and Kingsport Tennessee, and there on the front page of a paper was the grainy black and white photo of an elephant with a headline saying something about Murderous Mary being put to death. There I read the accounts—which turned out to be false—about her long record of trampling people and using her trunk to sling them around in addition to trampling tomato patches, and eating some old woman's pie that was cooling on a window sill. Nope, I could not make this up. There it was in the pages of that small town paper published in 1916. The photo of the elephant and the related stories pretty much filled that front page. Then when I finished reading, by chance I noted a little clip of news, in the lower right hand corner: "Two colored men found burned to death on railroad tracks." The dead men, it seems, didn't even warrant names in that part of the world back then.

I knew I had to write this story. How could a small town hang an elephant and lynch two African American men in one week? All I had to work from were those stories, and a few others, one explaining that Mary was not at all murderous—she had two abscessed teeth, and when her new trainer—who had never worked with animals—smacked her mouth with a stick in some effort to get her to move, well she swung her trunk, and he was knocked through the air only to land dead on the ground. That was useful material. An abused innocent elephant and two men brutally killed for no obvious reason.

The rest, I made up. I knew I wanted to write about power abuses, about brutal violence, I wanted to write about some kind of redemption and justice, because from what I saw in the paper there was no redemption and justice. I did know that the hanging of the elephant drew a crowd of anywhere from 6000-to 13,000, depending on which interview was quoted. And the crowd brought picnic lunches and cheered as the derrick normally used for moving train cars was positioned, the cables and chains put into place, and the elephant was killed. I knew I'd have to tie in a story about a man being lynched—I cut the number to one man for better streamlining of my plot. I knew I wanted to make that man a human being who loved and was loved. I wanted my story to hurt, and I wanted to somehow give it a happy ending.

What resulted was a script with this premise: Set in 1920's Tennessee, *Blood Sisters* tells of Grace Hanes' rebellion from her racist and Southern Baptist culture when she is forced to admit her daddy's involvement in the lynching of her friend's daddy. Additionally horrified by the public hanging of an elephant, Grace draws strength from the lynched man's daughter, inspiration from the spirits of the victims, and support from a Yankee reporter as she develops the courage to expose her daddy's crime.

You never know where a lead and a little research might take you. This script was a finalist in the Diane Thomas Screenwriting Competition sponsored by UCLA's Learning Extension Program and DreamWorks. The script also brought me an Ohio Arts Council Grant of $10,000, and it secured me an agent in Los Angeles. But it was never made. And for good practical reasons. Like all those crowds scenes and the need for staging the hanging of elephant, and all those animals to tend to. A period piece featuring lots of animals and crowds is quite expensive. And it's hard to find backers with big bucks, even in Hollywood.

Remember to keep your eyes and ears open. Good leads for story ideas can come from anywhere. One of my own stories was inspired by the news coverage of a "Mother's Day Brawl" at a Golden Corral. Yes, you can Google it. It's true. On Mother's Day, 2007 a young African American woman punched a middle-aged white woman who had referred to the African American woman's loud and unruly child as an animal. At one point the white woman shouted at the child to shut up, and the protective mom punched the older woman. Before long there was a brawl with lots of flying chairs and thrown napkin dispensers. The white woman's elderly mother suffered two broken ribs apparently from being hit with her own walker. Several customers went to the hospital, and a few went to jail, and the place was shut down for two hours. On Mother's Day. Well I had to tell that story. It wasn't my story, but I sure had a take on it.

That brawl was a result of racism and the conflict it can stir up. But that wasn't the story I wanted to tell. For the fun of it, I wanted to tell the story of the mother who had taken the first punch in defense of her child. And so a stranger's story became my story, a story that addresses issues near and dear to me, the story I had to tell. I'll get to the details of that in a later chapter on plotting.

So maybe you're tired of wrestling with your own demons. Maybe you want to write about anything but you. Consider some of the following options.

Any One Else's Story Up for Grabs?

1. Read your local newspaper every day for a week. Find some peculiar or awful or funny true story. Do a little research on it if needed. Then write out a story line. Put in your own reasons the story might have occurred. Imagine the consequences, how lives might have been changed by this event.

2. Eavesdrop. Take out your ear buds and tune your ears to conversation flying by around you. I once over-heard two middle-aged power walkers wearing office suits with good sneakers while on a lunch break talking their way down a park path. One said to the other: "I don't know how much of this self-improvement I can stand." And I was off with a story that resulted in a play about two middle-aged women in a yoga class on a cruise ship. A comedy of course. But anyone could take that line anywhere.

3. Love—at least look at—thy neighbor. You know someone has caught your attention. That guy with a mullet, he's always standing outside smoking. The goth girl with the piercings who daily walks the street with three dogs, and is perpetually on her cell phone. What's her story? And the retired man across the street who manicures his lawn though all seasons. He has a wife, but you've never seen her These are people from my street. Look at your street or dorm or apartment complex. People can indeed be strange creatures—if not strange, certainly interesting.

4. Take a look, really, at the people all around you that you don't see. Steven Frears' film, *Dirty Pretty Things,* takes a grim look at what goes on behind the doors of a nice hotel—it's not too posh, not seedy, just a regular high-rise hotel. Ultimately the film addresses the illegal trade in body parts. Many an immigrant will trade a kidney for a green card. Sounds grim, but it has a payoff at the end with the menial laborers getting their justice when they prevail over the corrupt men who have controlled them and say something on the order of: look at us, pay attention, we are the ones who clean your laundry, do your dishes, clean your toilets, and we have the power now. Try looking at the people you see, but don't see every day. The girls at your tanning salon—when I started looking at them I noticed over time that most all of them get pregnant, very pregnant. What's with that? Consider the postman, the men on the back of a garbage truck, the cable guy—well that's been done. You know, the routine people whose names you don't know. Take an interest, and what you can't discover about them, make up. There's a story.

Crossroads: There's not Always a Devil There

Crossroads is a term commonly known to mean a point of change. Legend has it that Robert Johnson met the devil at a crossroads to sell his soul for supernatural skill at playing the guitar. But a crossroads can be anyplace where an encounter with someone can stir change.

For another story idea try visiting places where people congregate, where they might meet others that might change them. Consider in particular places where people might be in a state of transition, or at least looking for a transition. If you'll first give some thought to your character, or characters, you might establish a bit of who they are, what they are looking for. Then put them somewhere where they might encounter a person or an event that will generate change, a story.

A classic, and overused location, is the side of a road where a hitchhiker gets in the car of a stranger. You could try this, but beware of clichés.

Other places to consider as potential places of change, transition, story might be:

A recovery meeting place (AA, NA, Over Eater's Anonymous, Anger Management)

A courtroom—you see plenty of this on TV, but aim for something fresh

A church revival—lot of things besides soul-saving can occur here

A speed-dating spot

A teacher/parent conference evening—with or without children

A law office where an estate is being settled—loads of potential drama here (There's an excellent student example of this in the chapter on setting.)

Other Notions Up for Grabs

Translations/Adaptations

While encouraging each of you to find and write the story only you could write, I have to admit that lots of films out there are adaptations of novels, short stories, and myths. So if you are at a loss for an idea, you can always find a short story, a fairy tale, or myth and adapt it. For example, that popular and frivolous film *Clueless* was inspired by Jane Austin's *Emma*. You don't have to write a period piece just because the original is a period piece. Consider *Scotland, PA* the hilarious take on the brutal story of the struggle for power in Shakespeare's *Macbeth*. In *Scotland, PA*, the battleground is a fast foot joint, one that with the curious logo of M—for McDuff's. This comic take on the bloody quest for power is completely fresh with its contemporary, and yes ridiculous, spin on the old story.

Rewrite a Fairy Tale from the Bad Guy's Point of View

There's a wonderful re-telling of The Three Little Pigs fairy tale, called *The Three Little Pigs: The True Story* by A. Wolf. The tale is told of course from the point of view of the wolf, where he explains the whole event was a series of misunderstandings, as all he really wanted was to borrow a cup of sugar to bake a cake. Have a look at the book if you like, then consider other fairy tales where perhaps the bad guy would like to speak out: consider the stepmother in Cinderella, the troll in Billy Goats Gruff; the giant in Jack and the Beanstalk. There are many stories just waiting to be told by characters that haven't yet had a chance to speak.

Consider Songs That Tell Stories and Show the Story

Find a song that tells a good story and show it with a series of images. But write the piece without the song as a soundtrack. Rely on images, motivations, and scenes to accomplish the narrative instead of just writing down the words to the song. Or if you are a songwriter, consider your own music video—there's always room for more on YouTube.

Mining Your Memory

All too often I have students who—in spite of being in a creative writing class—say things like, "I'm just not that creative." When I tell them to draw stories from their own experiences, they say things like, "Nothing's really happened to me that's interesting." And I say bullshit. If you've survived the elementary school playground, if you've survived puberty, high school, your parents, the battles of dating, you have something to say. If you look back closely enough, and if you go to the little bit of trouble to be curious about yourself—yes, you're worth it—you'll find the stuff of stories. So mine your memory for some jewels.

When was the first time you were surprised or changed by something?

List and describe places you have lived.

What are the good and bad memories about those places?

Who was the darling of your family? The trouble maker? Describe how so for both.

List what was important to you at five years old. Ten. Fifteen. Twenty.

Did you ever meet a stranger who changed you in some way? Or was it a relative? Describe.

How do your clothes define you? Or not?

What's one thing about yourself you'd like to change?

Finding Your Metaphors:
Seeking the Images That Say Who You Are

Maybe you haven't realized it, but when you are moving through this world, you simultaneously exist in an internal world along with the external one. For example, let's say driving down the interstate, you see a red Miata whiz by. You have a thought or feeling about it. Some of us wish we could afford a red Miata. Some might become envious, or angry that the smart little punk behind the wheel is breaking the speed limit. Maybe someone recalls the sports car he had years ago, wonders when he gave up the wild side for a more conservative path. Who we are, where we've been, where we hope to go, will determine just what we see when we observe that red Miata. The car flies by in a flash, but maybe we spend minutes, or hours thinking about the implications of a red sports car. Maybe the sight of that red Miata changes someone's life.

My point is to make you pay attention to the way we carry an inner world with us wherever we go in the external world. What's inside affects how we see what's out there; what's outside affects our interior worlds. Our minds continually oscillate between an awareness of what is out there around us, and the inner world where thoughts and feelings stir.

The following exercises provide very elementary and personal strategies for you to go inside yourself and see what is there. They may not lead to script ideas, and that's all right. The objective is simply a personal exploration for your own self-discovery. While doing these exercises, try to leave logic behind and let your emotions provide answers. We continually strain to be logical in how we live our lives, but often we do and feel things for reasons we can only call unreasonable. I'd like you to consider the idea of "psycho-logic"—a kind of logic governed by instinct, impulse, emotion rather than logical rules. For example, when we say a guy smells like money, we don't mean that literally, logically—the term is a metaphor and metaphor is a powerful device because it allows us to access the emotions and intellect simultaneously. So try playing with images and metaphors in these exercises as a way of perhaps sneaking up on your concerns and feelings. You may not want to share these exercises as they can be quite personal. But do them and keep them as a reminder of places you've been, as reminders perhaps of the little forgotten pieces of who you are.

Worst Place, Best Place

This exercise invites you to go to certain places you recall, and then by focusing on the five senses, you not only recreate the place, but also how you feel in the place. If you complete this exercise thoughtfully, honestly, the reader will go to that place with you and feel the sensations you are working to articulate. This is a simple, sort fill in the blank exercise that comes in two parts. It's personal and may be kept private. But keep it. You never know what dramatic scene or story can unfold. Just follow the prompts and fill in the blanks.

When I'm in the worst place I can think of I'm

I see

I hear

I smell

I taste

I feel

When I'm in the best place I can think of I'm

I see

I hear

I smell

I taste

I feel

The House Within

This exercise is designed to take you to an imaginative dream space within you. Give it time. Sit back; maybe even close your eyes. Imagine this house deep in your psyche. Go inside. Move down the hallway. Imagine opening these doors and discovering, not determining, what you find there.

Deep inside me is a place, a home where my heart thrives, sometimes where my heart hides. If you walked down the long hallway at the center of this place inside me you would find many doors of different colors.

Behind the blue door you would find

Behind the red door

Behind the black door

Behind the purple door

Behind the yellow door

And behind the white door far away at the end of the hallway

A Body of Water

This is the last of these self-indulgent exercises, and is optional, but give it a try if you like, and remember to be as precise with your images as possible. An image, remember, is something we know through the senses, something we can see, smell taste, touch. So when listing what might be lifted to the light in this exercise, avoid abstractions like hope, anger, love. Show us stuff: like old running shoes, gold coins, a skull, a Mercedes Benz. Anything goes here. Anything can rise.

If I were a body of water, I would be

If you took a golden net, scooped it through my depths and lifted it to the light, you would find:

Self- Portrait in Snaps

This self-exploration exercise shouldn't be rushed, should be executed carefully, and this one could be shared in class. The goal here is to examine your external world and who you are in it. Use your phone or get a disposable camera if needed, and set out to take a series of photographs that, arranged together, will provide a self-portrait. Anything goes here, but you must not take an actual photo of yourself. The images in the photographs will reflect and evoke who you are indirectly. Take 20 shots, and then edit the group down to 10-12 photographs. Arrange the photos as you wish and bring to class. You can easily mail them to yourself and project them on the screen in class.

Bear in mind, before a director sets out to shoot a movie, a step sheet is mapped out of the basic scenes and moments, a kind of blue print. So before you take off use that camera, make some notes here. It can take awhile to inventory all the things that might show something about you. List below some basic things that really must go in your self-portrait. And of course this can change. You are the director/camera here.

_____	_____	_____
_____	_____	_____
_____	_____	_____
_____	_____	_____

2. What a Script Looks Like, How It Reads

In this class you will learn how to write a reading or a spec script. It is not written for a camera, but for a reader, a producer or director who simply wants to see your story, to read good writing, to discover engaging characters or situations. The layout of a script is designed for a reader who, while reading for story, is also reading for a sense of how the film will look. There are specific cues that tell the reader when a new scene occurs, when action occurs, when characters speak. There will be a lot of white space on the pages of your screenplay. The space allows greater ease for a reader working to note scenes, action, speech. Given the layout of a script, you can plan on one page of script being the equivalent of one minute of screen time. Remember this when planning how much film you'll need to buy, how much money you have to spend.

A script is written on standard white paper, has a cover page, and is written in a standard 12 point font—no fancy gothic script. When submitting your plays for competitions or potential producers, you will submit it with plain front and back covers, in solid color index stock. The script will be held together with brass head fasteners placed in the three-holes punched at the left margin. Most writers use only two brads placed in the top and bottom holes. For those of you reading this text for a class and who are writing small scripts, most likely you can just submit your script with a paper clip. Later on in if you write a longer script, submit it in the standard format.

Now to the logistics of writing a script:

Screenplays are built on three basic parts:
1. Scene Headings (also called slug-lines)
2. Action—this is also where description occurs
3. Dialogue

Bear in mind in this class you are learning to write a "reading script" or a "spec script" rather than a "shooting script." You don't need to worry about camera angles at this point. Don't try to tell your reader or potential director how to direct the script. Many of you no doubt plan to direct your own script; guidance for knowing how to select and write choices for the camera can be found in a film/video production class. Also in a reading script you don't need to number your scenes as you would in a shooting script. Your purpose is to tell a story and to lay it out in a clear format so the reader can easily see where scenes begin and end, where description and action occur, and where characters speak.

Scene Headings

Scene headings are written in all caps and briefly announce where and when we are. Headings are very brief. No description is needed here, unless some detail is crucial. In a heading you simply need to establish whether the scene is outside or inside with abbreviated notes Type `EXT.` for exterior or outside shot and `INT.` for an Interior shot.

Next in your heading you write where we are, also in caps. For example:

`INT. COFFEE SHOP or EXT. FAIRGROUNDS`

Next in your heading, note whether it's day or night. No need for terms like DAWN, DUSK, AFTERNOON, MORNING; the exact moment can be worked out in description. Stick to NIGHT and DAY.

So a complete screen heading can look like this:

`INT. COFFEE SHOP - DAY`

Or

`EXT. FAIRGROUNDS - NIGHT`

Occasionally you can use the words SAME or CONTINUOUS or LATER when your scene takes place at the same time as, or just after a previous scene. This device is often used, let's say when you have a character moving from room to room and back to previous rooms in an apartment. A good example of this device can be seen in the student example below for the "Anyone But You" conflict exercise. Sometimes LATER is used in the scene heading to indicate a passage of time.

On occasion you may want to employ a secondary scene heading. Secondary scene headings refer to a specific place in the scene where some specific action occurs. For example, let's say you want to write a scene set in a coffee shop and then perhaps you want to focus in on a particular place in that coffee shop to show something happening that's not obvious to everyone. You would write the heading, then a bit of the action. If and when you want to move back to the general scene, let us know that with another heading. These little moves can be seen in the potential drama unfolding as follows.

INT. COFFEE SHOP-DAY

The usual specialty coffee place. A few STUDENTS with
laptops at tables. A few ADULTS reading papers.

A Middle-aged, well dressed professor type MAN walks in
eyes instantly on hot BARISTA GIRL, lots of cleavage, full
lips, black-rimmed bright eyes. She looks straight at him
as he steps forward.

                    BARISTA GIRL
          What's your pleasure?

She leans forward as if offering her breasts like biscotti
for his coffee.

He takes in the view, smiles.

                    MAN
          My pleasure?
          (beat)
          I do believe it's you.

She smiles.

                    BARISTA GIRL
          Call it my community service. I like
          to bring a smile to a stranger's face.

BARISTA GUY walks behind her, shakes his head and smiles.

                    BARISTA GUY
          She's an acting major, mister. Look out.

                    MAN
          I'll have a skinny latte. In a cup
          for here. Not to go.

Barista girl rings it up, takes his money.

                    BARISTA GIRL
          I'll have to go to the back and get a
          real cup for you.

She turns walks toward the back.

BEHIND THE COUNTER

Barista Girl leans to barista guy who is wiping down silver.

                    BARISTA GIRL
                    (whispers)
          Five bucks if his eyes aren't on my ass.

She bends showing a nice round ass, thong rising just enough above her jeans.

From across the counter, the man stares, a smile on his face.

                    BARISTA GUY
          You wench, I believe that's a five
          he's slipping in the tip jar.

She straightens lightly pats Barista Guy on the chest.

                    BARISTA GIRL
          Don't you love working with me?

She walks the walk back toward the Man.

INT. COFFEE SHOP-SAME

The man shakes his head.

                    MAN
          So an acting major?

She smiles leans closer.

                    MAN
          It looks like all your talent comes
          naturally to me.

Try to keep headings simple. If there is some specific information needed to clarify some key point about the scene, you can let us know with a parenthetical note. Let's say that in this titillating scene, later on, perhaps while the man sips his coffee and watches the hot barista, you might set it by writing:

INT. COFFEE SHOP - DAY (MAN'S FANTASY)

And here you would write the action of the fantasy. When the fantasy is over, you would write a new heading:

BACK TO SCENE

At first glance this business of scene headings can seem tricky if you are moving quickly from scene to scene, from present action to fantasy or memory hits. Just remember the goal is clarity. You want your reader to have good idea at a glance as to how many scenes there are to be shot. When a reader looks at your script he needs to know a few things quickly, and that is why the layout of a screenplay is particular. Scene headings are in all caps to quickly convey the crucial information to anyone who might shoot your script. For the same reasons, sounds in your script are in all caps. And the first time a character appears, the name is in all caps. The plan isn't designed to add hurdles for screenwriters, but rather to keep things clear and simple for the reader. More on all this later as you look at more writing samples and situations.

For now let's look at the second key element of your script.

Action

Now let's consider how you write the action or description—this refers to what is happening on the screen in terms of action as well as what objects, people and places are to be seen on the screen. Action will occur just under your scene heading and will set up and follow the dialogue.

Any action that occurs in dialogue will not be written in the dialogue section as it is in stage plays. Nope, you get out of the dialogue, go to the left margin and write the action, even if it's something simple as a woman touching up her lipstick as she talks. Action always goes to the left margin where it belongs.

In action segments you want to be precise and brief. Remember to use your white space. Space is easy on the reader's eye, and space allows a sense of time to occur. Break up your action and description sequences into small blocks—each block should be no more than five lines. In an action/description sequence, break and start a new block wherever the camera would shift its focus or something new occurs in the scene.

For example, if you are describing a pristine and elegant living room, you would write a new action block when a mouse scurries across the white carpet.

Remember the action/description sequences give only information that can be seen by the camera. You can't go into a character's mind and speculate what's going on there. Instead of saying what a character feels or thinks, you must show it. If a guy is worried, you can't write something like Sam sits in his living room worrying about how he will pay his bills." No one can see that. We just see a guy sitting in a living room, and judging from what's on the screen, we have no idea what is on his mind. So think, how would you show a guy's worrying about bills? Well, you might show him sitting at a table with a stack of bills piled up. Maybe a few have those big red "PAST DUE" stamps. You might show him flipping through the checkbook with a balance, let's say, of fourteen bucks. You could have him pacing, maybe avoiding a bill collector on his answering machine. There are numerous ways you can SHOW a particular worry instead of just telling us about it. There's a rule in other creative writing classes that when it comes to emotions, thoughts, feelings, you must "SHOW IT, DON"T TELL IT" That rule can be bent a bit in fiction, but it is unforgiving when you are writing a screenplay.

No doubt you'll be including characters in your action blocks. As I mentioned above, be sure to write a character's name or job title when he or she first appears. You will also want to describe him or her briefly, giving only the details crucial for us to have a sense of who the character is. There's no need to describe what a character is wearing unless the garment is significant to plot or theme. No need to give eye color, hair color, unless the detail is significant. No need for precise age, height, or build. You might note: good looking or goofy looking, or hot or dowdy--if that's important. But be brief and allow room for the director to make choices. This all cap rule of first appearances also applies to general people who happen to be in the scene. Or even a cat or dog. When a reader looks over your script it needs to be clear just how many and what sorts of people will need to be gathered up to make the movie.

As far as the grammar of action blocks goes, stick to present tense. And feel free to use fragments. No long-winded correct sentences needed here. Your goal is to be precise, quick, give the reader only the information that needs to be known to convey what is happening in the scene.

You can also be playful, as in the above when I wrote how the Barista girl seems to offer her breasts like biscotti for his coffee. A little metaphor or simile can do lots to affect the tone and spirit of your story. A little play with words can also show you are a writer who is confident and good at your game.

Note on Active Verbs Instead of Passive Voice

If you've been through a freshman composition class, you may recall the guidelines on passive voice—that is a use of "is"/"was"/"were" where your prose might become more vivid with "active" verbs. Consider this bit of description.

The morning sunlight is shimmering across the rolling hills of the countryside.

It's passive, wordy, flat. Try rewriting it to make the landscape feel more potent, alive. You don't want to bore your reader or waste the reader's time. Try instead:

Green rolling hills shimmer under the expanse of morning light.

That active verb "shimmer" makes the world you are creating come a little more alive.

Sound

Don't forget the use of sound in your action/description blocks. And always write your sounds that will be heard in the script in all caps. These all caps will alert the reader of your script to the sound effects that will be needed for the sound track of your movie. When writing sound, remember SOUND IS ACTION in a script. It has an affect on the characters in your script, and on potential viewers watching your movie. Sound can be tremendously useful in conveying tone, and meaning in your script. Sound can also be a motivating force for your characters. A DRIPPING FAUCET can lead the insomniac to desperate action. A man walking with SQUEAKING SHOES is a very different character than, for example, James Bond, whose shoes might make a SHARP,SMOOTH SMACKING NOISE as he seems to glide down a hallway.

In *The Short Series* movie, *Joe,* there is no dialogue. In this short piece about a guy in a mental hospital, whose only prized possessions are his well-polished boots, we don't need dialogue to understand his isolation and containment. The first sound we hear is the nice tight sound of his polished boots moving across the floor as he heads toward the TV room. We hear the sound of a nurse laughing in a conversation she is having on the phone—her mind happily engaged with some place that doesn't involve work, or patients like Joe.

A sound that recurs is the sound of keys on a ring as a nurse mindlessly plays with them, jingling them as she indifferently looks over the patients in the room. The KEYS JINGLE the sound of indifferent power. There's also the FUZZY TELEVISION NOISE of a documentary on the TV—yes, the outside world is somewhat incomprehensible, and unimportant to the lives of the patients.

In the quietly comic plot, another patient with an obsession for/addiction to his liquid antacid comes along and nervously sits near Joe. He pulls out the bottle and JIGGLES LIGUID as he shakes and shakes the liquid, mildly distracting Joe and making the viewers laugh in response to all that gurgling sound. When the bottle tips and spills on Joe's brilliantly polished black boots, we hear the sad, and yes comic, GLUG GLUG sound of antacid spilling on those shiny black boots.

Hearing the sounds we've been given in the movie, we know the tone of the film is light and that it isn't likely that Joe will go into a rage over his ruined boots. Nope, this is a happy movie about resourcefulness and finding choices when choices are few and the wrong choice could have severe consequences—like being locked away with those keys. The story ends with the sound of Joe walking smartly, happily once again walking in those shoes—now polished white, to match the antacid stains. All is well. And Joe WALKS SMOOTHLY, happily as he goes back to the TV room enjoy to peace of sitting with his newly shined shoes.

Since sound can function just as potently as action or dialogue, you want to give it notice. Sometimes sound alone can have the presence of a character—there are the "annoying character" sounds that can invade our lives: the dripping faucet, a barking dog, a crying baby, the indecipherable sounds of neighbors fighting. There are also the more cheerful sounds that can interact with a character in just the same way a person can: children laughing, fireworks, and the sound of the sea or wind in the trees. Don't forget that wonderful tool of sound to bring your story alive and make it jump off the page.

Dialogue

The dialogue parts of your script are centered on the page. To be clear—the name of the speaker is centered and the dialogue itself is tabbed in an extra tab space on left and right margins. See below for clarification. Screenwriting software will automatically center dialogue when you type the character's name in all caps. This really beats figuring it out with a regular word processor. Dialogue in screenplays, as in stage plays may include a bit of direction—that is a brief explanation of how a character says something: sadly, happily, cautiously. Although directions for how a character says and does things in a stage play is quite common, in a screenplay try to avoid these directorial intrusions that can involve clumsy and unnecessary adverbs. Try to let the context of the action, the character, and the dialogue itself imply the mood rather than coming out and explaining how a character speaks.

Avoid Writing Action within Dialogue

When you have a character doing action as he or she speaks, avoid writing the action into the dialogue. Get out of the dialogue, get back to the left margin and write your action. Small gestures, little telling actions may now and then be included parenthetically in the dialogue, but try to limit the use of parenthetical action in dialogue to only those moments where the action is judiciously timed and very telling.

O.S.—OFF SCREEN DIALOGUE

If you have a character in a scene who is talking and not actually present in the scene—let's say in the next room—this is called Off Screen Dialogue, and is written like this:

EXT. HANES' BACK PORCH-DAY

Clifford crouches over shelf, swipes belly of a fish, guts it.

                         GRACE (O.S.)
                I know what you did, Daddy.

Clifford slowly turns, faces Grace standing behind the screen door.

Voice over Dialogue

Voice over is the term used when a character is speaking who is not in the scene. Sometimes narration is provided in voice over, as in the opening of *American Beauty* when the protagonist establishes the context for the story about to unfold by announcing that he is already dead.

Voice over is also widely used in documentary, and the voice over provides a context or commentary for what the viewing is seeing. Voice over is used brilliantly in the short *Night and Fog*, where the narrator gives a historical and philosophical perspective on the graphic footage documenting the horrors that took place in the Nazi concentration camp of Auschwitz.

Voice over in a screenplay is often used to tell us what is on the mind of a character. It is often ironic with, let's say, the character appearing to be confident, but a voice over let's us know that internally the character is worrying about her breath, panty-lines, or if too much, or not enough, cleavage is showing.

One of the most engaging uses of voice over appears in the opening of *Adaptation* where Charlie Kaufman (Nicholas Cage), a screenwriter with serious writer's block, is basically beating himself up with his thoughts. Any writer who has stared blankly at a computer screen—and that would be all of us—can relate to this painful inner chatter that bounces around like a bucket of ping pong balls knocked from a shelf, just when we are trying so hard to focus and write something engaging, beautiful maybe, at least.

Frankly, a screenplay about a screenwriter with writer's block is one of the most common student writing clichés, but Charles Kaufman, who happens to be the true writer and director of *Adaption*, embraces the cliché with great humor. The blocked writer begins with, "I don't have an original thought in my head. My bald head." The bald head is funny, but his self derision gets funnier when he says in that strong serious voice, "Maybe if I were happier, my hair wouldn't be falling out."

One of the many reasons this voice over keeps our interest is it's funny, but more importantly, in this monologue of self-derision, there is no whining. Whining rarely wins anyone's interest. Our blocked writer is doing anything but whining, which is a weak way of expressing self-pity. Our writer is pissed. He's mad at himself, and he's so busy being angry at and frustrated with himself, the words are active, as if he were punching himself. But it never gets too serious. This little bit ends with him trying to goad himself into getting down to work by rambling into cliché: "Life is short. Today is the first day of the rest of my life." This line is followed immediately with "I'm a walking cliché." That's it for the self pity—too much self-pity tends to repulse. He rambles off with possible solutions for his unhappiness, and again he gets funny with thoughts of how he needs a girlfriend. He ponders what might make him attractive: maybe if he spoke Russian? Or Chinese? He ponders how maybe he would succeed if he were a screenwriter who spoke Chinese. The ironic voice over ends with him asking the old clichéd questions: "Why am I here? How did I get here?"

The clichéd questions take off with quite a visual answer. We see a montage depicting the creation of the planet earth, and then the fire storms and natural disasters that are all part of a developing planet. We see early life forms come and go. We see a primate stand upright and walk, then a quick cut to a baby emerging from a womb, and we can only guess it's the birth of this angst-ridden writer who has come from all this to sit and babble at himself.

The use of voice over continues throughout the movie to depict the humor of a successful screenwriter who is an emotional mess. There is much to be said of this movie that runs on a narrative that defies all "rules". There will be more on this when I discuss plot.

American Beauty uses voice over in the opening to frame the story we are about to see unfold from the perspective of our protagonist, who speaks from the great beyond. As the film opens with the establishing shots of a nice suburban all-American neighborhood, we hear our protagonist, Lester (Kevin Spacey), introduce us to his rather conventional and boring life as he gives us the surprising fact that he is soon to die. What's unconventional about this voice over is that our speaker is very calm, at peace, with his death. The story takes the cliché of a middle-aged man who, in a mid-life crisis falls in lust with a teenager, and through quirky plot devices and this voice over the story transforms a cliché into something profound with a peculiar and particular wisdom. Throughout the movie, the voice over of the soon-to-be-dead man keeps us mindful of a spiritual perspective of the mundane and often sordid desires of the human critter.

Voice over can also be used as a kind of internal haunting—let's say the voice of some authority figure looms in a character's head while the character is simply trying to move forward and do something. Any of you probably have the old words of your parents still humming in your heads, or maybe it's a former schoolteacher, a coach, or a loved one that got away. We hear voices in our heads all time; it's not necessarily an indication of psychosis. When you have a character hearing a voice inside, whether it's a memory, a dream, a guilty conscience, or spiritual intervention, you note voice over dialogue like this:

INT. BENJAMIN'S BEDROOM - DAY

Violet gathers her dead father's clothes from dresser
drawers. While the clothes are neatly folded, she further
straightens them before placing them in a box. She
addresses an old photograph of her father and her framed
on the dresser.

                    VIOLET
          Preacher says Mr. Carter can get some
          use out of your clothes. And I know
          you'd like 'em to go to somebody who
          could use—

She stops. Looks up.

                    VIOLET
          It just ain't right, Daddy. I mean you
          make me go to church. You tell me God
          has a plan for us all. But I don't see
          why God would let those men do all
          that—

She looks down, sees his shoes by the bed, picks them up,
fights tears.

                    VIOLET
          They didn't even give you time to put
          on your shoes. Can't you talk to God?
          Can't you tell him to do something? I
          pray. I pray everyday. I ask him to do
          something to make things right. Those
          men ought to be punished for what they
          did to you.

She looks up to the ceiling, dingy and cracked. Silence.

                    VIOLET
          Where's God in all this awful?

She looks up again. And again silence. She throws the
shoes in the box and carries it out.

EXT. VIOLET'S FRONT YARD - DAY

Violet carries the box to the road as if she's going
somewhere. She stops, puts the box down, crouches,
BREATHES.

                    VIOLET
          Can't you help me, Daddy? You used to
          tell me to pray to momma for comfort.
          And she was a comfort. She is a
          comfort in my dreams. But where are
          you? You just come to me in a dream
          and tell me to spit the rock out.
          What's that supposed to mean?

She looks up at the gray sky. Silence. A bird flies over.
Silence. She stands, looks down at the roadside littered
with rocks.

                    SPIRIT OF BENJAMIN (V.O.)
          The dead can't do a thing in the
          living world without the help of a
          human hand.

She looks back at the house, still, silent.

                    SPIRIT OF BENJAMIN (V.O.)
          David brought Goliath down with a stone.

Violet looks back at the road, picks up a rock, grips it.

                    SPIRT OF BENJAMIN (V.O.)
          The rock. Spit the rock out, and
          you'll go flying, girl.

Violet picks up more rocks, slips them in her pockets. She
looks back at the house. Picks up the box of clothes and
heads down the road.

In this scene we see and hear where Violet draws her strength to expose a horrible
wrong done in her small, racist town. She will take a terrific risk, and we see how
she is capable of doing it—not through faith in God as much as faith in the undying
love of her father.

Ad Lib Dialogue

This little dialogue trick can save you lots of grief when you have clusters of people chatting, and it can apply when characters are talking without restraint, over each other. It's for spontaneous improvised talk that's more like chatter than direct dialogue.

Even though technically ad lib is dialogue, it is written in the action part of your script. And it would appear in all caps, like this:

```
INT. SPORTS BAR - NIGHT

Frat guys stare up at football game on a big screen. AD
LIB football game CHEERING and CHATTER.
```

After this bit of action, you might then depict particular characters having a particular conversation in the standard dialogue format.

Montage and Series of Shots

A MONTAGE is a series of short, disparate images arranged to convey an idea or tell a little story in brief, quick moments that occur in various places and times. Often this device is used to convey the process of a couple dating and falling in love. You've probably seen this use of images to show a couple falling in love many times—you've probably seen the "love story" parodied, as it is such a popular device. We see them at the park, cooking dinner, sitting in front of a fire, cuddling under covers. The time and place varies. If you were to write scene headings for each moment, the script would be clumsy and would detract from the idea of fluid narrative that can be conveyed in montage.

There is also the scene-heading device, SERIES OF SHOTS. Frankly, the line between what is a series of shots and what is montage is a blurry one. Some say that a musical score usually underscores a montage, but this is not always the case. And some say a series of shots is when the main character appears in most all of the shots. I like to think of a montage as telling a mini-story, while a series of shots might show many disparate things occurring in a block of time. But then again, often this series of disparate things adds up to some kind of story, even if it's just to show how one swimmer in a lane beat the others racing, splashing across the pool.

Montage is a very important technique in film-making, in that it is a device that can convey an extensive amount of information in a very short time by using a series of images to tell the story of a place, a situation, or a relationship instead of depicting extended scenes. For your own exercise with montage, please try to avoid cliché. Remember your goal is to use a series of images that tell a story, and in the process lead to an insight or discovery of emotion about the characters or situation being described.

You might want to have a look at that very disturbing short documentary film *Night and Fog*. It can be found on the *Authority* volume of *The Short Series*. The director, Alain Resnais, chillingly uses a series of still shots and clips of Nazi film footage originally shot to document the Nazi's strategies for grand-scale execution. Through the series of images and clips—as well as the use of voice over—the director graphically recreates the horror that occurred in Auschwitz; a single image, such as mountainous pile of human hair evokes, a world of grief. Through one image we can experience a world of horrible action that occurred beyond the scope of the camera's frame.

In *Night and Fog,* a voice over narrator explains the story of the concentration camp at Auschwitz. He provides a historical overview to help viewers make sense of the horror being shown on the screen. Keep this movie in mind later if you consider shooting a documentary. The voice over rarely explains what's being seen on the screen—that would be a redundant and boring strategy. The voice over narration provides a context to help us understand the unbearable reality of what is being documented on the screen.

Through a series of images and clippings, the reality of the Nazi's cruelty is made experiential. We feel the cold calculation of the plan engineered for massive and efficient death. The film makes us feel the sorrow and horror of so many lives lost, and yet lets us know that such horrors, in time, are absorbed into the world of nature, of human experience. The image of the grass growing over paths where the doomed walked to their deaths conveys a broader level of horror by showing how nature continues to grow over and absorb the evil things a man can do. It's a powerful and wrenching film, and while I don't expect you to write or document such a disturbing story, much can be learned from studying the film's craft. Your task here is not nearly so daunting.

For a brighter, more inspiring example, you might have a look at the now classic montage scene in Peter Weir's *Witness.* Overall the film, a suspense thriller plot intertwined with a romance subplot, provides an excellent model of plotting. It's also so gorgeously shot, so artfully made that we are often so immersed in the beauty of the images, we forget we are watching a Hollywood thriller/romance. The premise features the detective John Book (Harrison Ford), who goes undercover in an Amish community to protect an Amish boy who witnessed a murder in a train station. While the basic story hinges on protecting the good guys while pursuing and punishing the bad guys, it's very much a character-driven plot that features the growth and development of John Book. In the opening we see that his character is a bit clumsy and sloppy in terms of the way he lives and in his relationships. He prides himself on his independence and is very much a lone wolf kind of kind guy who has trouble connecting, even with his own family.

Once Book goes undercover and changes his appearance to look like the Amish, he starts to change within. He soon learns that he has to rely on the Amish to stay alive –as well as solve the crime. The lone wolf comes to see the necessity of cooperation. In one of the finest montage scenes on film we see not only the necessity of cooperation, but the beauty and harmony of people working together to achieve a goal. John Book, who happens to be a fine carpenter, uses this skill to connect with the Amish who value such practical talents. A powerful bond is made when he assists in raising a barn. The shots of the barn going up depict beautifully choreographed movement where instinctually, almost silently, everyone knows their job and contributes to the final outcome: a barn, somehow miraculously raised by the orchestrated strength and skill of men working together. John Book, formerly so arrogantly self-sufficient, humbles himself to the knowledge and skills of a group of people he once considered a peculiar cult. His acquiescence to their wisdom and experience results in a growth that is spiritual. And that barn-raising montage provides a powerful metaphor not only for the internal changes at work in John Book, but also for the beautiful power of cooperation rather than bull-headed isolation.

Another classic and powerful montage can be seen in *The Godfather*, Francis Ford Coppola's multi-generational crime saga. When the patriarch godfather (Marlon Brando) barely survives an assassination attempt, his son Michael (Al Pacino), who was formally living a straight, mob-free lifestyle, decides to get revenge, and he carefully orchestrates the deaths of all the killers. He's a quiet man who keeps his planning to himself. But in one scene while he is technically becoming a godfather to his nephew in a church, we cut to the killings being done execution-style under the Michael's orders and back to the church ritual. We see the killings occur in a barbershop, a spa, an elevator, numerous public places. The public executions are juxtaposed with the very private spiritual ritual, showing the duality of being a godfather. In one scene, and through the efficiency of a montage, we see Michael become a protector of a child's soul, a sanctified godfather and another kind of godfather—a ruthless murderer, protecting his father and the family of crooks and killers.

There are many fine examples of montage and series of shots scenes used in popular films. Try noticing them. Watch them with a pen in hand to take notes of exactly how the shots are arranged and what is changed in the circumstances of the plot at the end of the scene.

If you want to use this strategy in your screenplay, write MONTAGE or SERIES OF SHOTS as a scene heading with a colon, and then and give a general statement of what we are about to see. Then below that list the series of images that will be shown. For example:

```
MONTAGE: GRACE AND VIOLET DEVELOPING FRIENDSHIP

--Grace slips out the back door of her house to meet
Violet waiting at the edge of the yard.

--They skip rocks together at a creek.

--They hold hands and walk down a railroad track.
```

```
--They untie a yelping puppy, bound with a chain, and
laughing run with it across an open field.
```

Often the series of images is listed as

(A)

(B)

(C)

But scripts are looking cleaner and clearer these days, so you might want to opt for the little bullets instead of letters, as I have done above.

As stated above, you may also use a SERIES OF SHOTS that doesn't really tell a story but uses a series of quick and various shots to convey action. This technique is often used for fast action/suspense. It can also be used to convey an idea. For example, in *Line of Fire,* where the potential assassin (John Malkovich) is closing in on his target—the president of the United States—we also see the parallel story of one of the president's security officers (Clint Eastwood) moving closer to identify the assassin before the hit. The series of shots strategy is excellent for building tension when you have two—or more—forces at work heading for a goal. When moving quickly from scene to scene, it's far more efficient to use a series of shots instead of employing the cumbersome and distracting scene headings.

Find below a comic and engaging student example of a conflict scene that employs the use of point of view and series of shots to illustrate the competition between a "mole" and boy who is out to win a whack-a-mole game. Setting, by the way, is another key element in this piece. It's set in a game room where children do indeed become mesmerized by the game at hand. The goal of winning something grows to huge proportions in a child's mind, as it does here. Also I like the playful fantasy switch to the "mole'" point of view. It's silly, but in a child's mind, he can certainly imagine the mole down there looking up toward him and plotting to defeat him. If you can access the dramatic, somewhat paranoid soundtrack of "Montagues and Capulets," you'll get even more pleasure from this playful look at a child's passionate quest to win. Matthew fist envisioned this piece as realistic film—shot with a real boy in a real place—but the script nicely lends itself to animation. More and more film majors have an interest in and talent for computer animation, so keep that option in mind for your scripts. Yes, "Whack-a-Mole" seems a silly idea, but the drama of winning a game can be quite serious to a child. If you'll bear in mind the musical score, the script is quite amusing. It works.
Have a look.

Student Example of Series of Shots, "Whack a Mole," by Matthew Rome

FADE IN:

INT. GAME ROOM - DAY

The room is filled with all kinds of classic children's games. Children run around wildly. BUZZERS and WHISTLES and other VARIOUS GAME NOISES echo and chaotically blend together with children LAUGHING.

The door to the game room opens. Behind it is sky-blue light that contrasts heavily with the dark game room.

The silhouette of a BOY, five to nine years old, walks into view of the glowing doorway and stands for a moment.

A gust of wind ruffles his hair. He takes three steps into the room and looks around at various games.

The Boy slowly walks in between the game machines DINGING AND BINGING AND BUZZING. He inspects and considers each one as he goes.

The Boy glances up, and from across the room, a sole Whack-a Mole machine catches his eye. Instantly, all his attention is drawn to it.

(Beat.)

Suddenly, all the sound and light in the game room fade away.

Except for a spotlight on the boy and a second spotlight illuminating the Whack-a-Mole machine in the center of the room.

The boy stares at the machine in pure silence.

(Beat.)

"MONTAGUES AND CAPULETS" beings to play loudly through the rest of the film, and the script moves in time with the beat.

The boy stares.

(Beat.)

SERIES OF SHOTS: WHACK A MOLE GAME TABLE

--Mechanical mole pop up and down various holes.

--The boy walks towards the machine.

--Moles pop up and down.

--The boy grabs up, studies the MALLET.

--MOLE.

--MALLET—CLOSER.

--MOLE—CLOSER.

--The boy whacks at the mole...

--Missing every time as mole ducks and surfaces.

--The boy panics. Sweat beads on his forehead.

--Mole continues to pop up and down.

--The boy wipes at sweat, leans closer to machine.

--Suddenly, the mole pops up in center hole.

--MOLE'S POV: The boy glares down at the mole.

--BOY'S POV: Stares at the hole.

--MOLE'S POV: The boy raises his mallet.

--BOY'S POV: The mole glares at the boy.

--The boy stands poised ready to strike. He swings. And
  he misses.

--The mole disappears and pops up in another hole.

--The boy swings again and misses, swings again and
  misses, swings.

--BOY'S POV: WHACK A MOLE GAME TABLE

--Mole pops up. Glares at boy.

--A second Mole pops up to join the first!

--The boy is horrified!

--The two moles pop up and down.

--The boy chases after them desperately, but can't keep
up.

--The boy stops, terrified!

--BOY'S POV: WHACK A MOLE GAME TABLE

--A mole pops out of every hole. Up and down! Up and
    down! Up and down!

--The moles disappear and the first mole returns, popping
  up and down.

--The boy watches, stunned. Angry, swings at the mole and
  misses, again swings and misses.

--MOLE FROM UNDER CENTER HOLE POV: The boy grows furious.
  He whacks to the left of the mole and misses, whacks to
  the right of the mole and misses, whacks at the center
  hole dead on with a solid THUD.

--Blackness. "MONTAGUES AND CAPULETS" ends.

                                        FADE OUT.

                    END.

Now have a look at a more serious take on how to use a series of shots, while
extensively employing point of view as a framing device, to tell a story. The writer,
Anthony Lopez, has an interest in the darker side of human nature, and here, again
through the eyes of children, we see how daunting the world can be. We also see
the ways children cope with having very little control of their worlds.

Student Example of Series of Shots Using Point of View by Anthony Lopez

FADE IN:

INT. HOUSE - NIGHT

BOY, seven years old or so, short brown hair, unusually skinny.

He RUNS from the dining room, afraid. Stands in living room looking around, BREATHING heavy, looks at Entertainment stand, CLICKS the bottom doors open and hides inside.

BOY'S POV: THE THREATENING LIVING ROOM

- Through the slit of cabinet doors

- Stuffed dinosaur underneath the couch, stuffing coming out chest

O.S. Sister's high-pitched SCREAMS, and SMACKING and BEATING noises

BOY'S POV: THREATENED LIVING ROOM

- Twelve pack beer bottles next to couch

- A single black ant crawling on carpet

- FATHER's cowboy boots, BARGE into living room, worn jeans

- Worn snakeskin belt, polished sheriff badge belt buckle threatens from Father's waist

- Father's calloused hands, thumbs loop and jerk belt

- Father SMASHES beer bottle on wall, his hands twitch

Boy looks at own hands, makes a fist.

Father sits down on couch. He looks at his reflection in the TV.

Father grabs another beer bottle.

Hesitates to pop top off, stares at his dark reflection in the bottle.

POPS top off and CHUGS beer.

Father grabs a framed photo from end table, photo is of a younger woman mid-twenties.

Rubs thumb over glass.

His reflection comes into focus, presses thumbs into glass until it CRACKS.

Watches blood seep through cracks.

Pulls photograph out of frame and sets it on couch.

Takes another drink while watching the WOBBLING ceiling fan.

Continues staring at WOBBLING ceiling fan.

Begins weakly CRYING.

BOY'S POV - THREATENING LIVING ROOM

- The ant crawls towards cabinet

- Father gets up from couch, walks towards the
  entertainment stand, stands there

- Scuffed metal plating around Father's boot

- Father SMASHES the ant, STORMS out of the house, SLAMS
  the door

INT. HOUSE - NIGHT

Boy crawls out of entertainment stand. Begins walking but stubs his toe on a plastic baby doll missing its hair. Boy stares at the baby doll for a moment Picks up doll, tries to squish its head with his hands, GRUNTING.

Begins WHACKING baby doll against TV.

Continues WHACKING TV, begins CRYING and SCREAMING, BREAKS baby dolls head off.

Boy looks down at baby doll's head.

Looks at TV screen, at his reflection.

Looks down at smashed ant.

INT. HOUSE DINING ROOM- NIGHT

Boy tries to duck-tape baby doll's head on.

With doll crudely duck-taped together, Boy walks into kitchen.

Notices broken spatula on the floor. Hears WHIMPERING.

Opens lower cabinet. Pushes cereal boxes out of the way.

SISTER, five, messy brown hair, curled up in a ball lightly CRYING.

Boy gives doll to sister. Tries to coax her out.

Sister resists, shuts cabinet door.

INT. HOUSE BEDROOM - NIGHT

Boy is in his upstairs bedroom, holding his stuffed dinosaur in hands, dinosaur is patched with duck tape.

Lots of human figures made from pipe-cleaners are strewn all over the floor. Some are wired together, holding hands

Boys sets a blue figure on top of dinosaur and plays. Boy puts a pink figure onto dinosaur's back and plays

Boy looks underneath bed, grabs a sheet of paper covered in drawings of the human figures.

BOY'S POV: CGI ANIMATION OF HAPPY PEOPLE

- Three figures holding hands, smallest one pink, the tallest red, and the medium blue

- Figures walk up a hill that goes up into the clouds

- All the figures have smiles on their faces

- The tallest figure helps the little ones climb up a tree
  at the top of the hill

- The figures see a green female figure with wings fly out
of the sun

- All the figures hold their hands up towards the winged-
woman

O.S.: Door SLAMS

BOY'S POV: CGI ANIMATION OF HAPPY PEOPLE

- The figures' smiles turn into frowns; the winged woman
  and the sun disappear

- A hole begins burning through the tallest red figure

O.S.: Wood floor CREAKING

Boy stands in front of door, reaches hand to open it,
stops and bends to look through keyhole.

BOY'S POV: HALLWAY THROUGH THE KEYHOLE

- Numerous holes in walls

- Dark doorway of adjacent bathroom.

- Sound of MOVEMENT in bathroom. FAUCET ON, then OFF.

- Sister's face slowly moves into light, cheek is swollen
  and red.

- Sister eases trembling hand on doorframe

O.S.: RUMBLING of foot steps in the house.

BOY'S POV: THROUGH THE KEYHOLE

- Sister jerks foot back, face fades into dark.

- Father's worn snakeskin belt looms by.

59

```
O.S.: Door SLAMMING

Boy shuts his door, walks to distant wall in his room,
places ear on wall. Waits for a moment.

Creeps to door, opens it, creeps into hallway. Floorboards
creak, he freezes. Looks at dark wood door almost black at
end of hallway.

Boy creeps forward into bathroom. Slips into bathroom,
pushes shower curtains back. Sister is huddled in bathtub.
Sister looks up, boy reaches out hand, helps her out of
bathtub.

Sister hugs brother.

Children creep into bedroom. Boy takes flashlight from
under his pillow, flicks in on, turns out light. Shines
flashlight on area around his sister

She walks over to bedside table, eases drawer open,
reaches inside. Pulls out an old worn storybook.

Boy climbs onto bed, she cuddles beside him. He opens book
to first page. Flashlight shines on title: Little Red
Riding Hood.

She smiles at Boy as she flips to first page of pictures
and text. Places her finger on first word.

                                          FADE OUT:


                        END.
```

Yes, quite a story can be told in just a few minutes if you carefully, carefully select your telling images and arrange them along with actions to reveal characters. You can create an engaging and powerful narrative based on the old reliable formula of conflict, crisis, and resolution, or as I sometimes state it: the how-to-solve-a problem story. The children here are faced with coping with a violent and grieving father. The story nicely shows how children draw on the resources of imagination, and each other, to find comfort. The problem for these children is not fully resolved—that would require a much longer story. But there is a complete story here, a story that depicts how another day of danger is endured.

Flashbacks and Memory Hits

Flashbacks are a favorite device for new writers, and are often used to provide rather long-winded exposition or background for what is occurring in terms of present plot action. Be careful not to let your flashback overwhelm the present story you are aiming to tell—unless, of course, that is your point. One could argue that the entire story of *American Beauty* is a flashback since the story is being told from the sweet hereafter. Flashbacks need to occur for a dramatic reason; something in present plot action triggers a memory, and then the memory has a dramatic effect on present plot action—in other words, it results in a change of mood, direction, or action. A flashback can be so brief it is sometimes called a memory hit, and it occurs dramatically within present plot action or within dialogue.

In the following scene a memory hit gives a glimpse of Clifford's childhood. Bear in mind, Clifford is a chronically angry man who is violent with his wife as well as anyone else he wants to overpower. He is the man who gets the plot rolling when he decides to lynch a man just for speaking to his daughter. As a writer I needed to figure what kind of background could result in such an angry, violent man. Going by my own philosophy that behind every horror story is another horror story, I decided that Clifford was isolated and beaten as a child. He was powerless to defend himself. Such a background would result in a man who liked to take advantage of his power and strength whenever he could.

So I wrote a scene where Clifford and his conspirator/friend are having a run-of-the mill conversation about the job they hate at a grain warehouse. The otherwise uninteresting conversation becomes interesting and loaded when I work in the flashback of young Clifford being brutally beaten by his foster father. The flashback gives a visual and visceral explanation of why Clifford has such a violent need for power. Clifford has chronic pain from a denture that doesn't fit correctly, and the denture is a constant reminder of his foster father, who knocked his teeth out.

Sure, I could have explained this in dialogue, but Clifford isn't the kind of man to talk about old childhood injuries. Clifford would never have the kind of self-reflection where he might think, "Hey, I'm violent because my daddy was violent." That would be very dull expository dialogue. Instead I use a memory hit to SHOW the pain that swirls inside of Clifford. The viewer then gains an insight into Clifford that Clifford lacks. In this way a viewer is participating in a character's story and isn't just sitting back and having the story told. You'll note in this scene I use a device called CUT TO:. This device is used as a transition when you have an abrupt change of location. Technically every scene could end with a CUT TO:, but they would get distracting. Use CUT TO sparingly, and use it only when there us a dramatic shift in local, as in a memory hit, or let say you are cutting from a conversation at someone's house, then want to shift to what's going on simultaneously at the airport, or to some other place across town. CUT TO: is always at the right margin of the page, and as you see includes the colon as a way of referencing the scene to follow. Cuts may end a page, but are not be used to begin a page.

There are occasions when you might want to consider different choices for cutting to another scene such as DISSOLVE TO: MATCH CUT TO: You might use DISSOLVE TO: to suggest the effect of a scene slowly fading away, and such a shot would establish a certain tone about the change. MATCH CUT: is used when the same object, or a similar object is used in two or more succeeding scenes or shots. They are used to quickly convey a passage of time or distance. For example, you might show a guy putting out a cigarette in an ashtray while he is waiting for someone, then use MATCH CUT: and show the ashtray now filled up with cigarette butts. This device would then indicate that the poor fellow has been waiting for quite some time and has quite a habit. In a student example, also by Matthew Rome, in the chapter on visual language below, you'll find an eloquent use of MATCH CUT: where the writer dramatizes how two lonely strangers living across town from one another have the same the very habits as they fill their loneliness. They should be together, but aren't.

For now, have a look at how CUT TO: is used as a transition for a MEMORY HIT.

INT. WAREHOUSE - DAY

Clifford sits on a feed bag, rubs his jaw.

                    FRANKIE
          Them fake teeth hurt?

                    CLIFFORD
          Got a smoke?

Frankie nods. Rolls a cigarette for himself, then one for Clifford. Watches Clifford adjust his denture.

                          FRANKIE
          I could whittle them down for ya. Fix
          'em so they don't rub a blister.

Clifford smokes, gazes out the door toward daylight.

                                            CUT TO:

MEMORY HIT: INT. BARN-DAY

YOUNG BOY CLIFFORD is HIT in the mouth by his FOSTER
FATHER. Clifford DROPS to the ground. Blood oozes from his
mouth.

Young Clifford feels for teeth in the blood. He fingers
them, slips them in his pocket. See silhouette of the
foster father coming toward him again the light beyond the
barn. HARD BREATHING.

BACK TO PRESENT

INT. WAREHOUSE-DAY

                          FRANKIE
          Hurts, huh.

At the end of your memory hit or flashback, don't forget to signal to your reader
that the flashback is over and that we are back in the realm of present plot action.
You note this by writing: BACK TO PRESENT or BACK TO SCENE so readers
are never lost as to just when and where we are.

Inserts

The insert or cutaway is used to bring something that's in the scene into focus in order to give the object dramatic significance. An insert occurs within a scene that has already been established with a scene heading. It's often used to zoom in on a letter, a headline, a bottle of pills, a bag of drugs, a box or briefcase that contains items crucial to the plot. For example in the scene below, Grace has stolen the cigar box that her father keeps close at hand. She has figured out that there is something in that box that is a kind of secret, something of great importance that her father guards. Grace has also come to believe in the possibility that her father might have been involved in the lynching, a fact that she doesn't want to believe because she knows it was her forced conversation with Benjamin Woods that led to her father's violence. When Grace discovers proof of her father's violence, she has to face her own complicity. The grim moment plays out below:

```
EXT. HANES BACK YARD - NIGHT

Grace clutches a cigar box to her chest as she runs from
the house. She glances back at the house, sees silhouette
of her mother move past the window. She runs, crouches
behind the trunk of a tree. She puts the box on the
ground, strikes a match, opens the lid.

INSERT-THE OPEN BOX

A clump of hair, a pocketknife, a few coins, and the
shriveled remains of a finger.

BACK TO SCENE

Grace slams the box shut, jumps up, shoves her fist to her
mouth, stifles a HIGH-PITCHED MOAN. She glances back at
the house, grabs up the box, darts across the yard and
runs down the dirt road.
```

Now a word of advice on inserts: don't overuse inserts to such a degree that you are continuously controlling the camera. Often you can note particular objects of significance just by referring to them in the action. Use inserts for those "AHA!" or "AHH" kind of moments, moments of precise and potent emotional significance.

There are many books out there that can provide guidelines for formatting just about anything you want to do in you script, but you have enough basics to get yourselves going. For now, have a look at the opening pages of my screenplay titled *Blood Sisters*. Observe how headings, action and dialogue come together to create a narrative that's visual, a story told in images that can also be heard, felt, experienced. Note how I begin with an establishing shot that lets us know we are in a rural setting. We also see pretty quickly that we are in a period piece, set in the early 1900s. We can see the "who," "what," "when," and "where" pretty quickly as well, with the setting showing caged animals in a time that pre-dates animal rights awareness; it's also quickly established that we are in a place that pre-dates civil rights.

The principle players appear, and basic relationships are established. As a reader you know where you are; you also have a clue as to where the story is going. I'll go into a closer analysis later. For now, just have a look to see how a script begins and flows.

When submitting a complete script to a reader, always cover your script with a title page. Centered in the upper middle of that page you type your title in all caps. Underneath, type your name and in the lower right hand corner, type your contact information. What follows is the standard model for the opening pages of a script. The sooner you are familiar with the conventions, the easier the writing of your scripts will go.

On page one begin your script with

`FADE IN:`

typed at the left margin. Then write your scene heading, then on to action. Be sure to use breaks to show shifts in where the camera might be, shifts in what is on the screen. Don't write in long paragraphs. Stick to bits of action/description no more that four to five sentences. And when the script is all over, also in the right margin write:

`FADE OUT.`

And at the center two or three lines below `FADE OUT`, type:

`END.`

Now let's look at the opening pages of my first screenplay.

BLOOD SISTERS

by

Jane Bradley

4138 Happyland Rd.
City, State, Zip
Phone:
Email:

FADE IN:

EXT. TRAVELING CIRCUS GROUNDS - NIGHT

Rural Tennessee, 1920s. Circus grounds in a field bordered
by woods. Railroad yard in distance. CALLIOPE MUSIC.

Small clusters of PEOPLE head toward the circus.

Scattered between railroad yard and circus, cargo cars
wait. One painted car depicts elephants rearing up. Clowns
and acrobats painted at center of the tableau. Lions rear
at corners. Across the top: "JIMBO JOHNSON'S BIGGEST
LITTLE CIRCUS SHOW."

EXT. CIRCUS GROUNDS - NIGHT

Midst of circus. Paths lit by strung lights, a few
torches.

A GIANT with a MIDGET on his shoulder strolls.
Periodically he dangles the midget over the crowd. The
midget feigns fear until placed back on the giant's
shoulder.

Caged animals outside: A black LEOPARD paces. MONKEYS
CHATTER above CROWD NOISE.

GRACE, BETSY, and CLIFFORD HANES walk through crowd.
Grace, a well-endowed girl of 14, follows mother Betsy,
30, attractive, but strained. Clifford, 35, a handsome man
with a face hardened by long-term anger.

Grace observes the leopard.

                    GRACE
          He don't like being in that cage.

                    BETSY
          He *doesn't* like being in that cage.

Betsy takes Grace's hand and pulls her along.

Crowd funnels toward entrance. Clifford buys tickets.

In near distance, a sign notes "Coloreds." A small group of AFRICAN AMERICANS enter, including BENJAMIN WOODS, 30, handsome, and VIOLET WOODS, 13, attractive like her dad.

INT. CIRCUS TENT - NIGHT

TRAPEZE ARTISTS swing in the air as Clifford, Betsy, and Grace waits in line.

A TATTOOED MAN inked with animals poses by the door. Betsy stares as he turns to flex inked, oiled muscles.

                    BETSY
          My goodness. It's an abomination.

Tattooed man exhibits chest bearing Rock of Ages tattoo. Pushing Grace forward, Betsy keeps eyes on the man. Grace bumps into Violet, who stands staring at a WOMAN TRAPEZE ARTIST swinging upside down on the trapeze.

Violet drops bag of peanuts. They lock eyes, smile.

                    GRACE
          'Scuse me.

                    VIOLET
          You didn't mean to.

Grace bends to help Violet pick up peanuts.

                    GRACE
          Violet. You ain't supposed to be over here.

                    VIOLET
          Better sight of the show here. We
          gotta sit back there behind the animals.

Grace looks across tent to Black audience section where a banner reads: "Coloreds." She notes Mary the ELEPHANT straining at chain to get at water barrel. Grace looks back to Violet, follows her gaze up to woman trapeze artist flying through air to grab trapeze.

                    GRACE
          Wish I could fly like that.

They watch woman swing, gain speed, release, flip through
the air to be caught by MAN TRAPEZE ARTIST.

                         BENJAMIN
              Violet?

                         GRACE
              Your daddy's calling.

Violet nods.

                         BENJAMIN
              We gotta go this way.

Grace looks at the cluster of African-American people
moving toward their section.

                         GRACE
              Which one's your momma?

                         VIOLET
              Ain't got no momma. She died.

Violet gives Grace a glance.

                         VIOLET
              Done told you that before.

                         BENJAMIN
              Violet, stick close to me.

Violet hurries through the line, takes her daddy's hand.
They disappear into the crowd.

Grace turns, sees Clifford, arms crossed over chest, a
leering grin, as he watches the scantily covered butt of
the trapeze artist descending on a rope.

Betsy stares at the muscled, tattooed man.

                         BETSY
              Leviticus says, "Thou shalt not make
              cuttings upon thy flesh--"

                         GRACE
              But that's Jesus on his chest.

                         BETSY
            Jesus belongs on the cross, not some
            half-naked man's skin.

Betsy pulls Grace to stay up with Clifford.

Clifford spots FRANKIE who is 30, skinny; one side of his
face droops. Frankie points to a space beside him.
MARY, the chained elephant, strains again to get at water.

TRAINER smacks her with a stick.

The Hanes sit next to Frankie, watch WOMEN on WHITE
HORSES.

                         FRANKIE
                      (To Clifford)
            Yer late.

Clifford nods, flexes his jaw, rubs at his chin.

                         CLIFFORD
            You bring a nip?

Frankie nods, offers a bottle. They sip and watch the
women.

Grace scans crowd, notices a section roped off, a sign
reads "Coloreds." Her gaze catches VIOLET.

Ladies on horses exit as Trainer pushes Mary into ring.

                      JIMBO JOHNSON
            And now, Mary, the two-ton pachyderm.
            Straight from the jungles of Africa.

Clowns boost WOMAN on top of the elephant. She rides,
waves. Trainer stays close, prod and whip ready.

                         GRACE
            She's got a big sore on her mouth.

                         BETSY
            Why do you always notice such things?

Trainer CRACKS the whip. Mary stands still.

                              TRAINER
            Down!

Mary kneels. The woman slips down the trunk, waves to
APPLAUSE.

Trainer CRACKS whip, jerks prod up. Mary stands still. He
CRACKS whip, raises prod. Mary shifts. Trainer CRACKS
again.

                              TRAINER
            Up! Damn you! Up!

Mary makes an attempt. Comes down. Trainer CRACKS whip,
SMACKS her with prod.

Grace notes Benjamin and Violet wince.

Mary rears up to APPLAUSE.

                            GRACE
          That man's hurting her.

                          CLIFFORD
          Quit being such a baby.

Frankie studies Grace's nice breasts.

                           FRANKIE
          Looks mighty grown to me.

Clifford elbows Frankie, grabs bottle, points to the ring.

                       JIMBO JOHNSON
          Now the largest living land mammal on
          Earth will do a little dance.

Clowns appear with ACCORDIAN MUSIC. Mary drops on all
fours, swings her trunk. Trainer CRACKS whip, SMACKS at
her legs.

Violet shakes her head as Benjamin pats her shoulder.
Mary moves back toward the water. Trainer SMACKS her mouth
with the prod.

Mary TRUMPETS/ROARS. Audience SCREAMS.

                              71

Mary grabs up Trainer, throws him down, tramples him.
MUCH SCREAMING. Clowns and Jimbo run.

                    JIMBO JOHNSON
          Get that animal under control!

OTHER TRAINERS crowd her with prods, torches. Someone
SHOOTS.

Mary TRUMPETS, tramples the stands. Crowd SCREAMS, runs.
One MAN lies dead, chest crushed.

Crowd bolts.

Mary runs, knocking down a pole. Part of tent collapses.

EXT. CIRCUS GROUNDS - NIGHT
Crowd rushes and scatters. Much SCREAMING.

                    VIOLET
          Daddy! Daddy! Where are you?

                    BENJAMIN
          Here!

Benjamin leads Violet clear of the crowd.

Mary runs past railroad yard, toward the woods.

Betsy cringes with Grace against one of the rail cars as
crowd rushes past.

EXT.DEEP WOODS - NIGHT

Mary rushes through woods. Crowd YELLS. HARD BREATH AND
FEET CRASHING BRANCHES. ELEPHANTS RUMBLING, TRUMPETING.
Mary breaks through woods to riverside.

Continued RUMBLING SOUNDS. Sudden SILENCE. YELLS OF MEN IN
CONQUEST. SILENCE.

Mary stands at water's edge, drinking. A crowd gathers
with torches, weapons, chains, a huge net.

A MAN stands with gaff. Clifford and Frankie wade in,
assist trainers in cornering Mary. Man lunges with gaff,
misses.

Grace spots Violet standing with Benjamin and other Blacks
under the trees.

The men whip at Mary with sticks.

> GRACE
> They don't have to hurt her.

> BETSY
> The Lord gave us dominion over the
> beasts of this world.

Grace runs to watch from distance with Violet.

> BETSY
> Grace!

Clifford smacks Mary's leg with a spiked stick. Mary
flinches, freezes.

Grace grabs Violet's arm.

> GRACE
> Let's get away from here.

The gaff comes down hard on Mary's back. Crowd YELLING
joins in to bring her down. She rolls in the muddy water.
Crowd throws net over her, chains her legs. Crowd CHEERS.

Violet and Grace disappear through the trees.

EXT. DIRT ROAD - NIGHT

Violet and Grace walk in the dark.

> GRACE
> It ain't fair. She had this big old
> sore. She was hurting. She was sad.
> She was so sad, she didn't want—

> VIOLET
> People don't think animals have
> feelings.

                         GRACE
         Momma just says the Lord gave us
         dominion over beasts of this world.

                         VIOLET
         Not to hurt 'em like that.

                         GRACE
         I found a new puppy at the dump. Want
         to come see it? Daddy says I can
         keep it if it lives.

                         VIOLET
         If it lives. I gotta get home. My
         daddy be worried sick about me.

Violet turns and hurries down the road. Grace watches
until she disappears in the darkness. Turns to head home.

EXT. HANES' FRONT PORCH - DAY

Grace sits on steps, tries to feed a sick PUPPY bits of
meat.

                         GRACE
             Come on, pup. Please. Just try
             eating something.

                         BETSY (O.S.)
         Gra--ace.

Grace makes a face, looks at the fried pie on a napkin.

                         BETSY (O.S.)
         Grace, you finish that fried pie yet?

                         GRACE
         Yes, ma'am.

                         BETSY (O.S.)
         Get in here and practice your scales.

Grace makes a face, shakes her head, cuddles the puppy.

                         BETSY (O.S.)
         And put that dog in the shed where it
         can die in peace.

                    GRACE
          I'm gonna save its life.

Grace breaks off a corner from pie offers it to puppy,
puts it back on the napkin. She looks out, down the road.

Benjamin Woods comes walking with a hoe over his shoulder.
He sees her, but looks straight ahead.

                    GRACE
          Hey there.

Benjamin nods.

                    GRACE
          You hungry?

                    BENJAMIN
          No, ma'am.

                    GRACE
          My daddy says you folks is always
          hungry.

                    BENJAMIN
          No more than most I reckon.

Benjamin starts to move on.

                    GRACE
          My momma made it. Won the blue
          ribbon. Makes 'em every week since
          she won that prize.

Grace rises with the fried pie wrapped in napkin.

                    GRACE
          I gave Violet one once. She liked it.

Grace goes to him.

                    GRACE
          Tastes like sugar and grease to me.
          Sticks in my throat every time I take
          a bite. Here, take it. It's rhubarb.

                    Got strawberry for a little bit of
                    sweet.

                              BENJAMIN
                    My Violet likes rhubarb.

                                GRACE
                    Go on. Take it.

Grace shoves the pie into his hand.

Benjamin looks at her house, then down the road.

                              BETSY (O.S.)
                    Gra-ace.

Benjamin starts to go.

                                GRACE
                    Wait. Give me back the napkin. My
                    momma counts these things.

Benjamin starts to unwrap the pie.

                              BETSY (O.S.)
                    Grace!

                                GRACE
                    Give it here and get!

Benjamin tries to give the pie back. Grace pushes his hand
away. He tries again. She pushes back.

                                GRACE
                    Just give me the napkin and go!

Betsy comes out on the porch with a handgun.

                                BETSY
                    You get away from my girl!

Benjamin throws the pie and napkin and runs. Grace kicks
the pie aside, picks up the napkin.

Betsy trains the gun on Benjamin. Grace rushes to her.

EXT. CIRCUS GROUNDS - DAY

Mary strains against chains. A TRAINER #2 HITS her with a
prod. HITS again. The lady who rode her, and the midget,
cry.

                    LADY
          Quit that! Somebody make him quit!

                    TRAINER #2
          God damn killer!

Trainer two HITS Mary

Giant grabs Trainer #2, SHOVES him. Trainer runs.

                    TRAINER #2
          He gonna pay for what he done.

                    LADY
          It's a female. Don't you even know
          her name.

EXT: HANES' FRONT PORCH - DAY

Betsy looks over Grace's clothes.

                    BETSY
          What'd he do to you?

                    GRACE
          Nothing.

                    BETSY
          You're hiding something.

Betsy takes hold of Grace's face.

                    BETSY
          That man upset you.

                    GRACE
          No, he didn't.

                    BETSY
          He did something, didn't he?

77

                              GRACE
                   He's Violet's daddy.

                              BETSY
                   Violet?

Betsy looks over Grace, takes her face in her hands again.

                              BETSY
                   Your daddy's gonna look into this.

                              GRACE
                   Not daddy. Momma, please.

Betsy grabs Grace's arm, pulls her toward the door.

                              GRACE
                   My puppy.

                              BETSY
                   Nothing you can do for that dog now.

Grace resists, but goes inside.

The puppy stares out. Dust lifts on the road.

End of scene.

This opening ten minutes of a script not only illustrates formatting, but the narrative establishes themes to be addressed in the story while also setting up the conflicts that will propel the action forward. We'll discuss the uses of openings in a later chapter. But for now, just note how characters are given dimension in a script through the dialogue and action.

 Once we've established the situation of the scene to unfold, a circus act, Grace's mother Betsy immediately establishes herself as hypocritical and judgmental with the way she eyes the oiled muscles of the tattooed man while declaring his appearance as an abomination. This is indeed a script about hypocrisy and harsh judgment, and the combinations of Betsy's gesture and words establish this theme while also establishing her character.

Considering a script runs a minute per page, I have our principal force, the protagonist Grace, the daughter of the man who incites the lynching, bump into her antagonist, Violet, the daughter of the man who will be lynched, the girl who will push Grace into facing and revealing her father's crime. Grace accidently bumps into Violet, also a bit of foreshadowing of how their paths will cross, and Grace's response is mixed. On impulse she politely says "'Scuse me," when she bumps into the Black girl—her first impulse is a good one, a civil one, that shows she has the capacity for thinking beyond herself. Then her training kicks in and she points out that Violet should go be with her own people in the segregated tent. These mixed responses hint at the conflict that will grow in Grace as she comes to wrestle with compassion for Violet while at the same time detesting the sight of Violet, who represents a reminder of the violence Grace's father can do.

Violet's father Benjamin's first line is to call out to his daughter—something he will continue to do, with great repercussions, throughout the script. His second line indicates that he knows to how to play by the racist rules of his community, and he knows the serious need to play by them. He tries.

When we meet Clifford, Grace's father, we see he's immediately put on the defensive by his friend Frankie, who without even a hello, gives the little verbal prod with "Yer late." The power dynamic is set between them—Clifford rubs his jaw, indicating some ongoing discomfort. Then he ignores Frankie's remark—a verbal way of taking control of the power dynamic—and he doesn't explain why he's late. He takes charge of the situation by asking for some whiskey, which Frankie promptly gives. Power struggles are established everywhere between races, men, women, parents and children. Even the giant dangles a midget over the crowd, threatening to drop him—all for the sake of entertainment, but still, the big guy really could harm the little guy.

This script hits the ground running with spectacle. There's much to engage us visually with the circus people, the animals, the lady on a trapeze and then the painful performance of Mary, who is so abused by her trainer she lashes out, tramples him and takes off. There's the initial inciting incident: violence begets more violence. The theme is established that controlling and abusing a creature will result in destruction. Grace is horrified by the abuse of the animal; again her impulsive response suggests that she has the capacity for compassion. All this and it's only five minutes into the script.

The next five minutes set up the major inciting incident. Grace is at home, being ruled by her mother. Grace is trying to tend a sick puppy, while her mother calls and calls for her to finish eating a fried pie—something Grace really doesn't want—and then she calls for Grace to come in and practice piano. Thematically Grace is contained and trained, much like the animals in the circus. And much like when the elephant was pushed too far, it lashed out, Grace will also take her frustration out on the first person who happens to come by: Benjamin, an African

American man who lives in a place and time where a bossy little white girl has the right manipulate him. Grace gets too close to him while basically forcing him to take something he doesn't want. When discovered by her mother, the woman instantly overreacts and suggests Benjamin who did something wrong. And in the racist world of the old South, this is plenty of reason to ignite Clifford's rage and send him on a path of destruction. And so the plot of containment/control, and the rebellion that results from brutality is established. There have also been religious references, and however self-righteous Betsy is, the idea of Jesus on a cross—even appearing on the muscled and oiled skin of a tattooed man—suggests there might be hope for some kind of redemption in this cruel world.

All the seeds of the story line are laid out in these first ten pages. Everything mentioned will develop in some way, and play out in the action and the ultimate story line.

Most likely you aren't writing a feature-length script, but even if you are writing a five-page script, be aware that in your opening you'll need to give visual and verbal clues as to the nature of the story about to be played out.

3. Building Your Characters

"In most good stories, it is the character's personality that creates the action of the story. If you start with a real personality, a real character, something is bound to happen."

Flannery O'Connor, "Writing Short Stories"

When I studied screenwriting through UCLA's Learning Extension Program, for the first semester we focused only on developing the kinds of proactive characters who had enough complexity and desire to generate the kind of plot that would engage a reader/viewer and keep that reader turning the pages of a 120-page script. We also had to map out, then write out the entire plot—I'm talking the major plot points, the action, discoveries, challenges, set backs, all the ups and down and twists and turns that keep a story interesting.

In that first semester no actual script was written, no scene heading, no carefully written action, no dialogue. It was at times exhausting, maddening, and it was, as I learned in time, the only efficient way to plan a script of that length. I also had to recall that when building a house, much time must first go into drawing out the blueprint, digging up the foundation, then building the entire foundation before anyone sets to painting the walls of a room. One who has ever worked as a carpenter know that you don't start building a house by hammering out one room at a time. The carpenter has to learn a few tricks first, things like how to properly hammer a nail, how to use a level, a power saw, and all those other crucial things that need to be mastered before anyone starts building walls.

This text does not ask that you start imagining a feature-length script. The process worked for me only because I had already written and published two books of fiction and had enjoyed the production of two of my full-length plays.

We're starting small here. You're going to learn how to be a lucid and powerful writer first. You're going to learn to create characters who can leap off the page, and to write scenes that grab the reader by the collar and pull the viewer into what John Gardner called a "fictive dream," a place created by a carefully calculated imagination, a place that is as smoothly engaging as a dream. It's good, clean, gripping writing that sustains a fictive dream. You want to pull a reader into your imagined world; you want them to be so convinced of that world, that they might laugh, gasp, maybe even cry at the scenarios spun from your head, hands, and heart.

While I won't be asking that you to start by imagining the kinds of characters and plot that can sustain a 120-page script, we will start by understanding what a character is. We often hear someone say of some quirky person, "Oh he's a real character." That little judgment doesn't tell us much except that perhaps the person is marked by distinct, possibly odd, eccentric, or perhaps immoral qualities. While some stories run on quirky character types, the richest stories run on characters who are multi-dimensional, perhaps contradictory. My guess is that if any one of you had to describe yourself with a single adjective, you'd be hard-pressed to do so, unless you said something broad like complicated. That might be true, but it doesn't tell us much. When you think of creating a character, most likely a type will come to mind: someone brave, or sneaky, or obsessive/compulsive, or lazy, someone who lives by integrity, someone who runs on vice. Such abstractions can be a start. After all, when we think of ourselves or others, we think broadly, as in "he's a good person" or a "bad person." But knowing people, creating people is much more complicated than that.

In order to think of the ways drama unfolds, or sometimes erupts, out of character, go beyond the single-quality character. No one can be defined by a single quality. Instead, think of a character as a whirling vortex of fragments revolving around a central core. Yes, we have a basic self, but it can manifest in so many different ways, depending on both external and internal conditions. I'm not suggesting that we are all quivering masses of personality disorders, but our personalities vary widely depending on various situations. For example, you are most likely one sort of person with a friend, another sort with a lover, another sort with your mom, and another sort with the cop who is asking for your driver's license. And all of those fragments of you are true.

Given all this confusion as to who we are, and the various guises we are quite capable of wearing, I'd found that a good way to know what a person is like is to get a sense of what they want. Think of what is wanted in terms of the basic verb that drives a character. Those desires can change of course. People in general are driven by any of these three things: the desire for love, the desire for money, the desire for power. Again, it sounds simple, but it's complicated. Some want all of it. Some want none of it. Some even just want a quick or slow, numbing way out of this world. And any one of these desires is enough to generate a character worth a story. The more you particularize what a character wants, the more particular, and engaging, that character will be.

For these exercises on character development, let's assume you want to write a narrative as opposed to a non-narrative experimental film. And while you could certainly tell the story of a city coming to life at dawn, or the story of a meal being prepared, or the story of a big cat stalking and catching its prey, let's assume you want to write a story about characters, people up to something.

A narrative involving character generally involves a character wanting something, or maybe a character content with something, as in the short film *Joe*. The film tells the story of a highly-functioning patient in a mental hospital, a place where no one has many choices. The film begins by showing Joe polishing his black boots and being very content with their polished perfection. Since, as I've said above, you can't have a story without trouble, within minutes something happens to Joe's shoes, and the plot hinges on Joe's reaction and *choice* of action. What we do and how we respond to challenge defines us.

The blockbuster *Jerry Macquire* begins with Jerry, a rather arrogant sports agent who is very content with his powerful position, with his skill at winning clients, and with his babe of a fiancée. By the end of act one, everything he assumes is within his domain falls away, and you have a story in motion as he struggles to regain money, power, and ultimately even love, which is to be a new thing he desires, real love, not just a trophy wife. In the end he wins not only the lost power and money, but he grows to want something more.

In Clint Eastwood's classic, *Unforgiven*, the story begins with the aging former killer, William Munny, wanting, and in great need of, money. We learn within the opening minutes that he was changed for the good when he married a good woman, and he settled down to raise a family, be a farmer. But in the opening seconds of the film, through the silhouette action of a man burying someone, and with a quick shot of the grave marker, we see the wife has died. As the real action of the movie starts, Munny and his two ragged children struggle against their bad luck with pig-farming, and are trying to separate the pigs with fevers from the healthy ones—a bit of foreshadowing of a plot that runs on a need to sort the bad guys from the good guys.

In this movie, a sheriff gratuitously brutalizes others for no good reason, and the "outlaws" like Munny bring justice to a town held hostage by the sheriff, who is a former outlaw himself. Minutes into the film our hero is wallowing in pig muck and The Schofield Kid, who happens to be the inciting incident of the plot, shows up to ask Munny to accompany him to go kill some bad guys to earn the reward. It doesn't take long for Munny to get on his unwilling horse, gather an old friend, and set out to be a killer for hire—but not for the greed of it. He wants blood money to provide stability for his children—an ironic plot that blurs the lines between heroism and villainy. *Unforgiven* tells the story of a vicious man who has the capacity to turn to good, who then can summon up all his brutal skills in an instant to bring some kind of justice to the very corrupt town of Big Whiskey, and then can turn back to a conventional life to raise his kids.

Your character should have a history—at least in your mind—and a built-in capacity to grow, or change in some way. But plots don't always unfold a positive change. The film *Capote* is based on the story of the research and the writing of the American classic tale of murder, *In Cold Blood*. While based on fact, the film used many fictional devices for building character, setting up motives with an inciting incident, and playing out how people are changed by both internal and external circumstances.

In the beginning we meet a successful and somewhat arrogant writer in New York who just happens on a news story about the murder of a farm family in Kansas. He calls his editor, says he'd like to go out there and research the event, to tell the story of how the slaughter of a family could affect a small town. And being a man who is accustomed to getting what he wants, he gets the trip along with his friend Harper Lee who'll do the research for him; she's a woman with the grace and good sense to open doors for Capote, an eccentric, vain and rather off-putting man.

So note, the first motive of our protagonist, the successful writer, is that he wants tell a good story. He has the capacity of good—he wants to tell the world the story of a small town rocked by murder. But when we look closer at the way his personality changes when he meets Perry Smith, the principal killer, we see how motive can change—and change us. Capote is no longer interested in the small town. He wants the killer's much more sensational story; he plans to take the opportunity to profit from the horrific misfortune of others.

He also has the capacity to be so selfish as not to see/or feel the pain of others; he certainly has the capacity to be indifferent. So the mixed motives of artistic ambition—he wants to tell a good story, and wants the fame and fortune that can go with it—these complicated motives result in him becoming entangled in the life of one of the killers. As he comes to Perry Smith, his motives only grow in complexity. He feels compassion for Perry, who suffered heart-shattering neglect as a child. Capote identifies with the sorrow of being a child abandoned by his mother, a child who has to find a way to make a life from nothing.

But there is something bigger than compassion that runs this ambitious writer. While listening to and identifying with Perry's painful story, Capote never loses sight of the need to get the book on the stands, and of the requirement to get all the dirty details of the murder of the farm family before Perry is put to death.

Most all stories revolve around a little (or big) growth of a character, or a little (or big) death. Characters can grow in wisdom, compassion, insight, or their morals, ethics. Or they can wither, become smaller souls as they make choices based on selfish desires.

In *Capote* we see a character development that is more like a little death of a soul than the growth of one. Capote lies to a man who has made himself completely vulnerable to Capote's interest—an interest that began as curiosity about another human being, but that turned into little more than self-interest. Perry Smith thinks the soft-spoken effeminate writer will surely tell a compassionate story of how a sorrowful childhood and a lot of bad breaks led Perry to be a man who could walk into a stranger's house and impulsively blast the brains out of a family for no good reason. Capote betrays Perry Smith. He misleads him about the narrative of the book he is writing about Perry; Perry seems to think the book will explain his sorrowful life and how it led him to kill. And while the book does do that, it graphically depicts the murders, leaving readers to feel more horror than sorrow for Perry. Capote misleads Perry about the stages of completion of the book, saying it's not complete when it is—this tactic keeps Capote from having to offer a draft for Perry to read. He also lies to him about the title of the book, saying he doesn't have a title yet, when he does have a title that boldly, firmly conveys Perry as a cold-blooded killer, not a victim of bad parenting.

By chance, Perry learns that Capote has already announced the sensational title for book, *In Cold Blood*, a title that makes Perry out to be a monster, not a broken man. In the movie, Capote goes on to revel in his success—and drink to the edges of delirium. In life he does the same, eventually drinking himself to death. We learn in the closing credits that Capote never finished another book after *In Cold Blood*. Perhaps he had a conscience after all. But the movie tells the story of how in the pursuit of the mystery behind evil deeds, we often slip into a little evil ourselves, and go down.

I'm not expecting you to sit down and write a plot driven by complicated and unruly forces such as we find in *Unforgiven* or *Capote*. But even in the smallest story, remember to give your characters dimension, a capacity for growth, diminishment, change. As you plan the journey of your protagonist, no matter how mundane, you want to bear in mind that the journey needs to progress through choices, discoveries, sometimes recoveries, and above all CHANGE. And you'll need to keep a few points in mind, as to what makes an engaging protagonist.

To begin, fictional characters are not identical to flesh-and-blood human beings, because readers wish to read about the exceptional rather than the mundane—if you are indeed writing about a mundane character, then there needs to be some exceptional quality about that character which will engage us as readers. Readers demand that "homeo fictus" (the fictional man or woman) be more handsome or ugly, ruthless or noble, vengeful or forgiving, brave or cowardly than real people are. In other words, they need a passion of purpose. "Homeo fictus" has hotter passions, colder anger. They travel more, fight more, change more. They have more of everything—including precise desires and conflicts, the kinds of desires and conflicts that generate a plot

'Homeo fictus" is an abstraction—or one might say, a vehicle—meant to act out and project AN ESSENCE, not the totality of human experience. They have complex motives and live lives with passions and ambitions. Even the dim-witted Homer Simpson has a passion or two: drinking beer and snoozing in a hammock. Intellectually challenged as such characters are, many viewers identify with their desire to avoid work, eat junk food, and maybe meet some babes.

But let's talk of some of the more dynamic characters in film. In the classic *Casablanca*, cool-headed and broken-hearted Rick wants to stay out of politics and just run a good bar. He was once crushed by an emotional involvement, and he never wants it again. Then naturally, for plot's sake, the woman who abandoned him appears and needs his help. Rick has to overcome all disappointments, pain, and desires for revenge to help her. He acts not only out of love for her, but out of a political conviction. He'll do whatever it takes to resist Nazi expansion. Even though Rick resides far away and long ago in the black-and-white world of Casablanca, he has passions, furies, and conflicts with which we can identify; we identify with both his internal struggle of the heart and the external struggle with the ruthless forces of Nazi occupation.

While it will take some practice before you write a script as engaging and seamless as *Casablanca*, you can aim to write a script featuring a character that readers can identify with and fully believe. *Spiderman* engages us, not only because of the cool animation, but because Spiderman is a very real character. He's just a guy, a high-school kid with all the geeky high school problems of being popular and being attractive to girls. And then he is a victim of a science project gone wrong when he is bitten by a genetically engineered spider. He's just a real guy with a real problem, albeit in an unreal world. Even animated super-heroes have back-story, have character. Superman has the everyday problems of being an immigrant, dealing with the challenges of living in a foreign world—no one in this new world of earth could ever really relate to his background, his weaknesses and vulnerabilities.

Your reader needs to have a strong sense that your characters exist and have lived full, or maybe failed, but certainly realistic, lives long before your film begins. With your film, something about your character's life is about to change.

Before you start writing your script, do some homework on your characters. And remember to use good orchestration for all your characters—in other words, don't make all your characters greedy or ambitious. And don't make your principle characters one-dimensional. People certainly aren't. Since you want to make us feel for and identify with your characters, they shouldn't be one-dimensional. Remember to make principle characters "round"—that is, multi-dimensional, and remember they will have a past, and just like real people, the past will still be with them.

In thinking about plot for your characters, think about giving them obstacles, both internal and external obstacles—this will keep emotional and physical action rolling.

Some writers suggest interviewing your characters. Make a list of questions and see how your imagined characters answer them. This is often a very useful strategy, as you are forced to let go of trying to control the creative process—a very good idea. Give your characters a say in the matter. Pose questions, and see what answers come floating up. Try it, but if it feels awkward, rely on the character profile sheet that follows.

Beware of Stereotypes

When all the reader's expectations about a character are fulfilled, when there are no contradictions or surprises in the character, you have a stereotyped character. If the old granny is a sweet lady who grows African violets on her window sill, bakes cookies for the paper boy, and drives her car only to go to church on Sunday, you have a stereotype. If the old lady is a retired police lieutenant who still likes to shoot at the local target range, or if the old lady is a bookish intellectual who secretly loves boxing, then you have a start on breaking free of stereotypes.

Now let's get started on developing the psychological, physiological, and sociological profile of your characters with a few warm-up exercises to help you to come to know characters, to develop them and then to depict them in such a way that your reader knows them as well as, and sometimes even better than, you do. In all of these exercises I want you to remember that we know this world primarily through our senses: sight, sound, smell, taste and touch. As artists we use any or all of these senses to convey an image. That is what an image is: something that conveys meaning through the senses. And film, well it's all about the visual. As writers we have to tell our stories through visual images and what characters say. Sight and sound. These are basic tools for building a screenplay. You're going to establish what the viewer will see and hear on the screen.

But a good filmmaker can certainly convey tactile sense; we feel this strongly in the tumbling soft rose petals in *American Beauty*. And with fine writing and cinematography the audience can even instinctively sense smell; most everyone in the audience cringes, and a kind of wince moves across the face when in *Slumdog Millionaire*, Jamal jumps in and goes under in that pool of excrement under the public outhouse.

But we're just starting out here, so let's use visuals and dialogue to bring a character alive on a page. Begin with the following writing prompts and fill in the empty spaces to see what characters you can bring alive. Then we'll see which ones you might want to develop and build a story around for your screenplay.

Character Building Exercises

Profiling and Showing Your Character

This character development assignment comes in two parts. Part I involves filling out a list of qualities about your character—the list is provided below. Part II requires you to bring your character alive a bit by showing him or her in a very brief scene. No need to write this in screenwriting format. Write as you wish.

Part I

Create a background for your protagonist; these bits of info most likely won't appear in your story, but they will be in your head as you write and will help assure that your character is helping you plot. Remember, plot grows out of characters as much as it happens to them. Provide the following details about your character:

Name:

Sex:

Age:

Looks:

Education:

Vocation/Occupation:

Marital Status:

Family/Ethnicity:

Diction (particular expressions/ways of talking):

Relationships:

Recreation/Hobbies:

Obsessions:

Beliefs:

Politics:

Sexual History:

Ambitions:

Religion:

Superstitions:

Fears:

Character Flaws:

Character Strengths:

Pets:

Taste in Books, Music, etc.:

Food Preferences:

Talents:

Nervous Habit:

Secrets:

Takes Pride in:

Part II

Now briefly bring your character alive. Write a one paragraph description of your character, using as much of the following as possible. This is called direct method characterization, in that you SHOW your character directly though:

Appearance

Speech

Action (a gesture as simple as scratching one's head will do)

Thought (you may allow yourself a little voice over, but be careful not to use this to have the character explain himself or herself—unless irony is at play.)

Reading between the Lines by Seeing the Unsaid Thing

In these exercises, consider how what we want shapes what we do. And what we do tells who we are. So consider motives and depict expressions of motives below. Feel free to change the gender for each prompt as you wish.

1. With the right make-up she could pass for eighteen, but you knew she was still a kid when

2. When I introduced my mom to my professor at the coffee bar, I could see she was up to her old tricks by the way

3. He said it was over between them, but it was clear it wasn't by the way he

4. She said she thought the older men who hit on her where she worked were pathetic, but you could tell she got pleasure out of it by the way she

5. He said he loved being promoted in the firm, that he'd do great things for it, but you could see the firm was the last thing on his mind by the way he

6. I could tell he was using again, maybe not at the moment, but I could see he was using again by

By Their Stuff You Shall Know Them

This exercise encourages you to use the personal living space of a character as a means for developing and delivering his or her personality. Before doing this exercise, walk into your bedroom, or a private room of someone you who won't mind you looking around. Do this alone, so you have no distractions. Stand there and look around while thinking like a camera. Is the bed made or a mess? What's on the floor? The desk? What's on the walls? What's hanging from the backs of chairs, doorknobs. Pretend you're a detective for a moment and draw conclusions about the personality who resides in that room.

If you'll do this carefully, you'll note that to a large degree we are the things we keep around us. Much can be concluded about a personality through the way that person keeps his or her private spaces. Train your eye to pay attention to any person's room—don't' snoop—just look at what is there. Medicine bottles carefully arranged on an end table say quite a bit about a character. Bottles of vitamins and supplements say something else. A dirty looking bong, and a little stash of weed, and a row of beer bottles all add up to a very different character. Got the idea?

Now create a setting for one of the following character types—or draw on the protagonist you would like the write about in your script. Furnish a place that reflects his or her character. The place can be any kind of local—a house, a specific room, an office, even a bed or a car. The description must incorporate enough characteristic things so that the reader can visualize the absent dweller accurately. If you share this exercise with readers, don't say which character you are describing. Your readers should be able to know the type by what you put on the page.

A wannabe rock star
A high school senior about to flunk out
A college grad going nowhere
A goth kid smarter than people think
A paranoid person
A man or a woman in a mid-life crisis
An old person who is patiently waiting for the big transition

Or make a type up and let us guess.

Before doing this exercise, so have a look at the following student example that demonstrates the personal spaces of a college grad going nowhere.

Student Example of *By Their Stuff, You Shall Know Them* by John Vigorito, College Grad Going Nowhere Fast

```
INT. BEDROOM - DAY
```

Early morning sunlight floods dingy window. On a futon is a tangled pair of khaki pants tossed across pillows, pizza box with one remaining slice, and a stack of magazines.

Clock on bookshelf next to window reads 7:29. On the book shelf: old video tapes, notebooks full of papers, a few comic biography books, and a paper Steak-N-Shake hat.

Near the trashcan, fallen Blake Littlefield's framed university diploma, a bachelor's degree in business, crookedly sits on the floor.

Movie posters, *Dazed and Confused*, *Clerks* and *Scarface* tacked on the wall.

TV stand next to bookshelf has flat screen TV on it with two rows of shot glasses from various states and beaches lined up in front.

A snowboard in the corner of the room.

A DVD rack full of comedy and action movies stands next to the TV.

A hat rack full of hats from various retail stores, restaurants and fast-food places.

On the desk next to DVD rack is a laptop, a few beat-up pocket notebooks, and scattered small scraps of papers with notes written on them.

```
INSERT: NOTE TAPED TO LAPTOP SCREEN
```

Bills

Electric: Steve owes $38
Gas: I owe Steve $42
Cable: Steve owes $26

Total: Steve owes ME $18

"awesome!"

BACK TO SCENE:

Behind the desk on the wall is a corkboard filled with
retail nametags. The name reads Blake—a few have
nicknames.

A chair with a dirty restaurant apron thrown across it.

On the desk is "Corndog Carnival" calendar with random
dates marked.

The alarm clock RINGS, reads 7:30.

                                              CUT TO:

EXT. CAR - CONTINUOUS

The sound of the RINGING alarm has turned into a JINGLING
cell phone alarm.

BLAKE, a mid-twenties guy stirs in the driver's seat of a
messy car littered with empty fast food bags, wrappers
cups and rental DVD cases.

Blake awakens with a jolt. He struggles to get his cell
phone out of jeans pocket and turns off the JINGLING
alarm. He moves in the seat and hears the CRINKLING of
paper. He reaches underneath himself and pulls out a half-
eaten taco in a wrapper that he tosses out the window.

Blake gets out of the car parked half in the driveway,
half in the yard of a cheap duplex. He stretches, looks
around then pulls out a cigarette and lights it.

                                              CUT TO:

INT. KITCHEN - DAY

Blake pours a glass of water from a water filtration
pitcher and puts the pitcher back into the refrigerator.
Shakes four Tylenol poured from a bottle into his hand,
pops the pills and CHUGS the glass of water.

                                              CUT TO:

INT. BATHROOM - DAY

Blake stands in front of a mirror in a beater. He brushes
his teeth, washes his face and then fixes his hair a
little bit.

                                                CUT TO:

INT. BEDROOM - DAY

Blake, in a beater, boxers and socks, rummages through
laundry overflowing from a double closet with no doors. He
pulls out a pair of black pants, slides them on.

He grabs a pack of cigarettes off of the desk, takes one
out and puts it behind his ear while tossing the pack back
on the desk.

He sits on the futon. The clock reads 7:49. He reaches
under the futon and pulls out a small multicolored bong.

He lights the bong and takes a long RIP. As he EXHALES he
sinks back into the futon as the clocks changes to 7:50.

He takes the cigarette from his ear and lights it.

                                                CUT TO:

INT. KITCHEN - DAY

Microwave BEEPS as Blake walks in now wearing a yellow
polo with a nametag and yellow hat.

He opens the microwave and pulls out a hot breakfast
burrito. He tosses the burrito on the counter because of
its heat and shakes his hand.

He pours more water from the filtration pitcher. Shakes a
giant vitamin from super-size bottle into his palm. He
pops the pill in his mouth and drinks some water.

He grabs the burrito and walks out with the burrito and
glass of water.

Microwave clock reads 7:59.

The Truth behind Closed Doors

This sounds more sinister than it is, but you can go sinister if you like. For this exercise you get to be a snoop, or if you're one of those truly polite people out there, pretend to be a snoop. There are many closed doors/drawers in even the most mundane of lives. And you can tell much about a person by what is not in open view. Go visit someone's refrigerator, a medicine cabinet, a junk drawer, and see what I mean.

Now pick one of the options below, list the things there, and let us take a guess at the personality of that person. Just fill in the blanks. And again, play with the gender of the prompts as you wish.

1. Okay, it was our third date, so it didn't seem too bold to have a look inside (pick one)

   a. the refrigerator
   b. the medicine cabinet
   c. the junk drawer in the kitchen
   d. the glove compartment
   e. the wooden box on the desk

   but I learned a few things from what I found there:

2. After my grandmother (or grandfather) passed, my mother made me be the one to go up in the attic and sort through what should be saved and what should be thrown away. I didn't want to, but I did it. But I slowly gained quite an education about family when I found:

and then there was the puzzling thing that will always leave me wondering, like:

A Mass of Contradictions

Think of those you know, maybe even of yourself. Yes we are for the most part a mass of contradictions. Sometimes shy, sometimes bold, sometimes generous, sometimes selfish, sometimes proud, sometimes shamed. And in spite of all these inconstancies, there are some things constant about us. Think of a character you'd like to write about. It may be someone you know, or perhaps someone you'd never like to know. It may even be based on yourself. In this two-part exercise, you'll first explore the unwavering aspects of a character. Then you'll play with the contradictions. Fill in the blanks with the name and gender you wish, and see what you discover about this character on your mind.

In spite of all many mysteries of _name_____, he/she could be

completely predictable in some ways. _____ never went anywhere

without_____. In his/her refrigerator there

was always, and at his/her bedside, there was always _____.

He/she couldn't help but cry a little at the sight of_____.

And if you wanted to get a laugh out of him/her, all you needed was

_____. He/she had a steady faith in _____.

And he/she was somewhat superstitious. _____felt that he/she was

where _he/she____ was in life because in a past life he/she was

_____. And he/she imagined that if he/she could do it

all over again, in a future life he/she would be_____

_____.

Now for part two. Explore the contradictions of your character.

(For simplicity, I'm using the pronoun "she" below, but just scratch out the "s" and write in "him" in place of "her" when necessary if you are writing about a male character.)

You could never be certain about the values of _____.

Routinely and without question she would give _____

to a homeless person.

Then with her own (pick relative or loved one) _____ he/she would

_____.

When it came to honesty you could count on her absolutely in regard   to

_____, when it came to _____.

As for intelligence, she was brilliant when it came to_____,

and a total fool when it came to _____.

She was quite the romantic in terms of_____,

but her cynical streak came out when _____.

In short, she was a whirling mass of contractions given her weaknesses for _____

_____ ,

and when it came to _____,

she was steady as a redwood.

Illustrating the Abstract Qualities of Your Character

Often when we first imagine a character and start to explain to someone what he or she is like, we begin with an abstraction. We say things like he's funny; she's vain; he's greedy; she's a do-gooder; he's ambitious; she's shy. But that is only a starting point. If you say an abstraction about someone, any attentive listener will want to know more, and by more, I mean details. If you want to tell a story and engage your reader, you need more of that general summary of a character or situation. You need scenes. And what makes scenes? Stuff. Actions, objects, sounds, speech. Scenes hold our attention with concrete things our minds and hearts can connect with, hang on to, experience. What's an image? An image can be created from just about anything that we comprehend through the senses—that is something we can see, hear, feel, smell, touch, taste. Images are the things our minds latch on to; they keep us engaged, make us experience what the writer wants us to experience through the characters or the setting.

When writing fiction, the writer can appeal to any of the five senses to evoke emotion by writing fine descriptive prose; smells and textures and internal feelings can be clearly described and thus made experiential for the reader. But in screenwriting, you'll be relying on visual images and sounds—sounds can include dialogue of course; they can also be sound effects. You'll be limited in the ways you can evoke or show feeling. Of course you can show someone sniffing a pot of chicken soup to convey the feeling of comfort; you can show someone sinking into a big down comforter and wrapping themselves in it to show sensual pleasure in relaxation; but note, those images that appeal to smell and tactile pleasure are SHOWN.

The following exercise is designed to help you conceive concrete images that will express an abstraction. Select from the list of abstract concepts below—or make up your own abstraction. Then make a list of things that will evoke that abstraction. Your list most likely will be more than a word or two. Allow yourself to write a bit of action or setting that illustrates an abstract concept. Your list will be a list of moments, maybe even mini-scenes. Good. With a mini-scene you are closer to writing a script. When you do this exercise at first, no doubt, clichés will come to mind. For example when we think of love, it's easy to think of hearts and flowers, kisses, hugs. But try to go further. Be original. The man who reaches and lifts a lock of hair from his girlfriend's face while she is busy chopping carrots at the counter shows an intimate act of concern, love. It's a simple, helpful, intimate gesture. When you're writing your list of concrete images that illustrate abstractions, allow yourself a few clichés to get warmed up, go ahead and write them, then get fresh and particular. Bring your list of images to class, and let us guess what abstraction you are aiming to evoke.

Abstractions Made Concrete

Select one or two abstract concepts that intrigue you; then make the abstractions experiential by writing moments that employ concrete images we can see and hear.

Lust	Envy
Risk	Nervousness
Old Age	Confidence
Poverty	Brutality
Wealth	Insecurity
Happiness	Loneliness
Innocence	Annoyance
Indifference	Boredom
Grief	Excitement
Deception	Temptation
Vanity	Arrogance
Weakness	Fear

Now here, sketch out a scene that would illustrate one of these abstractions at work. Then have a look at the student example that follows by Anthony Lopez. It's a scene that very effectively uses images and actions to evoke a haunting emotional experience that hums off the page through just what is shown. Although you don't have to write this exercise in screenplay format, it's a good idea to get a sense of how screenplays are formatted and how they read.

Student Example of an Abstraction Made Concrete
by Anthony Lopez

FADE IN:

EXT. CABIN - NIGHT

Alaskan woods, present day. Snowing.

INT. CABIN DINING ROOM - NIGHT

Cabin seems well-kept, very open and spacious. No
photographs anywhere, etc. Very basic.

LEE, late 30's, stocky, grizzly. He's drinking coffee from
a glass and eating toast.

Lee pours some Wild Turkey whiskey in his coffee, then
takes a swig straight and continues eating toast. He
doesn't look at his food, but watches the clock.

Clock 4:21 turns to 4:22

Lee pulls out photograph from wallet, hesitates to look at
it. Eventually decides not to and places it back in
wallet.

He takes a deep breath and SIGHS.

Finishes eating breakfast and collects his dishes then
moves onto the kitchen.

INT. KITCHEN - NIGHT

Lee does the dishes very thoroughly and puts them away. He
has only one item of every utensil, one plate, one bowl,
one glass, and a roughly hand-made pink coffee mug way in
the back of the cabinet that says "Best Dad Ever."

INT. CABIN BEDROOM - NIGHT

Lee sweeps/dusts his room though it doesn't really need
it. He has a single neat bed, a dresser and a TV.

He walks into the second bedroom.

INT. GUEST BEDROOM - NIGHT

A nondescript bedroom: single bed, a dresser. A closet
door stands open, showing a few empty hangers. Lee stands
in the doorway, takes in the room, SIGHS, turns away.

INT. BATHROOM - NIGHT

Lee looks at himself in the mirror. He messes with his
beard for a moment and then walks out.

INT. CABIN FIRST FLOOR KITCHEN - NIGHT

Lee grabs a custom-crafted dog bowl, and fills it up with
gourmet dog food.

He WHISTLES, and a little TERRIER enters. The dog looks
remarkably well-groomed. She has on a pink collar with a
heart-shaped dog tag. He crouches and plays with the dog.

                    LEE
          Just you and me, girl. Another day.
          Another night.

He smiles for the first time.

His eyes fall on the entrance to the basement. The door is
missing and there is only darkness. The smile leaves his
face as he stands up.

EXT. ALASKAN WOODS - NIGHT

A WOLF sits next to a tree. The snow has built up on his
fur. He seems to be staring at something.

A DEER dusted in snow stands at another part of the woods
and watches something.

Both deer and wolf watch a RABBIT chewing at its foot
caught in a trap.

A crisp sliver of moon shines above the tree-line.

```
INT. CABIN KITCHEN - NIGHT

Lee is still staring at the entrance to the basement. He
walks forward and stands in the doorway.

He lifts his foot, but hesitates for a moment. Then he
lets his boot drop to the first stair with a THUD that
echoes. He goes to lift his other foot but stops and
pauses for another moment. Then he lifts his foot from the
first step and turns back to the kitchen. He picks up the
dog and heads into the living room.
```

I admire this piece for the quiet, lovely writing and the freshness. The writer is conveying loneliness, no doubt. He also implies grief with that looming basement where something awful seems to have happened. The coffee cup, the empty bedroom suggest a child was lost. I also admire the way the writer chose to lift out of the domestic scene and put in a context of nature. It's a lovely shot of nature, but also ugly and violent. The domestic world is controlled and has its tenderness between the man and his dog. But it's all threatened somehow, by the lack of other people in those rooms. And that cold cut to the darkness and indifference of nature outside.

This little piece intrigues with a promise of the story beyond what we read on the page.

4. Conflict

> The cat sat on the mat' is not the beginning of a story,
> but 'The cat sat on the dog's mat' is.
> John Le Carre

The little scenario of the rebellious cat illustrates what story is all about. If not trouble, stories are fueled by potential trouble, instability. We are hooked into stories by the promise that something interesting can happen. And what makes something interesting? Change. The change may be as cataclysmic as an earthquake or as simple as a hamster that escapes his cage and thus creates small chaos in a suburban home.

Stories are fueled by trouble. You've heard them since you were a wee tyke. "The Little Engine That Could" wouldn't be a story without that big mountain as a challenge. Hansel and Gretel would be just two kids on a stroll without the cruel stepmother abandoning them and the threat of the carnivorous witch. Consider those idyllic worlds of functional families seen in *The Brady Bunch*, *Leave It to Beaver*, *The Cosby Show*. The plots of those 24-minute stories hinge on some kind of trouble. In one episode, "the Beaver" is implicated when his buddy lifts some change from his mother's purse; this action leads to doubt, trouble, but no big drama when it turns out that "the Beav'" is innocent after all. The moral dilemmas can be small, but do provide opportunity for tension, growth and change. So if you want to write a story, your best bet is to consider a problem. And remember, problems have their sources in a variety of places, ranging from deep within our hearts and minds to out there in the world on a battlefield.

Even those one-minute stories often shown in commercials find time to tell of conflict. For example, in a battery commercial, a grandson is whipping his granddad at a Game Boy—they are locked in battle, and the kid gets bored with easy successes until the boy's battery dies and the grandpa—with the stronger battery of course—wins. You've seen the mini-narratives: a frantic woman with tree roots growing in her sewer line is rescued by the Roto-Rooter man. A wife passes off a low-fat food product as butter to her oblivious husband. Another husband's obsessive devotion to his car threatens domestic harmony. Many products try to sell themselves by selling you on the idea that somebody—like you—wants something. That something might be sweeter breath or a secure retirement fund. The narrative makes the viewer believe that the desired something is out of reach, or perhaps its security is compromised. Such "dangers" and desires engage the viewer—and often the viewer's wallet. Compromise something, threaten to withhold or take something, offer something, and not only do you have a viewer's attention, but you also have a story about to unfold.

Before starting your script, try to reduce your idea to a simple story line—state what the conflict—what the problem is—and in just a few words set up what happens as a result of that problem. Even though you most likely aren't starting out with a feature-length script, have a look at the jackets on DVDs at your video store for examples of how complex stories can be reduced to log-lines, simple statements of the plot. Note how a storyline is reduced to a little hook that entices the viewer to want to see more. That hook most often involves a problem, or at least a problematic situation.

Before trying out the exercises offered in this chapter, consider the various realms where conflict can arise and play out. Conflict can occur in an internal landscape of your character's heart and mind, and it can occur externally in the realm of other people, institutions and events. Conflict can also occur in a spiritual, or if you prefer, an existential, space for your character. Most likely your conflict will play out in at least two of these realms. Internal conflict cannot be understood on the screen without external expression in the form of action and dialogue. And external conflict is more engaging if something internal or emotional is at stake for your character. Even Spiderman has an internal plot going on as he works externally to fight evil.

Whether you plan to write a script based on an internal conflict, or an external conflict, or if you plan the ambitious task of interweaving internal and external conflicts, it's a good idea to consider the various places conflict can start. Then try exploring how various domains of conflict can dramatically intersect.

Internal Conflict

Internal conflict draws on emotional and/or psychological tension. Two impulses press against one another, creating tension that is a kind of fuel that drives the character and the story. The conflict can be quite simple. Your character may want that big piece of chocolate cake on the plate and may also want to resist it; or your character may want a drink and want to resist it. Or other characters' interests might be at stake—your character may want to have an affair and yet want to resist it. Your conflict may also be a struggle to develop or recover a mental discipline or skill. In *Billy Elliot,* a boy who is expected to work in the coal-mine wants to be a ballet dancer. In *October Sky*, a group of Appalachian boys, also expected to work in the mines, want to build rockets. These internal desires quickly create a plot and action as other characters provide obstacles. The internal conflict quickly finds an external playing field. Another opportunity for conflict could be a situation where your character is suffering from a loss and wants to recover from that loss. The loss might be the disappointment or betrayal of a loved one, or perhaps the death of a loved one. Or your character may be trying to recover from lost pride, a lost skill, and a lost job. But the struggle with loss doesn't have to be a heavy conflict. The television series, *Seinfield*, offers many comic situations where one of the characters is trying to recover a lost object or a moment of lost dignity. In the comic Australian film *Strictly Ballroom*, the mother of a young man who wants to "dance his own steps" comically struggles to " keep on her happy face" while being driven to distraction by her son's rebellion. She struggles for poise when all about her, her hair, her make-up, her gestures, and her manner are comically deranged.

When a character's will collides with an obstacle that occurs WITHIN, as when duty collides with fear, love with guilt, ambition with conscience, and so on, you have inner conflict. Characters, just as real people do, often vacillate. Wracked by indecision, they have guilt pangs, fears, misgivings, doubts, second thoughts. In *Casablanca*, Rick certainly wrestles with his desire to reclaim his long lost love, Ilsa. And the plot soon reveals that he could have her. She loves him; she wants to leave her heroic husband and stay in Casablanca with Rick. But she also deeply admires her husband, doesn't want to hurt him. But she does want Rick. Caught between desire and duty, she tells Rick to make the decision for them. And he does. He overrides his personal desires and puts Ilsa on a plane with her husband because it is the right thing to do on a grander scale of human responsibility. And he risks his own life in the process. For a man who says he will "stick his neck out for nobody," he makes a terrific sacrifice. And as a result, *Casablanca* tells one of the greatest love stories in film while avoiding all romantic plot clichés.

Look closely at the protagonist of just about any movie, and you'll find inner conflict.   Even Bart Simpson has his moments of inner struggle—albeit they are very brief. Inner conflicts not only make characters interesting, but truly memorable. The viewer identifies with a character's inner conflict. Consider *The Matrix*, a futuristic fantasy of good versus evil. What hooks us, aside from the great special effects, is the story of Neo (Keanu Reeves), a man who is charged with the mission of liberating humanity from the matrix, a virtual reality system designed to enslave and destroy the human race. The external situation might be fantastic, but the emotional story of a man in danger of losing all he knows and loves—we can all relate to that. If your characters have no inner conflicts, your work will be a melodrama. Or something like a cartoon. Inner conflict confirms that the characters are involved, that something is at risk for them. As a result, the viewer identifies with that risk and so wants to see the actions unfold that lead to some resolution of the problem.

There are many avenues for internal conflict. The conflict may be as simple as a character trying to repress some urge. Or the conflict may stem from a larger, more abstract domain. For example, your conflict may concern a character who questions the nature or existence of God. In *The Green Mile*, prison guard Paul Edgecomb (Tom Hanks) is plunged into such a conflict when he meets a new prisoner on death row. The man, sentenced to death for murdering two girls, starts demonstrating his powers to heal. This incongruity of a murderer performing miracles upsets Paul's notions of God, good and evil, crime and punishment. Paul's world is transformed and he has to question his role in a newly mysterious world where justice eludes even those with the best intentions.

Or your character's conflict may be a philosophical quest for truth. This is tricky ground, and if you want to avoid preaching you'd be better off grounding your philosophical quest with a concrete problem. In *The Truman Show,* when Truman (Jim Carrey) sets out on a quest to know whether his life is of his own making or is driven by someone else's plan, the journey is sparked by his observation of the constancy of predictable events in his life. The old existential question of "is my life authentic" is a practical question in Truman's world, where his life indeed is media-manufactured project.

American Beauty, similarly, explores the existential question when Kevin Spacey's character, Lester Burnham, realizes that the reality of his life is in conflict with his notions of what he wanted his life to be—a life of genuine emotions, relationships, a life that externally expressed his internal needs. Lester struggles against his attraction to his daughter's high-school friend. The struggle with lust is intertwined with larger conflicts as Lester realizes there are more complex problems with how he lives. His life suddenly seems inauthentic—his actions, appearances, possessions are false indicators of who he is—or who he would like to be. The plot then runs on the story of Lester's existential mid-life crisis and his attempts to make each day an authentic manifestation of who he is.

Some might refer to his problem as a spiritual one—he feels suddenly empty, isolated, without purpose or hope. And some characters in this situation might find religion as a way of filling the emptiness. But Lester, like Truman, finds action. Both Truman and Lester are faced with giving up lives they've become accustomed to, but lives that have been imposed upon them by external circumstances. Their actions lead to a kind of death of old ways of being, but in exchange they lay claim to lives that are authentic to their needs, and thus they grow.

Such internal spiritual or existential conflict can lead to great stories, particularly when these internal conflicts find outward expression in social and political arenas. Internal conflict alone won't go far in a script. Unlike in fiction, where the narrator can dwell inside the head of a character, in film you generally have to show external signs of the internal struggle. In film often voice over is used to convey the inner struggles of a character, but voice over can go flat fast in a script and should be used judiciously.

As the fictionalized screenwriting teacher and author of *Story*, Robert McKee, says in the film *Adaptation*, voice over is death to the script. It's a comic line in the film, given that Charles Kaufman, the writer/director of *Adaptation*, uses voice over with great humor and irony throughout the script. The film opens with a black screen and the voice over of the fictionalized "Charles Kaufman" berating himself for his flaws as a man and as a writer. The voice over establishes the conflict driving the character and the plot. In the film, the character Charles has writer's block. Two forces are at odds within. In part, he has lost faith in his skills as a writer and in his appeal as a man. His self-critical impulses are in conflict with his impulse to recover his skills, his drive, and his belief that he can pull off his next project.

But if talking to himself were all he did, we wouldn't have much of a film. Few of us want to sit and listen to someone talk about their identity crisis—we go to movies to see the personal crisis play out. We wouldn't want to sit and listen to Charles Kaufman talk for long about his writer's block any more than we'd want to hear a cop agonize over the compromises he has to make on the job. We'd want to see it; we'd want to see Charles dramatize his conflict in the external realm of dialogue and action. And this discomfort is quickly shown in the scene where Charles sweats miserably with insecurities while trying to have a professional conversation with his agent.

External Conflict

Since internal conflict can't go far in a film without external expression, let's get on to considering the many ways external conflict can play out. External conflict often involves an outward expression of inner conflict. For example, if your character is trying to resist some urge or temptation, we have to see a concrete example of what tempts: the friends happily smoking or drinking, the forbidden love/lust interest. We will need to see an object or a person that illustrates the internal conflict by externalizing it. External conflict can also be seen in a challenge or problem offered to the protagonist that comes from external sources—from an authority, an institution, or a situation such as governmental upheaval or a natural disaster.

If an internal conflict is the fuel driving your story, consider how you might use external events to make that conflict accessible and experiential for your viewer. There are various playing fields for external conflict to be dramatized. External venues for conflict can be in the area of interpersonal relationships, areas of social convention or institutional rules. External conflict can also play out in more political or governmental arenas where one person's actions can save a life, affect a community or even change a world, as seen in films like *Life is Beautiful*, *Schindler's List* and *Gandhi*. When your get down to writing your script, you'll probably find that the conflict doesn't stay in one area; it transforms and becomes interwoven throughout the thoughts and actions of your characters. But for now let's consider the various playing fields for trouble.

Interpersonal Conflict

Interpersonal Conflict engages your character in conflict with others. Let's look again at *Adaptation*. Charles' inner conflict manifests in his relationships, as demonstrated in his conflict with his twin brother, a novice at screenwriting who finds the process both easy and pleasurable. Because of his writer's block, Charles is irritated and then threatened by the writing interests and successes of his brother. His inner conflict also destroys his love life. We see this development when Charles opts to go home and wrestle with his writing instead of kissing the woman who loves him. He repeatedly makes choices to focus on his writing problem rather than on a loving relationship, and the added stress of loneliness heightens his internal conflict. The external conflicts with those dear to him further fuel his self-doubt, and low self-esteem grows just at a time when Charles is under pressure to produce.

The interpersonal conflicts grow more complicated as Charles' insecurities complicate relationships with everyone he encounters until finally, in the last minutes of the film, the action escalates to a deliberately absurd level of conflict that is a comment on formulaic Hollywood plots. The personal struggle of Charles, the character, segues into a somewhat melodramatic conflict involving subterfuge, guns, and drugs, the kind of fast-paced action seen in Hollywood thrillers. The actual writer/director, Charles Kaufman, takes irreverent liberties with his script, deliberately pushing conventions to the absurd. What results is a wildly fresh narrative on the process of adaptation and translation—when an internal conflict is translated into external action, just about anything can happen.

In watching this film, you might notice how external conflicts are fueled by an inner conflict that leads to more external conflict, which then contributes to more inner conflict. And so the field of conflict oscillates between the internal and external worlds. Art imitates life in this way. Our inner worlds shape how we get through our day, and the external events of our world contribute to the state of our inner world.

Another example of this oscillation of internal/external conflict is seen in *As Good as It Gets*. Melvin Udall's (Jack Nicholson) conflict is primarily internal—he has an obsessive-compulsive disorder that creates havoc in an unpredictable world. His carefully devised system of survival quickly becomes upset when his waitress, Carol, (Helen Hunt) doesn't show up for work. Melvin is challenged to adapt to a situation he can't control. His trivial problems of not liking the neighbor's dog and not wanting an unpredictable breakfast lead to greater problems. The harassment of his neighbor inadvertently leads to his being forced to open his door and his life to his neighbor's needs. His insistence on the same waitress who always serves him breakfast, leads the control freak into the abyss of vulnerability—that place called love.

The plot unfolds simultaneously on internal and external planes. As his needs and behavior stir up external events, the events challenge him toward changes in his needs, as well as his behavior. Interpersonal conflict stems from a conflict between one character and another. Melvin wants Carol to change her actions to suit his needs, but in time she demands that he change his actions to suit her needs. He initiates his own journey toward change when he is forced to admit he needs another person, even if at the start she is only his waitress. But the journey occurs because others, his neighbor and his waitress, inspire, incite or demand some kind of change.

Many a fine story is set in motion when the protagonist is spun toward change by another character. Interpersonal conflict is often not only fueled, but can be sparked by another character. For example, in *Jerry McGuire*, Jerry's formerly complacent take on the world is rocked as his colleague informs him that he no longer has the power, the money and the prestige of the job he thought was secure. The external events force the once superficial Jerry to go in and make his inner journey toward learning to live from his heart instead of ambition. Enter the love interest. He loses his job, but gains a loyal woman—as well as a loyal friend. His interpersonal relationships teach him how to use the misfortune of losing a job as a way of gaining a conscience and a heart. As seen in *As Good as It Gets*, the protagonist is set on a path where the external world provides the relationships that provoke internal change.

Social/Institutional Conflict

Social/Institutional Conflict is usually related to both internal and interpersonal conflict. It involves an element of plot that overlays and fuels the more personal conflicts of your character. In the area of social conflict, your character finds himself or herself in conflict with a system or an institution. A classic institutional conflict film is *One Flew over the Cuckoo's Nest*, which tells the story of Randall McMurphy (Jack Nicholson), a man born to raise a ruckus, who is committed to a mental asylum. Given his love of fun and lack of respect for authority, he inspires his fellow inmates to rebel against the power-mad Nurse Fletcher. He wins the battle but ultimately loses the war against institutional rules. But his loss goes on to inspire the inmates to continue to rebel.

If you choose to write an institutional conflict story, you may be choose an abstract social institution instead of an actual building with barred windows and locked doors. For example, there's the high school institution, a place loaded with hierarchies of power and popularity. Films such as *Heathers*, *Clueless*, and *Welcome to the Doll House* all cleverly address the angst of high-school drama. Or may choose an institution that is a controlling and sinister opponent: the medium of television in *The Truman Show*, the giant utilities company in *Erin Brockovich*, the Nazi regime in *Schindler's List*, or the mind/world controllers in *The Matrix*. The antagonist in these movies is a clear and present force.

Many movies out there rely on social conflict for the plot. Such stories engage the viewer for many reasons. To begin, audiences love an underdog, the unlikely hero who is minding her own business until something arises that forces her to set her sights on a larger picture than day-to-day life. Many of us would like to think that the opportunity might come where we might stumble into doing something great, something to make the world a better place. The ambitions might be social, political or artistic. Erin Brokovich, while simply working to put food on her table, finds herself in a job where she can expose a corporate scandal that endangers a community. In the process of fighting for justice for her community, she evolves as a woman, grows in confidence, power and commitment to a world larger than her personal struggle for a paycheck. Often the social struggle fed by an inner struggle leads to a spiritual awakening. Once a person dramatically alters the course of daily life and sticks with it, profound change occurs. That change may be a process of growth toward greater life or a process of despair that leads to spiritual, if not physical, death.

Your plot may begin with a very simple desire and conflict that can lead to interpersonal, or political or spiritual change. In *Unforgiven*, William T. Munny

Munny (Clint Eastwood) needs cash to feed his family. So when an old gun-slinging friend shows up with a plan to shoot some bad guys for big cash, William has a life-altering choice to make. He goes. In an effort to save his family, he finds himself back in a way of life that he gave up in order to have a family. After trying to live by conventional standards, he once again finds himself breaking the rules by being a killer. But ironically by rebelling against the law (enforced by a corrupt sheriff) Munny finds a way to bring justice to a small town and finds a way to return to his children and give them conventional and stable lives. Michael (Al Pacino), in *The Godfather,* aims to be a good son and finds himself a ruthless killer. He can't avoid the social circumstance of being born to a mob family. His good intention of protecting his father results in him being a ruthless killer. Both Munny and Michael are deeply changed by choosing to break the law for a reasons they deem to be good reasons. If you know these movies, you can see how complicated life can be when we set out for a simple thing, and complexities abound.

Yes, much in our lives is quite trivial, forgettable, mundane, but to tell a good story, you might want to consider how mundane things can trigger magnificent events. We never know which day, which impulse, which random encounter with a stranger might change not only our notion of who we are, but also our relationship to this world. Which leads us back to inner conflict and how external events can profoundly challenge and change our interior worlds. In *Grand Torino,* a home owner (Clint Eastwood) simply out to protect his right to keep the local thugs off his lawn, finds himself embroiled in a battle no less deadly than the war he once survived in Viet Nam. He begrudgingly becomes the defender of neighbors he had formerly despised simply because of their race. Ultimately, the racist, disgruntled old man is transformed into something of a saint, only because he's out to defend what is right. The key factor in the plot is that his understanding of what is right is profoundly changed, and as a result, his motive, his action, and his identity are all changed.

Most feature-length movies have multiple layers of conflict and focus on a conflict that is interpersonal and social because these are the areas where conflict can be seen and heard. Think about it. How do we understand each other? It's very hard for us to get into the mind of a stranger, but we can deduce a lot by the way they interact with others, by where and how they define/express themselves in the social structure. It is by behavior that we know one another. As the cliché goes— actions speak louder than words.

As your characters work their internal conflicts out in the world of action, they will have many opportunities to prove something to themselves while dramatizing a story of change. Most stories can be distilled down to one of two kinds of change. There's the little growth story. And the little death story. American audiences tend to favor the little growth story, where a protagonist is challenged and ultimately prevails. The outer struggle, let's say against some evil, is often a catalyst for internal change. Consider detective John Book (Harrison Ford) in *Witness.* While trying to save the innocent Amish boy from being killed by corrupt cops, John has to wrestle a few inner demons. He has to learn he is vulnerable, that he sometimes has to rely on the help of strangers; this vulnerability manifests in the subplot of the illicit love story, which not only grabs the attention of the audience, but provides another layer of challenge and growth for the protagonist.

Many a good story stems from the conflict of a character trying to prove something to herself or himself, and external events both challenge and contribute to that process of self-discovery. In *Silence of the Lambs*, young FBI agent Clarice (Jodi Foster) seeks to define herself as a good woman, someone combating evil in the world. But her goodness is compromised when she comes to rely more on the help of Hannibal, the sociopathic killer, than on her crime-fighting colleagues. Hannibal, it seems, knows her better than anyone, and he reveals the insecurities behind her tough-woman façade. He also helps her to become the tough and competent agent she wants to be.

Clarice's conflict appears simple at the start—she has to get information from a bad guy in order to catch another bad guy. Her conflict is existential in that she wants to define herself as a good girl, a woman who struggles to combat evil in an unjust world that allowed the wrongful death of her father—as well as of all those lambs she once heard being slaughtered when she was a child. It seems that "good" people can do the "bad" act of killing innocent lambs. In turn, "bad" people like Hannibal can do good things like help Clarice do her job and find her strength.

In relying on Hannibal, Clarice finds herself on both sides of the line between good and evil, and the audience not only is engaged in the basic plotline of Clarice's effort to catch a serial killer, but also is drawn into the unlikely friendship between a cop and a cannibal. Relying on the help of a brilliant and charming killer, Clarice finds herself in a place of doubt as to just who she is. The script purposely blurs our notions of good guy/ bad guy by making Hannibal appealing and the doctor who cares for him despicable. All handbooks on how to combat evil, how to fight crime, are out. Clarice has to rely on her instincts, and a killer, in order to accomplish her goal. Conventional wisdom goes out the door when Hannibal becomes not only a greater aide to Clarice than her FBI boss, but at the end he becomes the only person in the script who is anything like a friend.

Clarice begins this movie running, alone. She is on her own in that FBI world. At the end of the movie, surrounded by her bureau colleagues, she is metaphorically alone again when Hannibal calls and offers the clue to his next victim. He is out there, but he is with her. At the end of the film the plot would seem resolved with the serial killer Clarice was after dead, and his intended victim rescued. But the movie hums like a dissonant chord at the end when Hannibal calls and connects with Clarice from a distance. It leaves us with a sense that all is not well in the end—the story and the sequel will go on.

Personal/Political/Philosophical Conflict

Maybe you're too young to remember that political slogan of the 70s, "personal is political," but you've certainly seen movies that embody this concept. Such movies fuse an inner spiritual/existential conflict with a political agenda. Gandhi's spiritual beliefs led to the liberation of a nation. Evita Peron's drive for self-preservation made her an unlikely and beloved leader of her country. Your character may have philosophical differences with a regime, as seen in *Life is Beautiful* or *Schindler's List*. Both films tell the story of how good men struggle to survive the nightmare world of Nazi expansion. Their conflicts begin internally but quickly become external as the men are forced into action. These men are in a political/social crisis that involves them risking their lives. They must wrestle with many inner demons as they work against the external ones.

Polanski's *The Pianist* takes the old story of good people struggling against bad Nazis and gives it a darker twist, where the protagonist is an anti-hero whose only dilemma boils down to how to save himself as he struggles in a world any sort of God seems to have abandoned. Based on a true story, the film tells the story of Wladyslaw Szpilman, a renowned concert pianist. His fame and status are suddenly of no consequence as Nazi forces invade Poland and begin killing Jews. The cultured man is reduced to an animal struggling to survive. Yes, he's an artist, educated, refined. He has all the conventions of a man shaped by his culture, but when his culture goes mad, all those acquisitions of culture are useless. Circumstances reduce him to a starved and filthy creature who clings to a can of pickles in the ruins of his world. Polanski takes the old story of good versus evil and implies the existential question of how a man is to be when he has no control over what he can be. Polanski's world has no heroes—there are no grand spiritual actions one aspires to—there is only survival. Our protagonist is no role model; he is a victim who just happened to get lucky and survive. Polanski offers no sentimental insights as to how we should be in a time of crisis, but instead shows what we are, animals in need of food and shelter, with the simple, primal desire to live another day.

Polanski's film takes a political situation of government-sanctioned genocide and raises an existential question of what it means, and what it takes, to be human in a world where humanity seems to have gone mad. Most likely you aren't ready to take on such an epic tale as how to survive a holocaust, or to take on broad philosophical ideas. You might find yourself preaching or "holding forth" too much, and viewer tend to what a story and not a sermon in their movies.

You can think on a smaller scale and still tell a rich story. There's many a fine story to be told based on the old "how-to-solve-a-problem" premise. When solving a simple problem, a character can often be forced to face complex and philosophical issues   I wouldn't advise setting out to write a script fueled by such broad abstractions as " what is the meaning of life," or " the purpose of humanity," or "who or what is God." But such questions can be subtly addressed through implications of actions and dialogue of your characters.

If you want to address such abstractions, start with a person who has a problem. *Children of Heaven* tells a powerful story of love, loyalty, endurance, responsibility, all those high-falutin' ideas, but the basic story is about what happens when a boy with good intentions loses his sister's only pair of shoes. Sounds trivial, but the story is a heroic tale of one kid's struggle to make up for one small oversight in his day. Little things can lead to big dramas.

Starting Small with Conflict

So let's get you started. The way to start is to think of a simple problem or desire that might propel a character toward action. Start small. And you can start small by steering your imagination away from feature-length films and considering the genre of short films. Here you'll find dramatic examples of small, concrete problems with vast ramifications. I would again urge you all to have a look at that collection of films titled *The Short Series*.

There's much to learn from studying short films before launching off to write a feature-length script. Let's consider again, the story line of that short film, *Joe* as it can teach you much about how a simple problem can bring a character alive on the screen. *Joe* is a low-budget, ten-minute film about a guy with a simple problem and very few options. Joe is in a mental hospital, and the only thing he can call his own, the only thing that gives him pride, are his carefully polished black shoes. He polishes them, slips them on, does a few proud steps, then walks his shoes down the hall to the TV room—where another patient promptly spills Maalox all over the shoes. What can Joe do? Yell and scream? Tell a nurse. Not much use in that. Punch the guy? Nope. That action most likely would get Joe heavily medicated or locked up. External events prompt an inner challenge, and Joe has to act. What does he do? He goes to Maalox man, and uses the Maalox to polish his shoes. White. Joe adapts—that's what one must do in a world fraught with accidents. Adapt or go crazy. Joe goes in and comes up with a solution for his problem. And at the end he looks quite happy with the change.

I should note here—this whole story is told without words. We see and hear the sound effects of the actions, and that is quite enough to tell the story. The "text" of images and sounds conveys the subtext of Joe's dilemma; we identify with him and share in his accomplishment, his change.

Another short to study for conflict on a larger, more social scale is found in the volume titled *Diversity*. Vin Diesel's *Multi-facial* offers a quick and insightful look at the subtle grip of racism in an actor's world. Vin Diesel wrote, directed and starred in this 25-minute film to tell his own story of being an actor who has trouble getting parts because producers can't get an easy fix on just what race he is. He can play a variety of ethnic types—Italian, Spanish, African American—but he never quite fits into a producer's notion of what works. We witness Vin Diesel play out several auditions, brilliant at all of them, but repeatedly he fails to get the part.

There is no resolution to this conflict, no solution to his problem; rather, there is insight offered through his monologue in an audition where he tells the story of his father's acting career and where is addresses the issue of race. The script doesn't preach. It informs us on the effects of racial bias, as we see the actor walking the streets, going from audition to audition, trying to be right for a part in a business where it seems he'll never be right for anything. This short did gain the attention of Steven Spielberg and led to Vin Diesel being cast in *Saving Private Ryan*. Both this film and *Joe* offer quick and tight illustrations of how a character with a problem can drive a story.

The exercises at the end of this chapter will serve as prompts to get you started by writing a little scene. Scenes are much like mini-stories in that something happens, something progresses in some small way. It's much less overwhelming to start by writing a scene rather than committing to a full story. Before moving on to the exercises, have a look at sample scene below. The scene tells a basic boy-wants-girl story, but in a particular way. And it accomplishes many things at once—it depicts characters and conflict, and it uses the text of dialogue, action, and description to evoke a subtext of what is going on within the characters. It illustrates how dialogue can work as action, and it also employs a thematic use of setting. You will be practicing your skill with all these elements that contribute to a scene. But for now, just have a look at the way a small scene using dialogue as action can work.

```
EXT.   FIELD IN MOUTAINOUS COUNTRYSIDE — DAY

BILLIE RUTH, good-looking teenaged girl in cut-off jeans,
skimpy t-shirt, stands barefoot and twirls a baton in a
field of Queen Ann's lace and purple thistle.  She works
with particular care given that one of her arms is in a
cast.

In near distance is a tar-papered shack, a beat-up Chevy
all but collapsed in a gravel drive.  Woods seem to be
growing toward the house as shadows lengthen under a
setting sun.

Billy Ruth marches in a circle, concentrating on the form
of her twirling and counting.  She pitches the baton high,
watches the gleaming silver, hears:

TRUCK RUMBLING, GRAVEL CRUNCHING on road leading up to her
field.

Billie Ruth turns. Baton falls, bounces on the ground.
```

Billie Ruth smiles and runs toward beat-up truck parked in
her dirt drive. TACK CALDWELL, handsome, tough, and cute
in a country-boy way, gives a cocky grin.

                    TACK
          Not bad for a cripple.

Billie Ruth leans into open window for a kiss. He gives
her a deeper, harder kiss than she might expect.

                    TACK
          Get in.

Billie Ruth looks into back of the truck, sees coils of
wire, cans, sheet metal scraps.

                    BILLIE RUTH
          What's this?

                    TACK
          Copper wire. Sheet metal. Good money in
          junk if you know what sells.

Tack reaches, gives her good arm a good squeeze.

                    TACK
          Bet I could get a quarter for that baton
          of yours.

                    BILLIE RUTH
          Worth more than that.

                    TACK
          I can get 'em a dime a dozen. I know where
          to look.

Billy Ruth throws baton. It sails, bounces, disappears in
the weeds.

                    BILLY RUTH
          Go get it if you want to.

                    TACK
          That ain't what I want.

Billy Ruth leans in closer to his face.

                    BILLIE RUTH
          Just what do you want, Tack Caldwell?
          Huh?

He reaches for her, but she jumps away. Walks into the
field to retrieve her baton.

                    TACK
          When you gonna grow up, Billie Ruth.

She walks back toward him, a sway to her hip, teasing
smile.

                    TACK
          Get in this truck, girl. I brought you
          something.

Billie Ruth runs around to the passenger's side, hops in
the truck.

INT. TRUCK — CONTINUOUS

Billie Ruth scootches closer to TACK, CRUNCHES paper
grocery bag between them. Tack takes bag in his lap,
pulls out a little glass-shaped jar of shrimp cocktail.

                    BILLIE RUTH
          Shrimp cocktail! You know I love these.

She gives him a kiss.

                    BILLIE RUTH
          I'm getting me a real nice collection of
          these little glasses back in my room.

Tack gives her a plastic spoon, watches her dig through
the red sauce, scoop up a tiny white shrimp, slide in it
her mouth.

Her pink lips glisten with red sauce. She licks her lips,
digs in for more. He shakes his head, reaches in bag,
pulls out a bottle of beer, twists it open, drinks.

                         122

                    BILLIE RUTH
          You ain't old enough to drink.

                        TACK
          Watch me.

He chugs half the beer down, gives her a big wet kiss.

Billie Ruth pulls away, wipes her mouth with the back of
her hand. Looks back at the shrimp cocktail glass.

                        TACK
          What you gonna do with all them little
          glasses you keep hid in your room?

Billy Ruth shrugs, looks back at her shack of a house.

                    BILLIE RUTH
          I don't know. Make a parfait.

                        TACK
          You don't even know what a parfait is.

                    BILLIE RUTH
          It's something you make with JELL-O.

She slides another spoonful of shrimp into her mouth.

Tack watches her chew, the little movement at her throat
when she swallows.

                        TACK
          When we gonna do it, Billie Ruth?

                    BILLIE RUTH
          What? Make a parfait?

He watches her dig out the last bit of shrimp in the
glass, grabs her arm and forces her to put the bite into
his mouth. He clamps down hard on the spoon, swallows and
smiles.

                         BILLIE RUTH

          Didn't your momma teach you no manners?

Tack pinches a little roll of flesh at the waistband of
her shorts.

                           TACK
          May I have a little bite of that, please?

                         BILLY RUTH
          I gotta get back in the house. Fix supper.
          Momma's drinking. You know how she gets when
          she's drinking.

                           TACK
          Yeah, she passes out in front of the TV.

Tack squeezes her crotch. She flinches.

                           TACK
          I want this. It ain't like you never done
          it before. I heard all about you and that
          Jenkins boy.

Hurt washes over Billy Ruth's face as she looks toward her
house.

Billie Ruth throws spoon in paper bag, considers tossing
in the glass, but holds on to it.

                         BILLY RUTH
          You don't know me. You don't know
          nothing about me.

Tack takes a firmer grip on her crotch and in a sudden
move is on top of her.

```
Billie Ruth jumps, drops shrimp cocktail glass out the
window where it CLINKS on the gravel.

                        TACK
          I don't want to have to fight you for it.

                     BILLY RUTH
          You don't have to fight me.  It's just--

He silences her with a hard deep kiss.

She struggles a bit.  Goes still, lets him kiss.

Tack pulls back looks at her blank face watching him.

                        TACK
          All right now.

He pushes her down in the seat, leans over her to kiss.

Billy Ruth SIGHS, closes her eyes and gives in as his hand
works at the zipper of her cut off jeans.

EXT. FIELD — DAY

Leaves shudder in the darkening trees as sun slips a
little lower beyond the mountains in the distance.  The
house seems to have receded into the growing darkness.
```

No doubt there is more to this story, but the scene depicts a dramatic and self-contained bit of drama in these characters' lives. A battle of wills rises, hits a crisis, a moment of surrender, and resolution.

There is much to note in how this scene is working in several ways simultaneously. First the issue of subtext. From the moment Tack pulls up we see his power. Billie Ruth drops her baton and runs to him. The dialogue suggests a playful power game between them. She is not totally weak—she can play the flirtation game. Her gestures and speech suggest that she likes him and wants his attention but also needs her own sense of control.

And note how dialogue reveals the personality of the characters. The way Tack speaks is confident, aggressive—as will be manifested later in his actions. Billie Ruth's dialogue indicates she is part child even as she is on the verge of being woman. She uses child-like flirtation in a very grownup game. Their power struggle will become physical.

Also note use of setting. The natural landscape of weeds and a barren field, along with the shack, indicates her isolation. The shack, which contains the unseen drunken mother, suggests Billie Ruth's emotional and physical poverty. We don't need to see the mother. Her physical absence speaks for her emotional absence. The woods and mountains in the distance reinforce Billie Ruth's isolation. In the huge natural setting, Billie Ruth seems small. The little scene works in itself, in that it tells a tiny story of a power struggle. But in reading the scene, we can see that a world of events proceeded this moment, and consequences will follow. The scene works and also provides source material for a larger story.

The following selection of exercises is devoted to getting your characters in motion by 130fueling them with conflict. Conflict can be a subtle thing, such as wanting the cigarette you know you shouldn't have. Conflict can be an emotional struggle, such as trying to get over and recover from a wrong done by a loved one. Or conflict can manifest externally in an argument or fight. Maybe some of you have a screenplay in mind that is fueled by an abstract idea; let's say you want to write about poverty, racism, self-destruction. Or on a happier note, maybe you want to write about love, spiritual presence in a material world, the innocence of children.

Do bear in mind though, your scripts can be fueled by ideas, but they run on the machinery of character and action. Try not to use your script as a platform for espousing your ideology—instead, bring ideas to life through characters, images, action. And you aren't going to have characters involved in action for long without some kind of conflict. It doesn't have to be big. Sure, it could be the conflict of surviving a war, a drought, a mean, possessive lover, or say, the conflict of saving a child from disease, ghosts, scary neighbors. But it can also be something more subtle, complex, or even crazy.

Not every moment in your script will be fueled by conflict. Of course you can establish your characters in a neutral state. In a simple scene, you can establish the context and the basic personality of your characters with setting, visual images, dialogue. But the character will spring to life only when he or she is put to the test, when he or she is forced to make a decision and ACT.

A character's response to obstacles, barriers, and conflict individualizes him or her, proves his or her characterization, and makes him or her real and distinct in a reader or viewer's mind. In order to get your character going, you do need good opposition, but this DOES NOT require a villain. The antagonist may be just as heroic as the protagonist. This does not mean villainous characters need to be ruled out—they have their place. The point is, they are not necessarily required for good opposition. What IS required for good opposition is well-motivated, rounded, non-stereotypical characters.

You may not know what's at stake as you write your script, but if you keep writing, your characters often tell you what's at stake. If you begin your project with well-conceived characters, often they take over and write the plot for you. Let them. In your first draft, anything goes that will keep you writing, keep the action and story moving forward. When you finish that draft, look at it. Ask what's at stake. What do the characters want? What are they willing to risk? How are they willing to change, or not?

Remember, whether you are writing a scene driven on internal or external conflict, you are using images to tell the story. Even an inner conflict needs external objects or events to give the problem substance, to help the viewer understand the inner conflict. Consider what your character wants and consider how you are going to show that an obstacle prevents the character from freely taking what is wanted. This strategy will help you develop character and get a sense of how external plot can grow from within a character. Once you begin your scene drawing on inner conflict, you'll quickly see that in film the line between internal conflict and the external dramatization of that conflict is, well, invisible. You have to show that inner conflict with stuff, people, events. For example, if a guy wants to resist smoking, you'll need to show the external temptation—others happily smoking, or free sample cigarettes that come in the mail. Consider the following suggestions for a character driven by internal conflict, and you will most likely find you are writing about an external manifestation of that conflict. Just remember, for these exercises the driving force of the scene is an inner desire.

Before, or if you prefer after, you've tackled some of these exercises, try having a look at some of the student examples offered at the end of the chapter for illustrations of how other students handled the exercises. Let those examples entertain, inspire, and challenge you.

Now have a look at the conflict exercises and aim for similar dramatic strategies in your own conflict scene. Try several. When thinking of an idea for your scene, you might do best to start with a small conflict. Yes, of course, many of you may have a feature-length script in mind and have already mapped the intricacies of your plot and subplot, but my guess is that most of you have a more immediate and small-scale project due. So think small for now. Don't burden yourself with attempting to write a fully worked-out script. Let yourself explore possibilities with a few scenes. Try out the exercises that follow as a way of flexing, finding your strength. Then, if you like, develop an exercise into a script and see where it leads.

Now get some characters fueled by desire and engaged in action. The following exercises can help you accomplish this. Pick a situation that intrigues you and write. Then read it. Read it out loud. If you like, have some friends read the parts. Watch them. Listen to them. Envision how your scene might work on the screen. Then rework it. Move on to another exercise and see what unfolds.

Conflict Exercises

Forbidden Fruit

This exercise is based on a simple desire. The desire stems from within and is expressed outwardly. Your character tries to accomplish something or tries to resist something. The struggle is fraught with temptation, resistance.

1. Write a scene where a character tries not to smoke or tries not to do a drug that is available.
2. Write a scene where luscious food is available and your character is under strict instruction not to partake.
3. Write a scene of sexual temptation.
4. Write a scene where a character finds a lost wallet or purse and struggles with temptation whether to pocket the cash or call the owner.
5. Write a scene where a strictly law-abiding character is tempted to break some minor law—such as running a red light at 2 a.m. when no one is around, or shooting a deer illegally; or if you wish, tempt your character with a more serious crime.
6. Retell the old Garden of Eden temptation—with a new twist.
7. Make up your own "forbidden fruit" and see how your character struggles to resist.

Mission Impossible

This exercise is inspired by an old and simple vaudeville routine where a clownish character is trying to shake loose a piece of tape stuck to his finger, and no matter what is attempted, the piece of tape manages to keep sticking—to another finger, to a piece of clothing, to some undesirable space. What results is a comic process of trying to solve the problem. Another classic illustration of a mission impossible is the assembly line out of control, where a character struggles to do a simple task on an assembly line, but the speed of the assembly line increases to a point where the character resorts to desperate measures.

Give your character a goal. Something must be accomplished, but what might be a simple task becomes impossible, forcing the character to desperate measures or perhaps even enlightenment regarding a way around the problem. Consider some of these problems and try writing the drama that might unfold.

1. The picture won't stay straight on the wall.
2. A mole continuously destroys a lovely lawn, thus driving the homeowner to an obsession.
3. A character tries to read a book on a bus while noisy strangers on ever-ringing cell phones abound.
4. A waiter or waitress tries to satisfy an impossibly demanding customer.
5. A professor tries to hold the attention of the class amid constant distractions.
6. Or you may draw on a problem in your own life and imagine the various comic or serious ways that problem can challenge. In the example below, a student chose to write about his pressing problem of trying to write a one-minute script. What results is a one-minute script.

Anything You Can Do, I Can Do Better

There's nothing like competition to bring out a conflict, and such conflicts can be told over a very short time frame and without words. Consider for example those commercials that tell a story of strangers competing to get ahead of each other's car on the highway—may the better engine win. And the better engine implies the owner of the engine is the better man. That's how products are sold; but that conflict is also how stories are told. Remember, how a how person competes reveals character—so use this. Reveal your characters through how they approach their competitors and, where relevant, the judge or audience. You might also note that you can load your competition with subtext—a hidden agenda. The competition itself may be a metaphor for an emotional or psychological competition—for example, two bartenders competing at demonstrating fancy bartending techniques may also be competing to demonstrate their manliness to a woman at the bar.

Here's a suggested list of venues for competition. Pick one or invent your own.

1. A competition for the attention of a guy or gal across the room
2. Competition at bowling, tennis, shuffleboard, foosball, darts
3. A debate to win over a crowd
4. Competition between siblings for parental approval

Remember, you can do just about anything you want here. The competition may be serious, or it may be a farce. The previously cited "Whack a Mole" script is a nice example of a farcical approach to this exercise.

That Obvious Object of Desire

For this exercise you need to bear in mind that just about every encounter between humans involves some sort of power dynamic at work. Our days are often a steady process of asserting, acquiescing, compromising. Whether we are negotiating lanes in traffic, requesting a raise, selecting a television program with our partner, or eyeing the last cookie on the plate, the question of who has the power comes into play. This exercise invites you to play with a power struggle between characters. We show who we truly are when we want something and someone is in the way. Our natures become pure once we are focused on an object of desire just out of reach. Write a scene where one character wants something that the other doesn't want to give. The idea is to convey character (personality) by how one requests, maybe demands, maybe tries to sneak access to the object.

Remember, ways of speaking, moving, or perhaps not speaking or moving, reveals the inner workings of character. Of course the object itself will do much to reflect who these characters are and what's at stake in their conflict. An argument over an ounce of cocaine will involve different characters, most likely, than an argument over the last can of Slim Fast in the fridge. Most likely. the moment you read the possible objects of conflict listed above, you visualized characters, scenes. A simple object can hint at the particulars of a life, as well as a world. Through your object and the struggle over that object, you want to convey as much of a world as possible.

Now pick an object. Pick your characters. Maybe a character is the object of desire Who are your characters? And why does the object matter? Your characters are particular. They have a past. Your scene, however, is concerned only with the present. But in the scene, we need to gain insight into where these characters have been and where they may go once this conflict is resolved.

You'll need to think about what the camera is seeing. When you write the first draft, most likely you'll have lots of dialogue and little action. Try to avoid the talking heads syndrome, where the camera shows one face talking, then the other, and then back again. Aim to have a bit more than just faces talking to each other. After you've written your first draft, look again. Is the scene visually interesting? What's in the scene? What little gestures are giving subtle insights into character?

It's a simple exercise, but it can be made rich, complex and challenging, if you're really interested. So pick a conflict you find intriguing, disturbing, amusing. Just make it real. Before you start, have a look at this clever example below. The scene illustrates how entertaining conflict can be.

Student Example of That Obvious Object of Desire
by Samuel Mentzer

```
INT. BAR - NIGHT
```

A semi-busy twenties-something place with pool tables and
a big round bar in the middle. Many neon signs, and the
room is somewhat smoky.

JET, a fit, clean cut young man, walks from group of
people playing pool towards the bar.

He steps up to the bar, leans on it, and glances to his
right side and then to his left.

Jet holds his gaze when he spots SHADOW, a young, buxom
woman with black and purple hair. She wears purple
lipstick and heavy black eyeliner, but is clearly
beautiful without it. She's dressed in all black, a low,
low cut sleeveless top and tight pants.

He licks his lips and shifts towards her, in one smooth
swoop he has moved past five bar stools to right next to
her.

> JET
>
> Guess what?

With her eyes closed, Shadow slowly turns her head to the
right and exhales a cigarette puff. She then opens her
eyes. She flicks her tongue off her teeth with a SMACK.

> SHADOW
> (flatly)
>
> What?

He flashes a white smile and speaks upbeat.

> JET
>
> We went to the same high school, Hilltower.
> Your name's Sidney. We had a few classes
> together. I'm Jet Berlin.

He sits next to her with a wide grin nodding his head,
waiting for her response.

She rotates her stool towards him. Her legs are crossed.
She looks down to the floor for a second, then back at
him.

                    SHADOW
          I don't remember you.

She turns back towards the bar and taps some ash off her
smoke. The neon lights reflect on the counter of the bar.
He breathes a LAUGH and smiles. He speaks in a reminding
tone, as if he is convincing her to remember.

                    JET
          I played halfback. I was homecoming king.

Shadow barely licks her lower lip. This motion turns into
her putting her front teeth over her bottom lip, slightly
biting down. She thinks for a split second, releases her
lip and turns her head towards him.

                    SHADOW
          I don't watch hockey.

She turns towards the bar and takes a sip from her mixed
drink.

Jet slightly jerks his head to one side and frowns. He
somewhat moves his head towards her as he responds.

                    JET
     Hmm?

One of the bartenders, DIMITRI, a swarthy good looking
young man, steps towards the two.

                    DIMITRI
          What can I getcha, bud?

Jet shakes his head and turns towards the bartender.

                    JET
          I'll have a rum and Coke. Get her
          another one of whatever she's drinkin'.
          Last name's Berlin, I'll be back in a
          second.

Dimitri nods. Jet gets up and heads to the bathroom.
Dimitri looks at Shadow, who is stirring the ice in her
drink with a straw.

                    DIMITRI
          Let me guess, you don't want that drink
          from him?

Shadow looks up from her glass at him. Shakes her head.

                    SHADOW
          Nope.

She looks back down at her drink. Dimitri speaks in an
uplifting manner.

                    DIMITRI
          Ya' know, you're really pretty. You
          should smile more. Enjoy your life.

Shadow looks back at him. He is smiling.

                    SHADOW
          I do enjoy my life.

                    DIMITRI
          Well you don't act like it. It seems
          like you're a little sad.

                    SHADOW
          Well, I'm not.

                    DIMITRI
Okay, so what do you do?

                    SHADOW
          None of your business.

He lets out a small laugh and smiles. She gives a quick,
pretend smile and takes another sip.

                    DIMITRI
          I'm Dimitri, what's your name?

                    SHADOW
          Shadow.

                    DIMITRI
        Really? That's cool. Very unique.

She slowly nods, opening her eyes a bit wider, and gives
another fake smile, this one held for a little longer.

                    DIMITRI
        Look, you've been sitting here alone for
        a long time. I'm not gonna lie, I find
        you very attractive. I was wondering if
        maybe I could buy your next drink?

He shoots her a grin and gives his head a quick tilt to
the side. She keeps her eyes on her cigarette.

                    DIMITRI
        C'mon, why not?

She puts her cigarette out and swallows. She speaks in a
somewhat annoyed voice.

                    SHADOW
            Sure, but don't think that you're getting
            in my pants. I don't date bartenders.

Dimitri cocks his head.

                    DIMITRI
        Well, isn't that rather closed minded?

                    SHADOW
        Does it matter? Not interested.

Dimitri rears back a bit. He composes himself and speaks
very calm, but matter of fact.
                    DIMITRI
            Fine. But ya' know, you just dress like
            that to get attention. You get attention,
            and you act like that? Whatever.

Shadow reveals a real smile. She stares at a bump on his
lip.

                    SHADOW
            Judging by the size of that thing on
            your lip, it looks like you've had too

much attention.

She winks and lets out a smooth, genuine LAUGH.
Dimitri stands up straight and CLEARS HIS THROAT with
dignity.

                    DIMITRI
          It's a zit. A pimple, okay. But thanks
          for noticing.

A drunk, middle-aged man speaks loud from a few stools
down.

                    DRUNK PATRON
          Hey, can I get two cement mixers and a
          dirty martini down here, Domingo?

Dimitri gives a false smile to Shadow then turns and walks
towards the customer.

Jet reappears and sits down on the barstool beside her.

                    JET
          Good thing I took my Flowmax.

He LAUGHS at his joke and then makes a puzzled face.

Shadow cocks her head and squints her eyes in disgust.

                    JET
          Where's my drink?

                    SHADOW
          Don't you think that comment's a bit
          pretentious?
                    JET
                    (louder)
          No, I'm not pretending. Where's my drink
          at?

Jet is looking at Dimitri who is near the opposite end of
the bar mixing drinks.

That Abstract Effort of Desire

This exercise is similar to the scene of conflict over an object, but the struggle is more complex, more subtle. This time, have one character want something abstract: love, respect, forgiveness, obedience, freedom, something we can't hold in our hands or lock in a safe. As in the previous exercise, the second character doesn't want to give in to the first's need or desire.

This exercise is similar to the previous one in that something important is at stake between the characters, and you are obliged to reveal the inner workings of the characters by what they do and say. Again, you'll most likely focus on the dialogue. But do remember to think in terms of actions. As this exercise is more complex and rich with psychological implications, you might push yourself to work with irony in this scene. Perhaps the resisting character could be saying "no," but he or she could be revealing the need/desire to give in through gestures, expressions, behavior out of sight of the opposing character.

In this scene you might find yourself committing to, identifying with, one character more than the other. That's fine. It's actually a good thing. If you identify, let's say, more with the young character than the older one, then most likely it's that character who will reveal mixed motives, complex emotions.

Try to think of this scene as "belonging" to one character or another. The scene "belongs" to the character most actively engaged in the drama, the one who has an insight, or makes a choice, or takes an action that results in change.

Conflict. Action. Change. This is the stuff of drama.

Now come up with a problem between characters that has to be struggled through, and maybe be resolved. Or not. Now this sounds like an assignment that may lead to serious drama, but it's also an opportunity to have a little fun, as exemplified in the student example below. It's a short complete script titled "Busker" by Vytas Nagisetty. I admire the way desire is shown and not told, and the way the desire changes as Busker changes. Music, rather than dialogue, will dominate the sound track, and given the fact that the music changes as Busker changes, we don't need any words to understand the plot unfolding here. Have a look.

BUSKER

By

Vytas Nagisetty

Vytas Nagisetty
1234 Music Row
Music City, NY
Phone:
Email:

FADE IN:

EXT. CITY SIDEWALK - DAY

Parked cars line the street in front of Bob's Bistro, a quaint restaurant in Downtown, USA. Sun moves toward setting in the distance. SOLO ACOUSTIC GUITAR underscores the scene. A sign in the restaurant window says HAPPY HOUR 4-7 P.M.

PEDESTRIANS pass by on the sidewalk. Some enter the Bistro. BUSKER, 30s, in ragged, unwashed attire, sits on a crate and plays the acoustic guitar about ten yards away from the entrance. His guitar case is open in front of him and contains some change and a few dollar bills.

BOB, 30s, steps out of the Bistro, walks down the sidewalk, and lights a cigarette. He wears a chef's jacket with a dish towel hung over his shoulder. He stays near the restaurant door, watching Busker from a distance.

A COUPLE approaches. They stop in front of Busker to listen. They stay for a moment, then smile at one another in approval and leave one dollar each in Busker's case. Busker nods a thank you at them with a smile. The couple leaves Busker, greets Bob, and enters the Bistro.

RICO parks his shiny car on the street near Busker and gets out. He looks fresh in the latest Sean Jean logo wear. He approaches Busker and stops in front of him, watching with a discerning grimace. Then he starts moving his head in time with the music, now grimacing even more. He snaps a Jackson out of his money clip and drops it in Busker's guitar case.

Bob finishes his cigarette and reenters the Bistro.

Rico leaves Busker with a gesture of light applause. He follows Bob into the Bistro.

EXT. CITY SIDEWALK - NIGHT

Night is just falling. The street is SILENT and the cars that once lined it are gone. Busker is standing up, stretching his legs. He organizes the small pile of cash in his guitar case into a wad and puts it in his pocket.

He puts his guitar away, grabs his crate and walks off
into the night.

EXT. CITY SIDEWALK - DAY

Busker is sitting on his crate in the same spot as before,
playing SOLO ACOUSTIC GUITAR. His case is open in front of
him and contains some change and a few dollar bills.

Bob steps out of the Bistro and lights up a cigarette. He
watches the traffic going up and down the street.

A YOUNG WOMAN approaches Busker and stops to listen. Bob
sees this but continues to act disinterested. The young
woman smiles at Busker and drops a dollar into his case.
She leaves him, passes Bob, and continues down the
sidewalk.

Busker starts up ANOTHER SONG. Bob finishes his cigarette
and approaches Busker. He smiles as he watches Busker
play. He looks off down the street in the direction of
the young woman. Then he gestures to Busker to come with
him. Busker STOPS PLAYING GUITAR and follows Bob.

INT. BOB'S BISTRO - NIGHT

The restaurant is nearly empty. Bob shows Busker to a
spot in the corner of the dining room. Busker sits down
on his crate and gets ready to start playing. Bob
gestures to wait and brings him a barstool to sit on.
Busker begins to play A NEW SONG.

EXT. CITY SIDEWALK - Continuing

A MAN walks in front of the Bistro, sees Busker in the
window playing, and stops for a moment to watch.

(Beat.)

The man enters the Bistro.

INT. BOB'S BISTRO - Continuing

Busker plays SOLO ACOUSTIC GUITAR. Through the window
behind him, outside PASSERS-BY stop to watch. NEW
ARRIVALS are seated as close to Busker as possible. The
restaurant starts to fill up.

Bob stands in a corner, watching the SMALL CROWD. He
smiles. AMBIENT CONVERSATION GROWS LOUDER. A CASH
REGISTER CHI-CHINGS INTERMITTENTLY. Busker's MUSIC GETS
DROWNED OUT BY THE NOISE.

INT. BOB'S BISTRO - NIGHT

The restaurant is SILENT and empty of customers. A WORKER
sweeps the floor. Bob and Busker stand near the cash
register and Bob hands Busker a wad of money.

A chalkboard on the wall lists food specials. Bob erases
the chalkboard and writes "Live Music on Saturdays."

Busker smiles. Bob and Busker shake hands and Busker
leaves.

MONTAGE - BUSKER'S GIGS

Busker plays SOLO ACOUSTIC GUITAR in the Bistro to a small
attentive crowd.

The restaurant empty, Bob hands Busker a small wad of
cash.

Bob erases the chalkboard that said "Live Music on
Saturdays" and writes "Live Music Nightly.

Busker smiles.

Busker and Bob shake hands.

Busker plays to a LARGE CROWD.

Rico is in the front of the crowd bobbing his head in time
and grimacing in approval.

The restaurant empty, Bob hands Busker a medium wad of
cash.

Busker plays SOLO ACOUSTIC GUITAR UNDER A HEAVY DIN OF
AMBIENT CONVERSATION AND CASH REGISTER CHI-CHINGS.

Customers LAUGH and CLINK bottles.

The restaurant empty, Bob hands Busker a fat wad of cash.

142

EXT. CITY SIDEWALK - DAY

SILENCE. Busker walks down the street with his guitar on
his back. His clothes are clean and new. He stops in
front of a music store and sees an electric guitar in the
window.

(Beat.)

He enters the music store.

EXT. CITY SIDEWALK - DAY

Busker walks out of the music store with the electric
guitar and a small amplifier. He no longer has his
acoustic guitar or case.

INT. BOB'S BISTRO - NIGHT

Busker plays SOLO ELECTRIC GUITAR OVER THE DIN OF AMBIENT
CONVERSATION AND SPARSE CASH REGISTER CHI-CHINGS.

A COUPLE seated near Busker try to converse. They gesture
to each other that they can't hear. The man gestures that
they should leave. They get up and leave.

CUSTOMERS get up to leave in succession.

Bob stands in a corner and frowns.

Rico sits near Busker grimacing, but his head is not
bobbing. He stands up, gives a cold nod to Busker and
leaves.

AMBIENT CONVERSATION AND CASH REGISTER CHI-CHINGS FADE
AWAY, LEAVING ONLY SOLO ELECTRIC GUITAR.

INT. BOB'S BISTRO - NIGHT

The restaurant is empty save Bob and Busker. Bob hands
Busker a few dollar bills and some change.

Busker frowns.

Bob shrugs his shoulders, does a little helpless gesture
with his hands.

EXT. CITY SIDEWALK - DAY

Busker approaches the music store. A sign on the door
says OUT OF BUSINESS.

Busker kicks a can in the street.

INT. BOB'S BISTRO - NIGHT

The restaurant is empty save the employees. Busker plays
SOLO ELECTRIC GUITAR. Bob walks up to him and gestures
for him to stop. SILENCE.

Bob frowns.

Busker frowns.

Bob and Busker shake hands.

MONTAGE - DENOUMENT

SOLO UNAMPLIFIED ELECTRIC GUITAR plays.

PEDESTRIANS walk up and down the sidewalk in the
afternoon.

Bob erases the chalkboard saying "Live Music Nightly" and
writes "French Onion Soup: $2.99."

Rico walks into the Bistro without a grimace.

A COUPLE walks down the sidewalk and passes Busker without
noticing him. He sits on his amp in his old spot and
plays his barely audible electric guitar.

                                        FADE OUT.

                              END.

Anyone but You

A simple strategy for conflict is to fuel that conflict with a character's desire to have something, but you might also consider a character's desire to avoid something, or someone.   We've all been there—placed in a situation with someone or something we can't stand, or at the least would like to avoid. The conflict only gets interesting when a character in this situation is required to bear up and handle it. Not much of a conflict can be developed if a character doesn't like a situation and promptly leaves. What peaks our interest is watching how dual purposes in collision play out. So draw from your own experience or imagine a situation where a character has to deal with someone or something they would rather avoid. Bear in mind, you need to have a reason the character has to bear up and adapt to a situation they'd rather avoid. It might be a motive as simple as the need to be polite. Or the need to keep the respect or attention of someone else involved in the situation; when a parent meets the less-than-perfect boyfriend or girlfriend of their daughter, the parent usually controls outrage out of respect and love for the daughter.   Or let's say a guy hates, maybe is severely allergic to, cats and when he goes to visit the woman of his dreams finds she has an aggressively lovable cat. How does the guy cope? How you handle the conflict is up to you. The situation certainly provides an opportunity for comedy, but it may also lead to a moment of disturbing drama. As you write this scene try to remember that drama builds; little annoyances build into bigger ones and force your character to adapt to heroic or comic extremes, or if you wish, to explode after a period of maintaining control.

Other possibilities for this situation could be:

1. Your character meets an ex-love at someone's funeral, someone's wedding, a situation where all are under pressure to behave.
2. Your character meets someone he has seriously betrayed.
3. Your character has to deal with a type of person she'd rather avoid—of another race, homosexual, a political conservative or radical, a religious fanatic, a nut of your choice.

Pick from these possibilities or make up your own, but first have a look at the student example that follows.

Student Example of Anyone but You Conflict
by Khadijah Aswad

FADE IN:

INT. LIVING ROOM — DAY

A huge teddy bear sits on the couch in a small apartment
living room.

Stacks of pizza boxes with different logos overflow the
garbage can near the couch. An infomercial for exercise
equipment plays on the TV, but the sound of MUSIC from the
stereo overpowers television volume.

INT. KITCHEN — CONTINUOUS

Pizza boxes sit on the counter. Dirty cups and plates are
piled in the sink.

Radio plays Christina Aguilera's "WHAT A GIRL WANTS."

AMANDA, mid-twenties, wearing sweatpants and an over-sized
t-shirt, paces, moving things around, accomplishing
nothing in her kitchen.

Doorbell CHIMES.

Amanda freezes, turns off the radio. Walks out of
kitchen.

INT. LIVING ROOM — CONTINUOUS

Amanda opens door, then puts her hand on her waist, taps
her foot.

PIZZA MAN, mid twenties, nice guy type, looks her up and
down, her oversized over-worn clothes, silly house
slippers.

                        AMANDA
            Finally! Took you long enough.

She motions for Pizza Man to come inside.

Pizza Man walks in, hands over pizza to Amanda as he eyes
the overflowing garbage can.

146

                         PIZZA MAN
             So you been trying the competition?

Amanda sets the pizza on the coffee table.

                          AMANDA
             I'm afraid of commitment.

She looks at Pizza Man, well-built, nice arms.
Puts on a pissed-off face. Points at the clock.

                          AMANDA
             It's been like, an hour? I thought it
             was going to be like the time my ex-
             boyfriend ordered Chinese. I was
             starving, and the guy never came.

Amanda pulls out money from her pocket as she speaks. She
points with the money.

Pizza Man bobs his head as his eyes follow the money.

                          AMANDA
             My ex-boyfriend had the same shirt. He
             used to wear it all the time. I
             remember this one time we went out and
             his friend wore the exact same shirt.

Amanda gestures with the money as she watches the Pizza
Man's eyes follow it.

                          AMANDA
             You wouldn't believe how embarrassed
             they were. Ah. You men.

Pizza Man's eyes are still glued to the money.

                         PIZZA MAN
             Excuse me, this story is fascinating, but
             I really need to go.

                          AMANDA
             Go? Well if you gotta go that bad you
             can use my bathroom. You know, one
             time my boyfriend peed himself 'cause
             he had to go so bad.

                            147

                         PIZZA MAN
            No, I have to get going.

Pizza Man holds his hand out, palm up.

                          AMANDA
            I thought you were going?

                         PIZZA MAN
            The total was $10.99.

                          AMANDA
            Oh here I am, holding on to the money like
            a mad woman. You must think I'm crazy. I'm
            not usually this forgetful. Here I am
            rambling on again. I'm sorry.

Pizza Man sighs, chews his lip.

Amanda hands him the money.

Pizza Man unfolds the cash.

                         PIZZA MAN
            That's two dollars.

                          AMANDA
            It's all I have. You see what happened was—

                         PIZZA MAN
            The total was $10.99.

                          AMANDA
            Just let me explain. My ex-boyfriend—

                         PIZZA MAN
            I get the point! I'm sorry, but no money,
            No pizza. Have a nice day.

Pizza Man grabs up the pizza and heads for the door.

Amanda sits on the couch and CRIES obnoxiously.

                          AMANDA
            He dumped me! Just like that. I suddenly
            wasn't pretty enough. What am I gonna do?

Pizza man sets the pizza back on the table. Backs away.

                    PIZZA MAN
          This one is on me.

Amanda stands and tries to hug Pizza Man. He backs away
from her.

                    AMANDA
          You are the sweetest man in the whole
          entire world.

Amanda grabs his arm and pulls him close to her.

                    AMANDA
          Do you have a girlfriend?

Pizza Man pulls away.

                    PIZZA MAN
          Well, I have more pizzas to deliver. You
          have a nice day.

Pizza Man walks out.

Amanda walks to her door and SCREAMS out:

                    AMANDA
          I'm not really crazy!

Amanda shuts door. She walks over to the couch and lies
down. She covers her legs with a blanket, then sets the
pizza box on her lap. She opens the box.

                    AMANDA
          They forgot the pepperoni. They can't get
          anything right.

She shoves a slice of pizza in her mouth.

                                        FADE OUT:

                         END.

This piece convincingly shows the kinds of mild nut cases delivery guys have to suffer sometimes. The writer neatly uses setting to convey the emotional chaos of our character. Also, that subtle bit of action with her moving around the kitchen and not accomplishing much reveals her kind of manic distraction. I admire that she didn't go over the top with this. Amanda is neurotic and unhappy, not completely bonkers. And the Pizza Man handles her with a bit of compassion, even as he hurries out the door. The writer avoided clichés nicely, and in just a few pages drew out convincing characters with motives that drive the scene.

Anywhere but Here

Yes, we've all been there. Stuck in a place or situation, and we'd rather be someplace else. In the film *Casablanca*, just about everyone wants to be someplace else. Their characters are revealed in the ways they adapt to, maybe even profit from being in Casablanca, or their motives, personalities are revealed in the ways characters resort to strategies for escape. I'm not asking for Casablanca here, but just a little scene where one or two characters are stuck in a situation. Plot and character are revealed in the actions and choices made by the characters. In the short film *Joe*, note how Joe adapts to the powerless situation of being stuck in a mental hospital. He could get hysterical when his prized black shoes are ruined—or he can adapt. In the short film Clown Car, on The Short Series volume *Trust*, two clowns find themselves out of gas in the desert setting of a dried lake bed. How they choose to respond to the situation reveals their characters and also reveals, perhaps, the author's idea on how we can always make choices even where the situation is beyond our control.

So think of a place where a character is stuck. The possibilities are endless. Consider one of the following situations or make up your own.

1. A broken elevator
2. A broken-down car
3. A plane in trouble in the sky
4. A check-out line
5. A small boat at sea
6. A public place during a tornado
7. A holding cell in jail with some dangerous or maybe crazy characters
8. A high school or family reunion with a spouse or partner

Star-Crossed Conflict

Write a scene where one character wants something from someone, while the other character wants something else entirely. This exercise is still about conflict revealed through action and dialogue, but the conflicts occur at two levels. And the motives of the characters are at crossed purposes. Try making up your own situation here. But consider one of the following examples to get you started or perhaps for inspiration:

1. A guy in a bar wants to hook up with a woman; the woman is in the bar because she needs a job. Or maybe the woman wants to sell the guy investment property. Or maybe the woman wants another woman in the bar.

2. A student wants a professor to raise his grade in a course, while the professor wants the student to go away.

3. A young first-time crook wants to rob someone, and the potential victim wants to know the spiritual/psychological/ social reasons this young person is opting for a life of crime.

4. One character wants to order and enjoy a meal in a fine restaurant, while the dinner partner, or maybe even the server, wants to use the occasion for a serious socio-political debate.

5. A homeowner wants to set up a home security system, while the security technician so loves the home, he wants to develop a friendship in order to be invited back into the place.

6. A hitchhiker wants a ride to Vegas, and the driver wants to save the wanderer's soul.

Now use one of these or make up your own scene of star-crossed conflicts and see where your characters go.

Student Example of Star-Crossed Conflict by Samuel Mentzer

```
INT. APARTMENT LIVING ROOM - DAY

DOYLE, a man in his mid-twenties, hunches forward on a
couch, playing a video game; GUNSHOTS and YELLS from the
game resound.

RITA, a young woman of the same age, whips open the door
with a smile.

                    Rita
          Let me just tell you, I had so much fun
          with Tracey walking today. We lapped the
          whole mall twice. Then we stopped, had
          some ice cream, and went around twice more!

Rita struts with exaggerated forward shoulder thrusts and
perches on the arm of the couch where Doyle slouches,
mashing the buttons of the controller.

                    RITA
          Zombie game, that's cool.

Zombie MOANS and automatic rifle SHOTS reverberate as the
Kinks song continues.

                    RITA
          I tell you what, mall walking has really
          changed my life. I know you don't care,
          but I frickin' love the mall, and what
          better way to exercise, right?

Doyle shouts in his headset

                    DOYLE
          Man down! Man down! No, by the beacon!

                    RITA
          Wow you suck. Anyway, I was thinking
          about doing something like buying incense.
          I'm feeling kinda Buddhist right now.
```

```
                        DOYLE
Oh, Rory is stopping by later.

Rita's eyes squint and she begins knitting her brow. She
lets out an angered SIGH.


                        RITA
     God. I hate him.

Rita gets up and quickly walks down the hall towards the
bathroom.

INT. APARTMENT BATHROOM - DAY

Rita looks in the mirror and moves her head side to side
slowly. She unbuttons the top of her polo shirt and props
her breasts up. She then begins to apply make-up.
```

This quick scene is quite efficient in conveying characters. He's absorbed in his game; she's absorbed in herself. This relationship is going nowhere. The writer nicely uses dialogue here to show how often in conversation we don't really talk to one another, but rather talk at one another, not really connecting while we stay self-absorbed in our own agendas.

Most everyone in my screenwriting class could relate to this couple going nowhere fast.

Show'Em, Don't Tell 'Em

"Good writers may "tell" about almost anything in fiction
except the character's feelings. One may tell the reader
that the character went to a private school . . . or one may
tell the reader that the character hates spaghetti; but
with rare exceptions the character's feelings must be
demonstrated: fear, love, excitement, doubt,
embarrassment, despair become real only when they
take the form of events—action (or gesture), dialogue, or
physical reaction to setting. Detail is the lifeblood of
fiction."

John Gardner

This exercise is designed to help you further reveal the inner workings of your
characters through what they say and do, how they appear to the viewer as well as
how they might appear to others in the scene. The exercise is much like the one on
making general concepts clear through concrete action, but this exercise is more
focused on character. Remember that good descriptive writing is much like the old
Catholic definition of a sacrament. It gives an outward and visible sign of an inner
spiritual, emotional, or psychological state.

Select from the list of general statements about the condition of a character, then
show the character and evoke the emotional state with precise description of
appearance, action and, if you wish, dialogue. The idea is to SHOW the intended
emotional state. You may select from the list, OR write your own summary of an
emotional state, then show it. And do please try to avoid clichés and stereotypes.

OPTIONS:
(Note a gender pronoun is provided, but change the gender as you wish.)

--She is nervous in public places.

--He hates being alone.

--He is a letch and a jerk who tries to hide his vices.

--She is a right-wing racist.

--He is obsessive/compulsive.

--She is the kind of woman who'll try anything for the thrill.

--He is most boring when he thinks he is being entertaining.

--She walks into any situation and tries to control it.

--He's fallen out of love and tries to pretend to his partner that all is well.

--He masks his insecurity by feigning supreme confidence.

--She's furious at her partner but tries to suppress it.

--He's an incurable romantic.

--She hates her job, but can't quit.

--He's having an existential crisis.

You can use this space to jot down notes for your scene, listing things that must be in the scene to convey the emotional state you are after, before getting down to writing the scene as a script.

Student Example of Show 'em, Don't Tell 'Em
by Vytas Nagisetty

INT. CORPORATE BOARDROOM - DAY

A nicely furnished room with a long wooden table, ergonomic
chairs, and all sorts of high-tech conferencing gadgetry. A
beautiful female CATERER, 20s, finishes laying out a display
of smoked salmon and caviar.

She bends over a tray of food when ERNESTO CASH arrives. He
is a dashing yet tacky man, 30s, sporting a purple silk
shirt, Bermuda shorts, a huge Rolex, Prada flip-flops, and
perfectly slicked-back hair. He eyes her rear and legs.

                    ERNESTO
          That looks fantastic.

                    CATERER
          Thank you, sir.

The Caterer turns around to see him.

                    ERNESTO
          Here's my card. Could you make sure
          that you send the bill to me and not to
          accounting? Those boys would kill me if
          I tried to expense something like this.

The Caterer holds up two cards that he's given her.

                    CATERER
          Sure. Oh, here, you've given me two.

Ernesto hands her a Montblanc pen from his pocket.

                    ERNESTO
          Do you want to put your number on the
          other one for me?

The young woman blushes. She writes her number on one of
the cards and hands it back to Ernesto without thinking
twice.

                    ERNESTO
          Keep the pen. It's for you.

She looks at the beautiful gold pen and then quickly moves
to leave before anyone else arrives.

                    CATERER
          Thank you, sir. Have a nice day.

                    ERNESTO
          Thank you.

Ernest looks at the card she handed him.

                    ERNESTO
          Amelia. I'll be in touch.

Ernesto mentally undresses her as she leaves.

EMPPLOYEES start to arrive. The CEO, JACK OLDMAN, takes his
place at the head of the table. Ernesto sits at his right.
After everyone has arrived, Mr. Oldman stands up to speak.

                    MR. OLDMAN
          I want to thank everyone for taking the
          time to be here. We've got some
          exciting news about a client that
          Ernesto has been reaching out to for a
          while now. It's a new job that's really
          going to take us to the next level. I
          don't want to steal his thunder, so I'll
          bring him up now to tell you the good
          news himself. Ernesto.

                    ERNESTO
          Thanks, Jack. Many of you here have
          done work on the Videoshop project. I'm
          happy to say that our rebuild of their
          website has boosted their sales
          tremendously. You should be very proud
          of yourselves. As a token of their
          appreciation, they've furnished this
          beautiful spread of food for us.

There's a MURMER in the crowd as everyone is surprised.

                    ERNESTO
          So please, before you leave, help
          yourselves. Now I'd like to tell about
          our new project with Videoshop. They
          just signed the contract this morning.
          It's going to be our biggest project
          ever. Ten million dollars! You heard
          me right. Okay, check it out. Here's
          what we have to do. We're going to make
          a movie out of the their website!

Suddenly the crowd looks worried and we hear a chorus of
DISGRUNTLED SIGHS. JULIE, the senior web designer, speaks up.

                    JULIE
          But we've never made a movie.

                    ERNESTO
          We've got the talent. I know we can
          pull it off. It will be a good
          challenge.

                    JULIE
          Ernie, we make websites, not movies. We
          don't even have a camera, let alone know
          how to use one.

                    ERNESTO
          We'll cross that bridge when we come to
          it. I'm confident that we have the
          capabilities. We'll have a kickoff
          meeting next week. If you've got any
          questions, bring them to that meeting.
          Now please, everyone, help yourselves to
          some breakfast. I've got to catch a
          flight to London, so I can't stay. But
          thanks to everyone for coming. Let's
          start getting pumped about this. And
          remember S.G.T.! Synergy Go Team!

Mr. Oldman starts to clap and the crowd follows in turn
while feigning smiles. Ernesto takes a bow and exits with
Mr. Oldman. After they leave, the employees turn around to
survey the amazing display of food. Nobody eats a thing.

There's certainly a potential sit-com in this cast of characters. The writer has found fresh ways to convey familiar office characters, including of course, the over-bearing office jerk. The fact that Ernesto has chosen to wear Prada flip-flops, Bermuda shorts and purple shirt—along with his oversized Rolex—to an office function says worlds about his arrogance, as well as his self-indulgent bad taste. We see he's a letch who has no shame whatsoever in the way he boldly moves his eyes all over the caterer and in the way he requests a phone number, certain that she will be pleased.

We also see that he is something of a con-man. He's playing both sides. He just wanted Videoshop to sign the contract so he could get his commission. Now that his commission is secure, it's small loot to call a caterer and set up a "let's feel good about this project and client" meeting. His tactics show him to be quite the liar. We just know that Ernesto's name is mighty ironic and that he is not a man to be trusted. A man who hands off Montblanc pens to pretty strangers has to have a hidden agenda and/or a shyster accountant who takes care of such expenses in a smooth way.

The writer is having fun here with having the characters speak in clichés. If you want to make a character unreliable in some way, just have them speak in clichés. We expect them from a guy like Ernesto. But when we get empty, clichéd phrases like "exciting news," "next level," and "don't want to steal thunder" from the CEO, Mr. Oldman, we figure this little group is doomed, not only by the insane project idea from the company man, but also by the lack of leadership from their boss.

When the group questions Ernesto's plan with the very real concerns of never having made a movie and not even having a camera, much less the know-how as to how to make a movie from a web-site, he sidesteps them with clichés and jargon. Remember that dialogue strategy: when you want to show who has the power over a conversation, let him dismiss the others' statement and plow ahead with the personal agenda. We can almost see the coldness in his eyes while he offers the cheering smile, saying things like "We'll cross that bridge when we come to it," and gives the final and futile cheer: "Synergy Go Team!"

No wonder no one wants to eat anything.

Point of View: Who You Are Frames What You See

In this exercise you are going to explore your characters further by focusing on what they notice in the world around them. It's common knowledge that when we walk out into the world, what we notice is largely selected by what is on our minds. For example, women who want to get pregnant, notice that there is a sudden increase in the number of pregnant women out there. A girl whose fiancée just dumped her is going to notice happy couples—everywhere. A man whose family has just lost everything in a tanking economy is going to notice the happy families tooling around in nice SUVs, and he'll get quite annoyed at all those—and suddenly there are so more of them—commercials for Carnival Cruises and family trips to Disneyland.

Think about yourself and the people you know very well. When you're having trouble making the rent, you notice all the other limitations in your life: those movies you'd like to see, the dinners out that others enjoy, those new hot jeans that your friends are wearing, your shoes that are gonna have to make it another season.

Life is a matter of what you are looking at.

The idea goes along with Forest Gump's mother's philosophy about life being a box of chocolates and you never know what you're going to bite into next. But here we are exploring the idea of choice. We choose what we see. We have proclivities to notice certain things given our needs, desires, fears, and moods.

Consider how this way of seeing applies to your self. I know when I'm down that I tend to see sorrowful things: the old lady in the supermarket, struggling alone with her walker to buy her groceries, paying with her food stamps. I see ragged children. I see scowling, lecherous men. I see my aging skin, my ragged fingernails. I see a living room that needs a paint job.

When I'm up, I see the older women at my gym wrinkled but still smiling, swinging their tennis rackets as hard as old bones will allow; I see the happy children out on my sidewalk, playing games; I see happy men jogging healthy and lean through the paths of Wildwood Park. I see myself running strong through the wooded. I see a great meal I've made to offer to my friends. I see myself typing quickly, smoothly at my computer, riding inspiration, making something new and real on the page. I see my clean, bright home, the wood floors, gleaming in sunlight. Mine.

Got the idea of how moods, needs affect what we see?

Think about characters and how who they are, what they do, shapes what they see. A shoe salesman sees shoes when he walks into a public place; a dentist sees teeth; a photographer sees light, lines, shapes. A child sees a lot of knees, feet, and big faces bending down. A child is also generally looking for something to play with, something to do with her hands. Now let's get to your exercise.

The goal here is to convey how who we are and what we do for our professions or passions shape how see the world. You want to illustrate the personality of a character by what they notice around them. For clarity and texture, use more than one character.

Put two or more characters in a situation and show us the differences in what the characters see. Write this as a script. When you introduce each character, describe him or her a bit. Then let us see what one character notices as compared to what another character notices. For ease and clarity in this exercise you may use POV, a device it's best to avoid in a spec script, but the POV direction might make your job easier within the scope of this exercise.

Now pick a place where a variety of characters might be: a plane, a subway, a doctor's office, a diner, restaurant, bar, a train station, a yoga class, any place you like. Now put characters in there and convey the personalities of those characters by what they notice. Come up with two or more characters who might see things in particular ways and write a brief scene indicating different points of view. What does each character notice? There's no need for decisive action or resolution in this scene. The goal here is to practice getting under the skin of various characters and seeing the world through their eyes.

For example, in a bar, the bartender sees very specific things, like the lack or abundance of tips, the dirty glasses backing up, the unattractive, flirty girl who keeps hitting on him for free drinks—she might see his nice eyes, arms, buns, while he sees her crooked teeth or a mole. A drunk at the bar might keep his eyes on his beer and really watch to make sure the bartender pours good hefty shots. An undercover cop walking into the bar would be eyeing up the young-looking faces.

You might write it something like this:

INT. COLLEGE BAR - NIGHT

The darkened place is packed with TWENTY-SOMETHINGS dressed
to hook-up for sure. Some cluster at the bar aching for a
drink while the lone BARTENDER, a good-looking, built guy,
struggles to serve all and take the money.

In the distance TWO GO-GO DANCERS do their thing while
STUDENTS dance and TWO MIDDLE-AGED stand and watch.

THUMPING music drowns out AD LIB CHATTER of drinks, chics,
hot guys, the usual bar talk.

A tipsy AVERAGE LOOKING GIRL who's not as hot as she hopes
sits at the bar, her too-heavy cleavage spilling out, her
overly made-up face a bit garish. She grins with bad teeth
and waves at the bartender, who looks her way, nods and
keeps hustling to catch up. TWO FRAT BOYS LAUGH and drop
shots in beers, guzzle them down.

AVERAGE GIRL'S POV: BARTENDER

The bartender's rear as he bends to lift tub of dirty
glasses and gives them to BAR BACK. The bartender's arm as
he reaches overhead for a wine glass. The bartender's smile
when he gives HOT GIRL a drink and she hands him a ten and
gestures to keep the change.

BACK TO SCENE

FRAT BOYS' POV: DRINKS

They watch bartender's hands as he slides fresh beers at
them, then fills shot glasses to the brim. Shot glasses drop
into the beers. Beers foam up, mugs lift, liquid swirling.

BACK TO SCENE

Bartender hustles to serve others near the average girl.

MIDDLE-AGED MEN'S POV: GO-GO GIRLS

TWO GIRLS' long lithe legs, bikini-clad butts wiggling,
smiling lips, open mouths, svelte tummy glistening in sweat,
bikini clad breasts bouncing, a rivulet of sweat runs down
cleavage, butt again, the crotch undulating under tight
shiny fabric.

Student dance to the THUMPING MUSIC.

AVERAGE GIRL: BARTENDER

He takes money from a COUPLE next to her. His profile, dark hair, just enough five-o'clock shadow, the lovely shape of his throat.

BACK TO SCENE

Average girl waves a ten, points to her empty wine glass, smiles. Bartender moves toward her.

BARTENDER'S POV: AVERAGE GIRL

Her thick hand with short, chewed nails waving ten-spot, her empty glass, the too-much, too-loose cleavage, her smile, the crooked yellow teeth.

BACK TO SCENE

Bartender fills the glass, takes the ten, starts to make change, she shakes her head, signals to keep the change.

BARTENDER'S POV: AVERAGE GIRL

That yellow-teethed smile again. Her writing a number on a cocktail napkin, pushing it his way.

BACK TO SCENE

He makes change, plops bills on the napkin, turns away.

Yes, it's a cruel world out there. But you could write a less mean scene. Let's say kids at an amusement park as opposed to the point of view of someone who works there. The carnies who work a fair see a whole different world than the kids who happily ride those rides and enjoy all the many frivolous things.

Before you proceed, you might want to have a look at a more extended way of showing different points of view in a single scene. The student example below tells a nice story of three different characters at a wedding reception. It neatly portrays and develops characters through what they focus on in a room. After reading this, pick your place, your characters, and evoke just who and what they are by what they see.

Student Example of *Who You Are Frames What You See* by Vytas Nagisetty

```
EXT. WEDDING RECEPTION - DAY

A JAZZ BAND plays Miles Davis' SEVEN STEPS TO HEAVEN at a
blazing tempo.  CLYDE, 30's and medium build, remains cool
as he walks the bass. DAVEY, a baby-faced man in his early
20's, sweats over the piano and SCAT WILSON, 60's, plays the
drums like he's about to fall out of his seat.

WEDDING GUESTS drink and dance.

Clyde calls out to Davey.

                    CLYDE
          Back to Latin!

On a dime, the band shifts from SWING to a LATIN GROOVE for
a couple of bars.

Wedding guests follow the shift in music with hotter dance
moves.

                    CLYDE
          Break!

Clyde and Davey stop playing while Scat plays a DRUM BREAK.
Clyde winks at Davey, who anxiously counts the bars.

                    Davey
                 (whispers)
          Five.  Six.  Se-

                    CLYDE
          Now swing!  Take one, Davey!

The band shifts back to SWING and Davey starts to SOLO.  The
crowd gives a BURST OF APPLAUSE.

DAVEY'S POV: PIANO KEYS

Fingers race over piano keys.  Drops of sweat hit the keys.

BACK TO SCENE
```

Scat and Clyde exchange grins. Clyde surveys the crowd.
His hands keep flying around the bass while the rest of his
body is completely relaxed.

YOUNG COUPLES crowd the dance floor.

An ATTRACTIVE COUPLE is dirty dancing. The WOMAN, stunning,
early 20's, wears a short red dress. The MAN, handsome,
early 30's, wears a bright silk shirt and massive Rolex.

CLYDE'S POV: STUNNING WOMAN

The woman dirty dancing spins and her short dress exposes
her thong.

BACK TO SCENE

Clyde nearly loses the bass line. He glances back at his
fingers to check his position but then returns his attention
to the dirty dancing couple.

CLYDE'S'S POV: THE HOT COUPLE

The man starts to slick his hair back as his partner grinds
on his thigh.

BACK TO SCENE

CLYDE LAUGHS. He looks at Davey.

DAVEY'S POV: PIANO KEYS

Fingers race over piano keys. Drops of sweat hit the keys.

BACK TO SCENE

Clyde looks at Scat.

SCAT'S POV: FABULOUS FOOD

SERVERS carry in a massive feast. One server carries a
large tray of lobster and caviar.

BACK TO SCENE

Clyde surveys the crowd again. His eye catches RENEE, a
pretty, athletic woman in her late 20's, who sits at a table
alone sipping on a glass of red wine.

CLYDE'S POV: RENEE

Renée gently wipes a drop of red wine off her full lips.
She looks directly at Clyde.

BACK TO SCENE

Clyde quickly looks back at Davey, who's WRAPPING UP HIS
SOLO. Davey glances up from the piano.

                    DAVEY
          Break?

                    CLYDE
          Yeah.

CLYDE looks over to Scat, who's still staring at the servers
bringing out food.

                    CLYDE
          Scat!

Scat looks up.

                    CLYDE
          Break!

Scat and Davey STOP PLAYING while Clyde launches a monstrous
BASS SOLO with his bow.

RENEE'S POV: CLYDE

Clyde's bow flying over the strings. Clyde's thinning
hair. Clyde's old wingtip shoes. Clyde's left hand, ring
finger with no ring. Clyde's cheap Timex watch.

BACK TO SCENE

Renée gets up and walks to the appetizer table. Clyde's
hunched over his bass, playing FAST PASSAGES IN THE HIGH
REGISTER. He looks up to see if Renee is watching.

CLYDE'S POV: RENEE'S EMPTY SEAT

BACK TO SCENE

Scat stares, jaw dropped, as servers bringing out several
racks of barbecued ribs. Clyde scans the room and sees
Renée returning to her seat with a plate of food. He ducks
his head back down and KICKS HIS SOLO UP A NOTCH.

SCAT'S POV: FOOD

Servers cut the rack of juicy ribs and plate them for
awaiting guests.

BACK TO SCENE

Scat calls out to Davey.

                    SCAT
          Head out! Head out!

Davey looks at Clyde, who's still soloing, shrugs his
shoulders and begins to play THE THEME FROM SEVEN STEPS TO
HEAVEN. Scat joins in on DRUMS. Clyde has no choice but to
drop his solo. He looks back at Davey like he wants to kill
him. Scat sees this and calls out to Clyde.

                    SCAT
          Let's take a break!

                    CLYDE
          Let's take a break.

The band WRAPS UP THE SONG. Scat gets on the microphone.
The crowd APPLAUDS.

                    SCAT
          Hey y'all thanks a lot. We're gonna a
          take a quick pause for the cause. But
          don't go nowhere—we'll be right back.
          Thanks.

Scat makes a beeline to the ribs table. Davey gets up from
his piano. Clyde plucks broken hairs from his bow.

                    DAVEY
          That wasn't too bad.

                    CLYDE
That was great, Davey. You sounded
great. And that song's a bitch. It
took me ten years to learn. You got it
in like what, two weeks? You make me
sick.

                    DAVEY
Thanks. Thanks a lot. You know I've
got the highest respect for you. That
means a lot coming from you.

                    CLYDE
Don't sweat it.
                    (beat)
Hungry?

                    DAVEY
A little bit.

                    CLYDE
I think Scat's got his eye on some
ribs. You might want to get in line
now if you want them. Looks like
they're going fast.

Davey looks at the ribs table. The crowd around it is
growing while the ribs are disappearing.

                    DAVEY
Good lookin'. I'll catch ya.

                    CLYDE
Later.

Davey heads to the ribs table. Clyde puts down his bow and
walks over near Renée, who is back at her table, still
alone. He stands close by but doesn't say anything to her
for awhile.

                    CLYDE
How's the caviar?

Renée munches on caviar spread on a cracker.

                    RENEE
Delicious. You guys sound great.

                    CLYDE
Thanks.

                    RENEE
How long have you been playing?

                    CLYDE
Since I was five.

                    RENEE
That's a long time.
                    (beat)
I mean, five's pretty young. You don't
look that old. I didn't mean it like-

                    CLYDE
No worries. No offense taken.

                    RENEE
Good. What's your name?

                    CLYDE
I'm Clyde.

                    RENEE
Old school. I like that name.

                    CLYDE
Just an uncle's name.

                    RENEE
Must have been a special man for your
momma to give you his name.

                    CLYDE
I took a lot of heat on the playground.

Renée offers her hand.

                    RENEE
  Well I'm happy to meet you, Clyde. I'm Renée.

He shakes her hand.

                         CLYDE
          Renée.
                    (beat)
          What brings you to this auspicious occasion?

                         RENEE
          My boyfriend is the groom's brother.

                         CLYDE
          I see. He's a really lucky guy.
                    (beat)
          The groom I mean.
                    (beat)
          Though I'm sure your boyfriend is a very
          lucky man, too.

                         RENEE
          Did you just put your foot in your mouth?

                         CLYDE
          I guess so. Oops.

                         RENEE
          To answer your question. Yes, he is a
          lucky guy.

She shoots Clyde a seductive smile over her shoulder.

                         RENEE
          A very lucky guy.

CLYDE'S P.O.V.: RITA'S LEGS

Renée's well-defined calf muscles flex above her high heels
as she walks away.

BACK TO SCENE

                         CLYDE
          Nice to meet you. I'll see you later.

Clyde stares after Renée, who has disappeared into the
crowd. Davey arrives with a plate of food. He talks with a
mouthful of caviar and crackers.

                    DAVEY
          I don't get why people go ape-shit for
          this stuff. Caviar. It's like salty
          baby food. Or like salty, fishy, baby
          food. What's the big deal?

Clyde watches ANOTHER HOT WOMAN step up to food table.

                    CLYDE
          When was the last time you ate baby food?

                    DAVEY
          Point taken.

(Beat.)

Clyde breaks his gaze from the hot woman.

                    CLYDE
          No. Seriously. When?

Clyde keeps a straight face for a few seconds and then
starts LAUGHING. Davey starts LAUGHING, too.

This little sketch very succinctly reveals how who we are, what we care about, shapes what we see in a room. Davey loves his music. Skat's into food. And Clyde, well he likes the ladies. And if any of these three interests is likely to shape a story, it will be the interest in the ladies. Clyde makes his effort. And while we don't get a little love story, we do get a bit of movement. No, Clyde doesn't get the girl, but he does enjoy a little taste of her flirtation. And that's a good thing. But just like caviar, such an encounter may not be for everyone.

A flirtation that goes nowhere with a good-looking woman may not be every man's idea of a pleasure—some might consider it a frustration. Davey, for example, has little interest in women or appreciation of caviar. He doesn't notice the lady, and considers caviar as no better than baby food.   When Clyde, being the sensitive guy he is, calls Davey down on his sloppy metaphor, Davey doesn't question his point. But Clyde pushes with his "when was the last time you had. . ." question, and with that question hanging in the air, we wonder when was the last time Clyde was with a woman. It's not a heart-breaking question. It's an amusing question about the little pleasures that come close, are in reach, and are sometimes unappreciated, and sometimes—sigh—slip by.

5. Visual Language and the Image: Think One Frame at a Time

> "Images haunt. There is a whole mythology built on this fact: Cezanne painting until his eyes bled, Wordsworth wandering the Lake Country hills in an impassioned daze. Blake describes it very well, and so did the colleague of Tu Fu who said to him, 'It's like being alive twice.'"
>
> Robert Hass, "Images"

One of the many reasons we go to movies, aside from general entertainment, is that we enjoy being immersed in those big images on the screen. Watching a movie involves more than our being engaged in the characters and the action We get to go somewhere, inhabit another experience through the images on the screen; the resulting feeling is indeed as if we are living another life, as if we can be "alive twice." In movies we can experience all the risk, danger, romance, lust, adventure, vicariously feel the successes, defeats, joys and sorrows. Movies offer feelings for which we do not have to pay—that's one of the many reasons we like them. Not only do movies need to contain ideas, which give significance to characters and events, but the ideas must be experienced; they must be felt, or the movie, whether it's narrative or experimental, will fail. And how do we make ideas experiential? The use of images.

When you hear the word image, the first thing you think of is something visual. Don't forget that movies—in spite of all that talking—are a visual medium. We like our images on the screen big and clear, because it's through these images we are transported to other places, times, adventures, passions, even to poetic/spiritual experiences. We spend loads of money on bigger and higher-definition screens.

We spend big bucks on the IMAX movie, and we still get excited about the chance to watch action in 3-D.

But an image can appeal to more than the eyes to convey meaning/feeling. An image is something that conveys meaning to any of the five senses. Just think of a memory and you'll set all sorts of images to work. Most of us summon up memory with visuals and words. But just try this now; think of a memory that appeals to your sense of smell—the scent of your mother's purse, the scent of your dad's cigar. The scent, perhaps, of honeysuckle, the scent of a particular beach you love, a lake. Now recall tastes: your mom's fried chicken, your dad's grilled steaks. And don't forget texture. Every mother remembers her baby's skin, the warm soft fuzz on the top of her baby's head.

In film you have two basic senses to manipulate to evoke meaning/feeling: visual images and dialogue or sounds. Using these two avenues carefully, you can evoke other senses so that the viewer might "feel" the soft down of a comforter laid over someone who has just been rescued from a freezing forest, or you can lead the viewer to perhaps "smell" the rot when you show, let's say, a garbage bag of fish guts and heads scattered on a kitchen floor by a family dog. In our imaginations, the senses all interconnect. By strongly appealing to one or two senses, the whole sensory network can be triggered and spring to life.

There's another aspect to the image that makes it a valuable tool. An image communicates by simultaneously appealing to both our rational thinking and our emotional response. Think of that vivid image that recurs in *Slumdog Millionaire*. Little boy Jamal has to find pleasure and a few coins in whatever way he can. When he's locked in a public outhouse while crowds gather nearby to greet a famous movie star as he steps off a helicopter, Jamal is desperate to get out and take a photograph to the movie star to have it autographed. Something as pathetic as a signed photo of a film star would be a remarkable treasure to this boy, who has little of what he needs to live and much less of those frivolous things that give us joy. He raises the photo high in the air, holds his nose, and leaps down into the pool of shit that gathers beneath the outhouse.

After a quick cut to the eager crowd scene we see Jamal again, now completely covered in shit, still raising that clean photograph high in the air, and running with no shame, running with only sheer will and hope to win the treasured autograph. The crowds part at the stench of him, and he pushes on to his goal. The actor signs the photo with no comment on the ambitious and shit-covered boy. Jamal wins. This is such a strong image that it becomes symbolic of Jamal's tenacity and the hope that will always drive Jamal until, ultimately, he wins the love of his life—not to mention the fortune that results from being the unlikely winner of the game show. We will return to this image of Jamal smiling victoriously in spite of the fact that he is literally covered in shit again and again in the movie, as the grown Jamal moves toward his larger goal of rescuing the love of his life. The shit-covered boy who runs full of hope and with no shame toward his impossible goal—that's the essential Jamal, an icon of what audiences love to see, the underdog—and here, the slum dog—who emerges victorious from a gruesome battle for life.

And so you see, in discussing the image, we slipped into symbol—while discussing character. It all works together. Through images Jamal becomes something more than a boy; he becomes a force, a symbol of perseverance toward achieving a goal. With carefully selected and arranged images you can make your characters larger than life; you can make them into forces, personalities that viewers will remember and talk about for years.

This use of a use of a reoccurring image to convey a character's personality is frequently used in film; it's a vivid and powerful device. In *Cinema Paradisio*, a Sicilian boy, Salvatore, is known for his complete adoration of movies. He is just as enchanted by the reels of film whirring on the projector as he is by the projected images on the screen. He is encouraged and mentored by the projectionist who is ordered by the local priest to cut out the snips of film depicting physical romance— this includes even the innocent things like embraces and kisses. The boy so loves both the physicality and the projected images of film that he collects these little snippets as if capturing bits of life and saving them from ruin. These bits of film create havoc in his home; they also contribute to a passion that will result in the boy growing up to be a famous director. And yes, those snippets of film will appear again, when Salvatore assembles them into a short movie that serves as a loving tribute to the projectionist, the only man in that village who understood the boy's passion for life and film.

Chocolat also uses a reoccurring image to establish and develop the character of a single mother who seems to have supernatural skills when making her confections of chocolate. She tends her simmering pots of chocolate much as a witch who watches her cauldron of magical brews. We hardly see this character without some sort of chocolate in her hand or at her side. She is the essence of chocolate with her silky dark hair and alluring dark eyes. She is tempting; she is sweet; she is satisfying, and even somewhat addictive. And just as a fine piece of chocolate can change a sour mood, she transforms the cranky little town.

But when it comes to defining and developing characters through the use of images, no movie does it more cleverly and delightfully than Jean-Pierre Jeunet's *Amèlie*. Before the opening credits roll up, we have a voice over pointing out the quiet magic of random things. The voice over—and the camera—point out how in a single moment various mundane activities and events of great consequence can occur: a blue fly capable of beating its wings seventy times a minute lands in Montmartre; a breeze shaking an outdoor café table makes two wine glasses dance; a man returns to his office from his best friend's funeral to erase his friend's name from his address book; the sperm of Raphael Poulain makes a dash for his wife's egg; nine months later, newborn baby Amèlie slips into this world. This vivid and comic montage juxtaposes trivial events with birth and death to establish an idea once stated by Oscar Wilde that "Life is far too serious a thing to ever talk seriously about." We know from the start that this will be a comic tale about the serious value of THINGS. The opening also sets up the idea that this will be a story of random events and how they can sometimes have a ripple effect, as in the chaos theory premise that the movement of a butterfly's wing can have far-reaching consequences. And yep, this premise will play out in the plot. More on that later.

For now let's consider how the major players of the story are introduced. As the opening credits roll, we see a montage of Amèlie's childhood. We see the various ways the curious and cheerful girl entertains herself: she plays puppet games with her hands and fingers; she wears a cherry like an earring; she makes wine glasses sing with the wet touch of her finger; she blows a leaf to make it hum; she spins coins and arranges dominoes in a neat row, then enjoys the ripple effect of knocking one down. Hmm, we most definitely can infer that this is to be a story about consequences, the ripple effect of the slightest action. The writer has suggested this twice in the opening minutes of the film, and not through a voice over explanation, but rather with pictures, with an arrangement of a series of images that SHOWS what the story is up to. Bear in mind, voice over can be a useful tool, but what will engage the viewer most is what is seen on the screen. In movies, even more so than in fiction, meaning is best shown rather than explained or told.

In the next series of montages we are introduced to the significant people in Amèlie's life, and we come to know the charming and quirky personality of Amèlie. We meet Amèlie's father, a rather stern doctor, through his likes and dislikes. We SEE his character emerge by watching how he interacts with the things he likes and dislikes in his day-to-day world. He dislikes peeing next to someone at a urinal, and he dislikes the critical looks of strangers passing by when they pause to stare at his poor fashion choice to wear socks with his shorts and sandals. He likes tearing off wide strips of wallpaper, and he likes cleaning and reorganizing his tool box. When we meet Amèlie's mother, a school mistress, the first thing we are told is that she has delicate nerves, and we SEE a comically played facial twitch; she dislikes having her hands touched by strangers and dislikes pillow marks on her cheek in the morning; she likes figure skaters and cleaning out and reorganizing her purse.

When we are introduced to Amèlie, the first thing we are told is that she desires to be hugged by her father. We see the small girl, her eyes wide with longing and adoration as her father checks her heart rate—his touch buffered by the stethoscope. Unfortunately, her father only touches her for her monthly check-ups, and the occasional bit of intimacy makes her heart race so rapidly that the good doctor/father declares her unfit for school—and thus we are introduced to the lonely life of Amèlie. Homeschooled by her well-intentioned but cool-hearted mother, the little girl entertains herself with imaginary friends. Her only real friend is her goldfish Blubber, but we are told the poor fish is so stressed by the neurotic family environment, he becomes suicidal and frequently leaps out of his bowl and causes the girl to have screaming fit—it's comic—while dear dad comically tries to retrieve the fish, which somehow slipped under the stove. The ensuing family chaos that results from the suicidal goldfish's flights leads to the fish being dumped in a stream and Amèlie left more alone that ever.

She's given a new amusement, a camera, to help her through her solitary days. For a while she's content with going about the neighborhood and taking pictures. Amèlie's pleasure in taking precisely framed photographs of mundane things in the neighborhood suggests that this sweet little girl approaches the world with great sincerity and whimsy, much like the writer/director. As a child she likes framing and arranging her world with a camera lens; later in the story, she will take on the role of director of the people in her world. She will manipulate events that will change everyone's life, including her own.

We are told she dreams her way into adulthood, and when we see the grown Amèlie (Audry Tatou), we observe another montage of what the young woman likes as a way of quickly giving us a character profile of the lovely, and still lonely, young woman Amèlie has become. We discover her "likes" have shifted from dreaming and taking pictures to going out to the theatre, where she enjoys watching other peoples' faces in the darkness, and looking for little details in the films that others don't notice, things like the little scratches and marks on the film that are completely irrelevant to the story playing out on the screen. Her propensity to observe all things is a key and telling detail about Amèlie. She has a sharp and compassionate eye. She enjoys watching people and notices details in the world around her that others tend to overlook. Since she was a girl trained to accept loneliness without self-pity, and to rely on her own imagination and curiosity for entertainment, we see her grown into a self-sufficient and reasonable young woman, but she lacks the skills to connect to others—she'd rather watch them. The one glimpse we have of her sex life is one of comic disinterest, as she stares up at the ceiling while her partner huffs and puffs over her.

Amèlie prefers other simple, private pleasures. We see her plunge her hand into a sack of lentils and smile at the feel of them engulfing her fingers. She enjoys cracking the hard surface of crème brulée with the back of her spoon. She likes skipping stones. She likes watching her neighbors from her window. She uses a little telescope to see the details. We get the view through her telescope; we experience how her eye can zoom in for the tiny, telling details when she zooms in to watch a sickly old painter who lives in an apartment below. She watches him touch his brush to his canvas, lightly stroke the face of a woman in a crowd scene. While sharing in her voyeuristic moment of watching the artist, we share in her precise and quiet pleasure in watching the details of this world. We SEE that she is a sensual young woman, but a very reserved woman who, it seems, will always be alone.

But ten minutes into the film, her life changes. While doing her before-bed ritual of watching the news and washing her face, she becomes engrossed in the news story of the death of Lady Di and drops the top from her bottle of cleanser. She bends to the floor to discover a loosened tile—a tile loosened coincidentally by the dropped bottle top, which was dropped because Amèlie was distracted by the death of Lady Di. Behind the loosened tile she finds a box, a little metal box filled with a collection of objects placed there by a boy some forty years earlier. The discovery of a mysterious box for the imaginative Amèlie is something akin to the discovery of King Tut's tomb. The box contains only simple things: a photograph of a young man with a soccer ball, a little race car, and various trinkets that could only be of value to the child who put them there.

After finding the box, Amèlie sits in bed and plots how she will find the owner of the box and will return it. And she declares that if the man is happy to have the box of memories returned, she will devote her life to doing good things. And if he isn't pleased, her only thought is: oh well.

And so the plot takes off, leading Amèlie to venture out of her apartment and get to know her neighbors, leading her on a quest to open herself up to strangers, including—and bear in mind, this happens in the first fifteen minutes of the film— the romantic interest. She comes across a man digging out castoff photos from a coin operated photo booth—yes, someone else with an interest in things framed. It's the biggest ripple effect of them all—she encounters the "love at first sight" love of her life.

The film is full of a cast of characters who are very particular about what they like and don't like. They are defined in many ways by these things. The film is immensely popular not for the little love story it tells, but for the way the director uses quirky and vivid images to evoke emotional significance for each character the film presents and to give meaning to the simplest of things. The inciting incident of the plot hinges on the discovery of a random things, a box, filled with objects selected and treasured by a boy who once lived in Amèlie's apartment. Her mission to return it to the stranger leads her on a path of affecting and improving a great many lonely souls—including her own.

In this film characters are very much defined by the objects they treasure. These objects are very private and personal treasures, made valuable only because the characters tend to deny themselves the love, lust, pleasure, adventure, the life they crave. Amèlie's mission is to do or provide the necessary things that will push the characters beyond their self-imposed limitations. No one could have anticipated the popularity of the garden gnome Amèlie steals from her father and sends off traveling the world with her flight attendant friend. The gnome sends postcards from his exotic destinations back to Amèlie's father and thus inspires him to get out and see the world in the way he craves, but doesn't allow himself. In the end, the gnome is returned, and then the father sets out to see the world. No wonder then that the traveling gnome was picked up by Travelocity to promote the travel industry. The gnome is everywhere; the gnome became a cultural icon of the pleasures of tourism, with few knowing the humble French beginnings of that famous gnome.

Movies have given us many cultural icons, with one of the earliest and classic ones being *The Wizard of Oz*. Made in 1939 and one of the earliest color productions (along with *Gone With the Wind*), *The Wizard of Oz* was a breakthrough movie with its use of color to reinforce the magic of the land of Oz compared to the dreary black and white world of Kansas. Think of the main characters and you'll associate key props that both indentify the characters and move the plot forward. Dorothy has her dog Toto, a thing that gets the Kansas conflict going when he inadvertently annoys the evil neighbor, Miss Gulch, who hits him with a rake for chasing her cat, and threatens to call the sheriff, and then tries to steal the dog away. Dorothy's love for Toto illustrates her loneliness as an orphan living on a farm with well-meaning relatives and only farmhands for friends. Toto is more than Dorothy's prop; he will do much to move the plot forward with his tenacity and strong will. He embodies qualities that become Dorothy's strengths as the story unfolds: defiance, loyalty. He also embodies the three things her friends in OZ desire, smarts, heart and courage.

Toto is part prop and part character, but consider the inanimate objects that hum with meaning. Let's start with those ruby slippers—every little girl that sees the movie wants a pair of those slippers. They provide magical protection; they can even provide magical transportation, and, well, they're just so shiny and bright and enticing. Every little—and big—girl loves a new pair of shows. And these shoes give Dorothy power with their protection. They are the means of getting her down that yellow brick road—another thing in the script that has leapt from screen to cultural icon for a clear, bright path to a goal.

We hardly meet a character in this script who doesn't have a prop in hand or a prop they desire. Uncle Henry and Auntie Em have their faulty incubator and baby chicks to save and the farmhands their wagon to repair and their tools and their pigs to tend. The shyster traveling fortuneteller/wizard has his crystal ball, his magical wizard head/throne contraption, and finally the hot air balloon that becomes his final means of transportation. The evil Miss Gulch has her bicycle; she can ride it through the tornado to trade it in for a broom when she transforms into the Wicked Witch in Oz. Glenda the Good Witch has her wand. While Tin Man, Scarecrow, and the Cowardly Lion all want abstract things—a heart capable of compassion, brains, courage, qualities they already have—they do in the end receive the objects representing these qualities: a shiny plastic heart placed appropriately inside his hollow tin chest, a diploma, and a medal for valor. Abstractions made simple and concrete. Children love such things, and viewers of all ages will remember such things.

Think of your favorite movies, and consider the images that instantly surface. Steven Soderbergh's *sex, lies, and videotape* is a hypnotic, voyeuristic film that tells of how the lives of a frigid housewife Ann (Andie MacDowell) and her philandering husband John (Peter Gallagher) are disrupted and transformed by a visit from John's old fraternity buddy, Graham (James Spader). Graham, it seems is a changed man who no longer enjoys lying or manipulating women to sleep with him. Impotent, he now can only get his thrills while watching video tapes of women who talk about their sex lives. His primary possessions are a video camera and his collection of tapes. It isn't long before Ann and her sister Cindy, a bit of a sexual predator who happens to be sleeping with John, discover the tapes and choose to tell their own sexual stories for Graham. Soon John discovers that his wife had made a tape, and after watching it he realizes there is much more to his wife than he thought; he also realizes that she is leaving him behind. All of the characters are transformed by the videotapes. Cindy realizes John is a jerk and insults him. John realizes he isn't the all-powerful stud he thought he was. And Ann, who discovers the affair between her husband and sister, is empowered by making the tape—as well as having sex with Graham. She leaves John on a note of strength and fury, and she moves beyond her frigidity and reach to Graham for the easy affection and passion that she had formerly denied herself.

American Beauty, a film lush with images, also uses videotape as a motivating factor for key characters. The primary plot tells the story of a middle-aged suburban husband Lester (Kevin Spacey) who hates his marriage, his life, the man he has allowed himself to become. His effort to change his life collides with a similarly alienated, disgruntled and seemingly all-American family next door and results in his death. The collision course of a plot line is marked by powerful images that simultaneously enthrall and disturb. There are roses, of course, carefully grown, pruned and arranged American Beauty roses. They are shockingly perfect, brilliant red, and if you know your roses, you'll know that the American Beauty variety has no scent—it's devoid of the very quality we generally associate with roses, an intoxicatingly lovely smell. When the unhappy protagonist, Lester (Kevin Spacey), fantasizes about the promising sexuality of his high-school daughter's friend, he sees a hypnotic shower of rose petals fall from her where she floats above him on the ceiling; the soft, luscious petals quickly start covering him, seemingly drowning him in intoxicating sensual pleasure. The use of roses in the film is one of the finest examples of how a visual image can trigger our sense of touch, and oddly, even smell.

Another recurring image in the film is marijuana, another intoxicant, and it is the unlikely element of a friendship to develop between a middle-aged, middle-class man and a lonely and brilliant young man. The friendship opens both of these emotionally sequestered characters to one another as well as to themselves—they both grow and change, and their changes ultimately result in the death of Lester, a death which, as indicated by the voice over at the beginning and end of the film, seems to be more of a liberation of a life than the end of one.

And then there is the video camera, and the young man who likes to watch the world through that lens. He likes to tape people of interest to him, but he also likes to tape things, simple things that ring of powerful significance, things such as the odd, surreal plastic bag that's caught up in the gusting breeze. It's a mundane thing, a disposable thing, that when caught up by specific and yet random forces becomes somewhat magical, even spiritual—much like the human critter which is also mundane, disposable, and yet, in some specific moments, something somewhat divine.   And yes, there's been much fun made of that plastic bag—I've seen more than one parody of this moment rendering it as a pretentiously poetic device. And yes, I've grinned a bit at those parodies, but when I first saw that odd image in the film, I was transfixed and somewhat amazed that the director, Sam Mendes, had pulled off such a transformation of meaning in such a simple everyday thing.

A thing, an object, can always be more than it appears; a thing, like that box of some little boy's objects found, can set a plot in motion. Consider that famous ring that corrupts souls and generates wars in the *Lord of the Rings*. Yes, the ring first appeared in Tolkien's trilogy, but it became a cultural icon of evil once we saw it up close in that seductively, softly brilliant gold. We see it again and again, slipped on, yanked free of fingers, safely resting on a chain around some nervous hobbit's neck. Pretty much every trinket store across the country sold that ring.

Another treasured object that is so important that it almost serves as a character is the jewel known as the "Heart of the Ocean" in *Titanic*. I won't spend much time discussing this blockbuster, but it does warrant some mention, given it was the most nominated film in history and won a record number of eleven of its fourteen academy award nominations. We all know the love story set on the doomed ship, but I'm more interested in discussing the subplot concerning the quest for that jewel. The pretty-much-priceless piece is given to Rose as an engagement gift from her fiancée. Given that he maintains control of the jewel for most of the trip, the jewel is actually something more like bait than a present. The dashing and cruel fiancée only appears to be wealthy. With most of his family fortune gone, he offers the jewel to Rose, and assumes she will bring a family fortune to their marriage. But it seems she's in the same financial boat—I couldn't resist. With her own family fortune gone, she is pressed by her aunt to marry the man who only seems to have money. The diamond, in short, is a deception, used in an attempt to trade for another deception.

As the real love story grows between Rose and the poor but big-hearted Jack Dawson, the significance of that jewel dwindles. What was once guarded in a safe and only brought out to adorn the wife-to-be, becomes somewhat trivialized as the ship starts going down. The fiancée stores it in his jacket pocket as the chaos grows, not a very secure place when the ship is rolling about. Later in the chaos, he finds Rose and places his jacket on her, in part as a way of protecting her, but also as a way of laying claim to her. But Rose and the jewel slip loose from his grip once again. He'll never recover it, and even the several recovery crews sent out to search the ruin at the bottom of the sea never recover it. Once Jack is gone and Rose lives on, the great mystery of the story becomes whatever happened to that jewel, a symbol of ostentatious wealth, a reminder that humans, like jewels, can be bought and sold.

It seems Rose was wearing that jacket and unknowingly had the jewel at her side as the ship went down. By some miracle it remained in that pocket as she nearly drowned in those icy waters. When the old woman in the end reveals to the viewer that all along she has been in possession of the jewel, we aren't too surprised. The love story that has unfolded reveals that she is a passionate and reckless romantic. No surprise when she climbs, with her bare feet and brilliant red toenails, the railing of the recovery ship, only to toss the much-sought Heart of the Ocean to the dark sea. This object, and what she does with it, says worlds about the woman. For all that urging for her to marry into money, she truly never gives a damn about material things. The jewel, just like all those doomed passengers, can sink to oblivion, and the heart. . . . well, you know how the song goes.

In writing your script, don't underestimate the importance of things. Just the way we can make certain judgments by what a person wears, we can infer all kinds of meanings by the props they keep around them, what they hang on to, and what they let go.

At this point you've learned about how to develop a character, have one character interact with others and through action, speech, implied feelings and thoughts, change, be changed. You've learned by now to write dialogue that is convincing, fresh, not exceedingly expository, dialogue that is not pedestrian, cliché, but rather is the best of the dialogue your characters could say, dialogue that at its best is memorable, clever, maybe even wise. Now let us consider how to paint or portray our characters by using, really using with focused attention, what will appear on the screen.

But we don't spend the big bucks to see a movie just to hear a story told. We drink in those images, all that color, texture, movement, shining, shimmering, or intriguing with dappled light and shadows. While I'm not asking you to think so much as a director or cinematographer—they will do all that work for you—you do need to remember you are providing the blueprint of a story that will be told, in spite of all that movement, one frame at a time.

I don't mean to suggest that you really write your scripts one frame at a time, but do think about the minutes, the seconds that you have to work with to keep a viewer's attention on the screen.

If you watch a lot of television, you might underestimate the task of telling a story with interesting visuals, not just words. In most primetime television, the camera moves from face to face as the characters spout the expository dialogue that tells us just what kind of crime occurred, who might have done it, who might be to blame and why. The many variations of *Law and Order* and *CSI* have intrigued audiences for years, but not with their sterling dialogue. Viewers are more drawn to the who-done-it and how-will-we-catch-them plot lines. And of course there is always the gratuitous eye-candy, cops, lawyers, and investigators running around in hug-the-butt and feature-the-cleavage clothes. Whatever works.

Sit-coms also stick with the camera moving from face to face as the talking-head characters gush, complain, manipulate and emote in response to whatever silly challenges or embarrassments come their way. Some of these can be quite clever. *Friends* and *Seinfield* were highly successful programs that pretty much feature a bunch of friends sitting around and talking.

In a movie you should do better than this. We've been brought up on so much run-of-the mill, day-to-day television; it's easy to forget that filmmaking is an art as well as entertainment. You can do both.

In the comic mockumentary, *Waiting for Guffman*, a film made on the shoestring budget of writer and star Christopher Guest, we are instantly introduced to a cast of characters who are indeed *characters*. And in seeing them, we know them at first glance by the way the writer has chosen to describe them. The film opens with a town board meeting where local "important" people are planning a celebration of the 150th anniversary of the small town of Blaine. When the first issue being discussed is a thoughtful place for the port-o-potties for the old people who will attend the festival, we get the tone of the piece. It's to be a comic commentary on small-town folks with over-blown notions of their importance.

Our inciting incident takes off when the oh-so-fey and oh-so-serious dramatic artist, Corky St. Clair, plans a casting call for a theatrical tribute to the town. When we first see Corky we are maybe stunned, but certainly amused by his look: thick, short-cut, combed-forward bangs, the "artistic" mustache/goatee, lots of hand gestures and a dramatic polka dot shirt. He introduces himself as a man well-experienced in New York theatre who decided he needed a change, so he came to Blaine, where he thought he might be a construction worker and wear one of those what he calls "flowing" hard hats, and chaps. Between the lines we can see him practicing for a gig with the Men at Work group and happily dancing to "YMCA." His dialogue is full of over-the-top and oh-so-serious theatre jargon, and in spite of the weird hair-cut, he completely engages us. The film is a parody of community theatre, and it gets right to the hopeful hearts of small town folks looking for a bigger life on the stage. The humor in this script hinges on the incongruency of how silly the characters appear while taking themselves and their "talent" so seriously.

In a series of vignettes we meet the players in this ensemble cast. Ron and Sheila are a married couple who consider themselves the worldly ones of the town, as they run the travel agency. He's too tanned, and she's too made-up, with those weird '80s teased-up and sprayed bangs that rise like some plastic tidal wave off her forehead. For the audition they dress alike in garishly bright workout clothes and do very serious breathing and stretching exercises while they wait their turn to show their talent act, a goofy, campy thing that has Corky sighing with delight, while the musical director for the show looks nothing but appalled.

Then there's Libby Mae Brown, the Dairy Queen counter girl, a stringy-haired, skinny and tough little thing who manages simultaneously to chew gum and smoke, while telling us in all seriousness the details of her job: making cones, burgers, cokes. Her audition would be pathetic if it were not so comic; she sings off pitch, struts her skinny stuff around in a tight and worn-out dress. She flirts with all she's got for the casting team and ends with a split made ridiculous by her scrawny legs and her feet in white pumps worn only by poorly paid teachers of vacation Bible school.

And finally we meet Dr. Pearl, the dentist who is comic at first sight, with his geeky face, oversized thick glasses that cover half his face, and his teeth, oh those teeth, all yellowed and crooked, peeking out to baffle us when he smiles. He tells us he's always been quite the comic. And ironically, unintentionally he is comic, but for his looks, not for his clever jokes. When he retells an old Johnny Carson joke, it's so flat he has to explain it to us. And he's the only one laughing.

It's a silly and engaging script for the ironic and clever dialogue, but also for the writer's eye for detail. Try having a look at *Waiting for Guffman* or *American Beauty*, or any critically acclaimed movie—*Citizen Kane* uses details that provide exquisite clarity in terms of characters' personalities. In most any movie, train yourself to study the way details about physical appearance or gestures reveal the nature of characters. In *Waiting for Guffman* we know these comic characters by their hair-dos, their clothes, the little gestures they make with their hands. While they are something closer to caricatures, almost cartoon-like creatures, they are very much real in their desire for recognition and their fifteen minutes (or more) of fame. And misguided as they all are about their talents, they are very earnest in the pursuit of their goals, making them lovable as well as laughable.

When writing your characters, pay close attention, not just to any detail, but to significant details. In the classic little writing handbook, *The Elements of Style*, William Strunk, Jr. wisely notes this insight about details. Keep his advice in mind when writing anything, whether it's a postcard or a screenplay:

> "If those who have studied the art of writing are in accord on any one point, it is on this: the surest way to arouse and hold the attention of the reader is by being specific, definite, concrete. The greatest writers . . . are effective largely because they deal in particulars and report the details that matter."

Let's really think about the difference between detail and significant detail. You don't need to give every vital statistic about every character in your script, only the significant details that reveal something about the character, details that might play out with some meaning in the script.

For example in my script *Blood Sisters,* I introduce three main players in the story very quickly. I don't want to clutter the movement of images as I establish my characters in the tawdry setting of a circus with caged animals and circus freaks roaming the grounds. So I introduce the family of three in two descriptive sentences:

```
GRACE, BETSY, and CLIFFORD HANES walk through the crowd.
Grace, a well-endowed girl of fourteen or so, follows
mother, Betsy, 30-ish, attractive but strained. Clifford,
mid-thirties, a handsome man with a face hardened by long-
term anger.
```

Note that I didn't go into details of height, weight, eye-color, as these details are not significant to the story. I describe Grace as a well-endowed girl of fourteen or so because I want to point out that she is on the border of being a grown woman fully aware of her powers as a woman, and fully aware that she is grown enough to rebel against her parents. I want Betsy and Clifford both to be attractive so we can guess that at some time they were physically drawn to one another, but the wear and tear of marriage, and life in general, has beaten them. Betsy is strained, suggesting she bears up under the steady anger of her husband. And I want Clifford's handsome face damaged by the anger he carries around. A basic theme of the play addresses the damage that repressed anger can unleash. I want to show a hint of that strain and anger on their faces the first minute you see them.

Now consider the tools that will bring your story alive. A camera and a screen—a giant moving canvas where images play out to draw the viewer into the fictive dream. And this fictive dream begins with you staring into space and summoning up characters, actions, things that all add up to a story that strangers will want to hear—and see.

Exercises for Fine-tuning Visual Language

> "Writers don't need tricks or gimmicks or even need to be the smartest fellows on the block. At the risk of appearing foolish, a writer sometimes needs to just stand and gape at this or that thing—a sunset or an old shoe—in absolute and simple amazement."
>
> Raymond Carver

Good descriptive writing gives an outward and visible sign of an inner psychological, emotional, spiritual state. And your good descriptive writing will depend on every single word you choose to put down. It would be wonderful if writing were always this free-flowing experience where a writer channels some kind of life in some other plane and just has to hurry and write it down. There might be some fleeting moments like that, but most often we stare, trying to summon up people, places, words, things. Then sometimes, bam-- we get lots of stuff, and we write late into the night, we are so on a roll. But before you take that written piece to share with your classmates, your writing buddies, or your teacher, look at it. Test every word to see if it holds, if it means what you want it to say. Writing is a process of calling up or down a storm of words, but we also have to pick through the results in the end. We CHOOSE what stays and what goes.

Consider your own clothes, your look. What does your choice in clothing say about you? Or not? Consider your mom, your aunt, the lady down the street. The middle-aged woman who wears high-waist jeans and a sparkly Christmas tree on her sweatshirt is a whole different breed from the middle-aged woman who wears low-riding, tight jeans and a tattoo on her well-toned and tanned bicep. The college guy who wears tight, black, skinny jeans, converse sneakers and rock band t-shirts and is always carrying a skateboard is a whole different kind of fellow than the guy who wears three-layered popped-collar shirts, Abercrombie jeans and deck shoes. Don't forget the basic props some always carry. I'll admit, I always have a bottle of water and a tube of Mac lipstick on hand. It could be a pretention, but I do use them constantly, even when no one is around. Scary maybe, what that might say about me, but it does say something.

Let's say you have a character who can't go anywhere, not even into the shower, without the cell phone at hand. What might that imply about the character? So do consider in your character sketches below, what stuff might always be around.

187

Pick a Person You Know and Show Character through Appearance

Pick a person you know, either closely or at a distance. Now note the significant details about them. And play psycho-analyst for a bit.

Name

Age range

Hairstyle

Typical shirt, jeans, skirt, slacks, whatever they typically wear.

Shoes

Basic Props

What do you make of him or her?

Now Make Up a Person, a Possible Protagonist, and Show Character through Appearance

Name

Age range

Hairstyle

Typical shirt, jeans, skirt, slacks, whatever they typically wear.

Shoes

Basic Props

What do you make of him or her?

How an Old Prop Can Start a New Plot

Consider movies where plot grows from something as simple as a character's relationship to an object. There's the cult classic, the low-budget, post-apocalyptic film *A Boy and His Dog* (1975), which features Vic (a young Don Johnson) roaming a wasteland with his grumbling, telepathic dog. They find trouble in an underground society of women who want Vic's sperm. It's a darkly comic tale of tough choices, as you might guess. On a lighter note, there's *Bridget Jones' Diary.* The lonely Bridget (Renée Zellweger) comforts her loneliness with her diary—along with cigarettes, sappy TV shows and bad underwear. But it's her diary that reveals her interior world and the sorrow there that gets her going on her quest to find a man.

Consider the following and sketch a quick plot. Or make up your own.

A thirty-ish year old woman and her high-school yearbook

A guy and his porn stash

An older woman and her recipe box

A man and his tool box

A hipster and a vinyl collection

A failing actor and old promotional photos

A former beauty queen and her crown

A former rodeo rider and his belt buckle

How a New Prop Can Start a Plot

This exercise is inspired by the old device of starting a story by having a stranger show up to spin an old world into something new. Such plots are often seen in fairy tales: Aladdin finds a lamp; Hansel and Gretel find an edible house. And there are the contemporary fairy tales. In *Eternal Sunshine of the Spotless Mind,* Joel (Jim Carrey) and Clementine (Kate Winslet) find a machine that can erase all memories; in *Being John Malkovich,* street puppeteer Chris (Kevin Spacey) finds a portal into the mind of the man Malkovich, who certainly leads a more interesting life. On a more serious note there's *The Red Violin*, with a more somber and convoluted plot that shows how the lives of many characters across centuries are changed by the arrival of one singular and remarkable violin.   And of course there's that familiar magical gold ring that moves from hand to hand to stir up a war worth a trilogy of tales.

Consider the following and sketch a quick plot. Or make up your own.

A driver finds a very old, sickly woman collapsed on a sidewalk in front of an urban cemetery. (This one actually happened to me. See what you might do with it.)

A young volunteer for the Katrina clean-up crew finds a voodoo doll.

A young, neglected teenager finds a musical instrument tossed by a dumpster.

Anyone finds what seems to be a human bone in a field.

Anyone finds an unlikely thing (or person) in a recycling bin.

Writing a Montage or a Story without Words

For your own exercise with montage, please try to avoid cliché. Remember, your goal is to use a series of images that tell a story, and in the process lead to an insight or discovery of emotion about the characters or situation being described. Remember, and maybe reviews that classic montage scene in *The Godfather* where Mikey is officially becoming a godfather at a christening in a church, while simultaneously becoming a ruthless godfather in the mafia world. The previously discussed short film *Joe* is an excellent example of how a story riding on desire, conflict, and resolution can convey finely-tuned character development and tell an amusing, even enlightening story without words.

It is also possible to make an entire short film that is essentially a montage, but tells a larger story. The student example "Strangers Not in Paradise," at the end of this chapter, does a very fine job of telling the story of two lonely people who walk right past one another and back to their loneliness. The student example, "Busker," which you read in the earlier chapter on conflict, relies only on music and shots to tell the story of a musician brought down by too much ambition too fast. Have a look at these scripts and consider how the story is playing out without words, then consider writing your own story without words.

Your purpose here is to tell a little story to your audience with a series of images, still shots and/or little clips of action. There's to be no dialogue. Rely on images alone to tell your story.

Now have a look at the suggested options for a montage. Or make up your own idea.

Options for Montage Stories

Montage can be used to tell a min-story such as the example of a couple falling in love; it can also be used to present a slice of life where no plot is involved, but rather the viewer sees a series of images that result in an insight into the topic or situation being depicted. Take a look at the suggested options, or make up your own situation to depict. At the start, you will no doubt be drawn to clichés—write those if that's what it takes to get you going. Then push yourself for freshness; try to be particular and original in your choice of images. Your best strategy for avoiding stereotypes and clichés is to stick to a subject that you really know, or to do your research. Try staking out a place; watch it, see what routinely happens, who routinely comes and goes; then tell the story of that place. Know something about your topic. You can always interview a person of interest, follow him or her around all day to get a realistic view of how a day is spent. Take your time; be honest; try to write the piece only you could write.

Mini-Story Situations

--a couple falling in love (if you must) or a couple falling out of love

--a character slowly becoming an alcoholic, or healing from alcoholism

--a character learning an athletic skill

--a character going through a makeover—say from nerd to dude, or from frump to babe

--a city coming to life at dawn; a natural setting coming to life at dawn

--a bar from morning to peak business hours to closing time—a day in the life of a bar

--a student going off to college or a first prom

--a wedding day or the day of a funeral

--the renovation of a house

Slice of Life Portraits

--a day in the life of a bakery, a bowling alley, a flea market, or any place of interest to you

--a day in the life of a drunk, a fitness fiend, a hunter, a mom, a student, a small child

--a day in the life of a cop, a paramedic, a fireman (resist melodrama)

--a day in the life of a groundskeeper, a maintenance man, a maid

--a day in the life of an object, a piece of furniture or equipment

Have a look at the student sample below by Matthew Rome. It is a complete story told without words and employs excellent use of montage to how two lonely young people are locked in their loneliness even when they cross paths. They are so caught up in their narrow worldviews, and most-likely less-than-great self-esteem, they don't see each other or the possibility for change.

Student Example of a Story without Words
by Matthew Rome

STRANGERS NOT IN PARADISE

By
Matthew Rome

M. Rome
231 Lonely Strangers Ct.
Toledo, OH 43611
Phone:
Email:

FADE IN:

INT. LONELY GUY'S CAR - DAY

LONELY GUY, 20s or 30s, plain-looking, generic hair-cut,
wearing an ordinary shirt and tie, with a class ring on his
right hand, drives down the road, listening to the radio.
He stops at a red traffic light and looks to the car on his
right.

LONELY GUY'S POV - TEENAGERS
A group of FOUR TEENAGERS are all talking and gesturing.

BACK TO SCENE

Lonely Guy smiles a sad, half smile. He looks to the car on
his left.

LONELY GUY'S POV - COUPLE

A COUPLE is kissing as they wait for the light to turn
green. Lonely Guy continues to stare at them.

The couple stops kissing and the woman driver notices Lonely
Guy staring and points. Her car takes off. The guy in the
passenger seat gives Lonely Guy the finger.

BACK TO SCENE

A loud HONK snaps Lonely Guy from his surprise and he
accelerates. Lonely guy turns up the volume on his stereo.
Unsatisfied with the
 MUSIC on the radio, he begins playing with the tuner.

INSERT - TUNER

Lonely Guy's right hand, class ring visible, eventually
settles upon a LONELY SOUNDING SONG.

                                        MATCH CUT:

ANOTHER TUNER - SLIGHTLY DIFFERENT

The SAME SONG continues to play. A girl's hand leaves the tuner dial.

INT. LONELY GIRL'S CAR - DAY

LONELY GIRL, mousey and girly, approximately same age as Lonely Guy, wearing a pink blazer and skirt, drives down a neighborhood street. She pulls into a parking lot along the side of an apartment complex and pulls into an empty spot.

Lonely Girl pulls down her visor mirror and puts on some lip gloss. She smacks her lips together and stares at herself in the mirror. She gives herself a slight frown before putting up the visor.

INT. LONELY GIRL'S APARTMENT - LOBBY - DAY

Lonely Girl enters the apartment lobby and walks over to the mailboxes. She uses a key to open her box and takes out the mail.

INSERT - JUNK MAIL

--Various bills.
--Publisher's Clearing House "You may already have won
  $1,000,000."

                                        MATCH CUT:

DIFFERENT JUNK MAIL

Publisher's Clearing House. Coupon Packs.

INT. LONELY GUY'S APARTMENT LOBBY - DAY

Lonely Guy stands in a noticeably different apartment building lobby looking through mail. He shakes his head, looking disappointed. Lonely Guy walks past a group of PEOPLE standing and chatting in the lobby. They pay no attention to him.

Lonely Guy pushes the "up" arrow for the elevator and with a DING the door opens. A WOMAN walks off the elevator. Lonely Guy smiles at her, but she doesn't notice and keeps on walking.

Lonely Guy walks onto the elevator, and the doors close.

CLOSED ELEVATOR DOORS

                                        MATCH CUT:

SLIGHTLY DIFFERENT CLOSED ELEVATOR DOORS

With a DING, the elevator doors open.

INT. LONELY GIRL'S APARTMENT - OUTSIDE HALLWAY - DAY

Lonely Girl steps off the elevator into the hallway. She
walks down the hallway towards room "202," passing a nicely
dressed MAN along the way. She smiles at the man. Without a
pause in his step, the man gives a slight nod of
acknowledgement and continues past her.
LONELY GIRL opens her apartment door and steps in.

INT. LONELY GIRL'S APARTMENT - DAY

The clean apartment has a definite "girl's touch" to it.
Lonely Girl tosses the junk mail onto a coffee table near
the couch. She sets down her purse and takes off her blazer,
placing it on a hanger inside a near-by closet. Lonely Girl
grabs an apple from a basket in the kitchen and washes it
off. She polishes it on her shirt.

She walks over to the phone and answering machine and takes
a bite of her apple with a LOUD, CRISP CRUNCH.

INSERT - PHONE/ANSWERING MACHINE

A girl's finger hits the "New Message" button.

                                        MATCH CUT:

SLIGHTLY DIFFERERNT PHONE/ANSWERING MACHINE

An electronic voice sounds "You have *no* new messages."

A CRUNCH sound from a potato chip.

INT. LONELY GUY'S APARTMENT - DAY

Lonely Guy's apartment is noticeably more messy and unkempt than Lonely Girl's, though certain similarities between the two apartments exist, such as how they are arranged, where certain items are kept, etc.

Lonely Guy stands next to the phone/answering machine with an open bag of potato chips. He chews a chip and reaches in for another. He puts it in his mouth and CRUNCHES it.

He plops down on the left side of the couch with an audible SIGH. He reaches to the coffee table, where a small stack of mail lies, and picks up a remote control. He kicks off his shoes, puts his feet on the coffee table and turns on the TV.

INSERT - LONELY GUY'S TV

A NEWS program is on.

BACK TO SCENE

Lonely Guy flips the channel.

INSERT - LONELY GUY'S TV

A CARTOON is on.

BACK TO SCENE

He flips the channel again

INSERT - LONELY GUY'S TV

OPENING SCENE of *City of Angels* is on.

BACK TO SCENE

Lonely Guy flips the station again to a SPORTS PROGRAM. He watches it for a few seconds, then flips it back to *CITY OF ANGELS*.

INSERT- LONELY GUY'S TV

CITY OF ANGELS continues.

MATCH CUT:

LONELY GIRL'S TV

The same scene from *CITY OF ANGELS* plays.

INT. LONELY GUY'S APARTMENT - DAY

Lonely Guy picks up the remote and shuts off the TV. He
reaches up and wipes away a tear from the corner of his eye.
SLAPS his face to snap himself out of it. He stands up and
walks to the fridge. He opens it up and looks inside.

INSERT - FRIDGE

The fridge is mostly empty. Inside are a few cans of Pepsi,
some leftovers, a box of cold pizza, condiments, milk, and a
few other odds and ends.

BACK TO SCENE

Lonely Guy reaches in and pulls out the milk and sets it on
the table.

INSERT - MILK ON TABLE

A carton of 2% milk sits atop the table.

O.S., the fridge closes with a THUD.

                                             MATCH CUT:

MILK ON TABLE - SLIGHTLY DIFFERENT

A carton of skim milk sits atop the table.

INT. LONELY GIRL'S APARTMENT - NIGHT

Lonely Girl opens a cupboard above the sink and pulls out a
dish. She sets it on the table next to the milk. She opens a
counter drawer near the sink and brings out a spoon. She
places it on the table, then arranges it as a place setting.

INSERT - TABLE

The bowl and spoon sit next to each other in an orderly
fashion, with the milk slightly off to the side.

                                        MATCH CUT:

TABLE - SLIGHTLY DIFFERENT

The exact same setting as above.

INT. LONELY GUY'S APARTMENT - NIGHT

Lonely Guy grabs a box of previously opened Cap'n Crunch
cereal off the top of his fridge. He pours it into the bowl,
but only a few pieces of cereal fall out.

INSERT - BOWL
A few pieces of dry Cap'n Crunch cereal are scattered in the
bowl, not enough to eat.

                                        MATCH CUT:

BOWL - SLIGHTLY DIFFERENT

A few pieces of dry Cap'n Crunch cereal are scattered in the
bowl, not enough to eat.

INT. LONELY GIRL'S APARTMENT - NIGHT
Lonely Girl stands holding an empty Cap'n Crunch box over a
bowl of cereal. She SIGHS. She tosses the empty box in the
garbage can, grabs her coat, picks up her purse and her
keys, and opens the door to her apartment.

She walks through and closes the door behind her.

                                        CUT TO:

INT. LONELY GUY'S APPARTMENT - NIGHT

LONELY GUY tosses on his jacket and grabs his keys from the
coffee table. He opens the door to his apartment.

He walks through and closes the door behind him.

EXT. KROGER - NIGHT

The night is dark except for the few street lamps in the parking lot and the Kroger sign. The parking lot is fairly empty. Only a few cars sit parked near the entrance.

Lonely Girl gets out of her car, heads into the store

Lonely Guy's car drives in and parks right next to Lonely Girl's car.

The car shuts off, the door opens and Lonely Guy walks towards the store.

INT. KROGER - NIGHT

The store is empty of customers.

SOFT MUSIC plays in the background from the store's speakers. Lonely Girl walks down an aisle, looking at various cereals stacked on the shelf. The shelves look picked-over.

A MAN, holding a box and walking as he studies boxes on the shelf, bumps into Lonely Girl as he passes. Lonely Girl looks at the man. He wears a Kroger name tag, is clearly a stocker. Lonely Girl gives him a brief, forgiving smile and the stocker continues to walk.

Lonely Girl continues to scan the shelves.

She sees an empty space, sees it's where the Cap'n Crunch cereal should be.

INSERT - SHELF LABLE

The shelf where Cap'n Crunch should be is almost completely bare, except for a lone box, high up, in the center of the shelf.

BACK TO SCENE

Standing on her tiptoes, Lonely Girl reaches up to grab the box of Cap'n Crunch. She gets it in her hands, but just as she pulls it down, the box slips from her grip and falls to the ground with a THUD.

Lonely Girl starts to bend down to pick it up, but before she can:

INSERT - BOX ON THE FLOOR

A hand wearing a class ring grabs it off the floor, picks it up.

BACK TO SCENE

Lonely Guy holds the box in his hand, and Lonely Girl is standing next to him. Lonely Guy studies the shelf long enough to realize he holds the last box of cereal.

                    LONELY GUY
          Here. I think you dropped this.

Lonely Guy hands the box of cereal to Lonely Girl.

                    LONELY GIRL
     Yeah.

Lonely Girl takes the box from Lonely Guy.

                    LONELY GIRL
     Thank you.

Lonely Guy smiles.

                    LONELY GUY
     My pleasure.

Lonely Girl smiles back at him, hesitantly turns and walks down the aisle.

Lonely Guy watches her walk away for a moment, then looks back to the shelf.

Lonely Girl stops, turns back for a brief look at Lonely Guy, who doesn't notice. Then she continues walking out of the aisle.

LONELY GUY waits a second longer, turns, smiles to himself and begins to walk toward the opposite side of the aisle from which LONELY GIRL left.

INT. LONELY GIRL 'S APARTMENT - NIGHT

Lonely Girl, dressed for bed, finishes her last bite of
cereal. She picks up the bowl and spoon, washes them in the
sink and leaves them to dry.

She walks back to the table, picks up the box of Cap'n
Crunch, walks over to her fridge and reaches to put it on
top. She stops for a second, looks at the box, considering
something, smiles, then puts it on top of the fridge.

INSERT - FRIDGE TOP

A lone box of Cap'n Crunch sits atop the fridge.

                                        MATCH CUT:

SLIGHTLY DIFFERENT FRIDGE TOP

Cap'n Crunch box on its side, empty.

INT. LONELY GUY'S APARTMENT - NIGHT

Lonely Guy tosses the empty box in the trash. He opens the
fridge and pulls out a can of Pepsi. He opens it with a SNAP
and HISS and takes a sip.

Then he pulls out a leftover box of pizza. He opens the box.

INSERT - OPEN PIZZA BOX

There are two pieces of cold, leftover pepperoni pizza.

BACK TO SCENE

Lonely Guy closes the box and carries it, along with his
Pepsi, down the hall towards his bedroom.

INT. LONELY GIRL'S APARTMENT - BEDROOM - NIGHT

Lonely Girl, still dressed for bed, delicately takes the
many stuffed animals off her bed and places them neatly on
the floor. Lonely Girl takes special care with each animal.
Once the last animal is removed, Lonely Girl turns down the
covers on the left side of her double bed and climbs in.

Lonely Girl reaches down and picks up a fuzzy teddy bear slightly bigger than the rest. She squeezes the teddy bear tightly, gives it a kiss, then lets out a lonely SIGH.

Lonely Girl reaches over to the bed stand next to her, turns off the light and turns on her radio.

A LONELY SONG PLAYS (the same one as in the beginning) as Lonely Girl cuddles close under the covers with her teddy bear.

INSERT - ALARM CLOCK

The face of the alarm clock is lit up in big red numbers "9:59 PM"

                                        MATCH CUT:

ALARM CLOCK - SLIGHTLY DIFFERENT

The same LONELY SOUNDING SONG PLAYS. The big red numbers "9:59 PM" flip to "10:00 PM."

INT. LONELY GUY'S APARTMENT - BEDROOM - NIGHT

Lonely Guy lies asleep on the right side of his double bed. Lonely Guy has the covers cocooned around him, leaving the left side of the bed completely bare except for Lonely Guy's outstretched arm and an empty pizza box.

INSERT - LONELY GUY'S BED

An aerial view of Lonely Guy's room and bed. Lonely Guy sleeping on the right side.

                                        MATCH CUT:

LONELY GIRL'S BED

An aerial view of Lonely Girl's bed. Lonely Girl sleeps on the left side. LONELY SONG FADES OUT SOFTLY.

                                        FADE OUT

                        THE END.

This quiet story is a sad little realistic piece that would be simple to make in that primarily we are in two easy-to-manage locations: two apartments. I find this writer to have been quite clever in the use of match cuts to show the similarities between two strangers in their daily routine.

It's a lovely story, and well-crafted. But there are a of couple glitch spots if this script were to be made. One is getting the rights to use *City of Angels* in a script—not an easy or a cheap thing to do. In the writing, in theory, it works, as the movie parallels our story of two lonely strangers. But in practice, there's a problem. If you were to make this movie, you'd probably want to show something else the two strangers have in common. A book perhaps. Or maybe they both keep fish and talk to the fish. *City of Angels* is a film about romantic longing. There are many ways the theme of romantic longing can be played out.

Also, there's the matter of the Kroger parking lot. It would be tough to get a release from the chain store corporation to use their space. Lots of legalities involved. You'd be best to make friends with a local independent grocery store owner. Getting the release for shooting there would be a simpler process. And the store owner would probably enjoy the extra attention—and business.

When writing your script, it's good to let go of some of the practical details of possibly having a script made into a movie. Don't worry about everything, until it's time to worry over a particular challenge. Do each little task in its turn and you'll have a script of quality in the works.

6. Dramatic Dialogue

"What we've got here is a failure to communicate."

Cool Hand Luke

No doubt you've heard this line before, but perhaps you don't know where it comes from, being it was used most recently by the smooth-talking Everett (George Clooney in *Oh Brother Where Art Thou)*, who always remains cool-headed and well-groomed while running from the law with his comrades, fellow convicts on the run. The ironic line was made famous by Luke (Paul Newman), the "natural born world shaker" who repeatedly infuriates his prison warden, the "Captain," with his cocky attitude and his successful escapes. Luke's use of this line appears late in the story, just before the climax, and it is a mockery of the Captain, who uses the line earlier in the movie when he explains to the other prisoners why he has been so harsh in his punishment of Luke. His line is a bit different. He says:

"What we've got here is...failure to communicate."

The context of the line, as it is first delivered in the film, is when the Captain has just captured Luke after a brief escape. The Captain, who seeks to make an example of Luke to the other prisoners, warns with a smile, "Now I can be a good guy, or I can be one real-mean sum bitch." When Luke mocks his arrogant pretense of benevolence, the outraged Captain lashes out and punches Luke, who then falls and rolls down the hill. While Luke remains slumped in the culvert by the roadway, the frustrated Captain recovers his composure and delivers the line, pronouncing his judgment of the problem: that violence is necessary, given Luke's failure to understand the one-way nature of the power hierarchy in the prison. The line is an opening for a warning speech directed to the other prisoners who are watching. The Captain goes on to say "Some men you just can't reach. So you get what we had here last week, which is the way he wants it... well, he gets it. I don't like it any more than you men."

Yeah, right.

The theme is restated during the final action of the main plot. As evening falls, Luke's third escape from prison brings him to a country church, where he seeks shelter and makes his last, despairing attempt to communicate with God, whom Luke holds responsible for making Luke what he is. Quickly surrounded by the flashing lights of police cars, Luke's prison buddy "Dragline" wants to surrender. Laughing, Luke goes to the window — either to concede defeat, size up the enemy, or taunt his captors one more time — and when he speaks the familiar line, the posse instantly shoots him. Certainly a failure to communicate there.

The line denotes mockery and arrogance. When the Captain first uses it, the line conveys an understatement of reasons for brutality; it's almost sweet-talking in the way we've often seen Southern villains depicted—as in *Deliverance*—smiling, laughing at they while they proceed to torture and kill some unfortunate soul. We also see a little glimpse of this cruel irony in *Pulp Fiction*. The line says worlds about the cold-heartedness of the Captain, in that it conveys how he's having a bit of fun with his own cleverness as well as his cruelty.

When Luke uses it just before he is shot with the blast that will result in his death, he also reveals an arrogance, but not of the cruel kind. He's a bit naïve. But the Captain is no regular authority figure; he's a man aching for a reason to hurt Luke in the worst possible way. It's a clever line that provides a deadly understatement of the danger at hand. And even though the line is pretty much the same one spoken by different characters, it's implied meaning is as different as the two men who speak the line. When you write dialogue, ideally it should be so particular in expression, rhythm, vocabulary, that we should be able to guess who is speaking the line without having to see the speaker. And bear in mind, context can be everything. A simple line like "I'm satisfied" can have a world of meanings, depending on what character is saying the words, and why.

A Failure to Communicate Exercise

On the note of "we have a failure to communicate," write a scene where you deliberately show that in spite of an effort to communicate, the result is a failure. It's a terrific way to establish character quickly, as at least one of the characters has a motive to communicate, and it just doesn't work. So come up with two characters; give them a motive—something they would like to communicate—and then, given the nature of their characters, show how the communication fails. The following exercise nicely shows how a couple, in emotional trouble but still hanging on, fails to communicate. Being drunk certainly doesn't aid in their communication skills. Still they make an effort to connect; however, their own individual agendas keep them from engaging with the other's needs.

Student Example of a Failure to Communicate
by Nathan Elias

EXT. APARTMENT COMPLEX - NIGHT

MONICA and SVEN stagger out of Monica's car. She walks in
front of him, up the stairs, dangling keys. He follows close
behind. At her landing, she struggles to unlock her door.
DROPS KEYS, picks them up, tries again.

> MONICA
> I don't know why it won't unlock. I
> tried everything.

> SVEN
> Be slow, patient. You'll get it.

> MONICA
> Unlock, damn you!

> SVEN
> Here, give me the keys.

> MONICA
> Wait, I almost got it.

> SVEN
> You're drunk. Give me the keys.

They playfully fight over the keys until they stumble over
each other and fall to the ground, LAUGHING.

INT. APARTMENT, KITCHEN - NIGHT

Sven sits at the kitchen counter, not paying attention to
Monica changing out of her clothes as she scurries around
and heads to the bedroom. Zoned out, he tries to light his
"dugout" for a hit, gets nothing. He stares at it, rotating
the metal cigarette between his fingers.

Monica comes into the kitchen in her underwear, grabs a
glass of water, walks out. The bedroom door SHUTS behind
her. Sven puts the dugout in his pocket, heads into the
bedroom.

INT. APARTMENT, BATHROOM - CONTINUOUS

Sven walks into the bathroom and leans over the edge of the
bathtub. Monica follows, sits on the toilet and PEES.

                    MONICA
          Are you okay?

                    SVEN
          I'm drunk.

                    MONICA
          Do you need something?

                    SVEN
          Can I bum a smoke?

She reaches around to the toilet tank where an ashtray
overflows with butts, grabs a pack of cigarettes and a
lighter. She hands him a cigarette and the lighter. He
lights up, still leaning over the tub, while she wipes,
FLUSHES, yanks up her panties, and sits looking at him.

                    SVEN
          Hey, are you okay?

                    MONICA
          I don't understand why you like to
          hurt me.

                    SVEN
          How do I hurt you?

                    MONICA
          One minute you say I'm your girlfriend;
          the next minute you won't touch me.

Sven straightens, sits on edge of the tub.

                    SVEN
          When did I not touch you tonight?

                    MONICA
          All night, Sven. Nobody there knew we
          were together. When that guy said we
          look cute together and asked if we were

dating, you didn't even say anything.
                    (beat)
Are you embarrassed of me? Do you know
how many guys tried to hook up with me
tonight?

                    SVEN
You're completely wrong, Monica.

                    MONICA
How? Where were you when those two guys
had me cornered in the hallway?

                    SVEN
Where were you when I was outside having
a fucking panic attack in the street?

                    MONICA
Jesus, kid. Get over yourself. There's
nothing wrong with you.

                    SVEN
How can you say you love me when you don't
know a thing about me?

Monica gets up, reaches for a cigarette. Sven slowly stands.
She tries to light a cigarette, but her hands shake. He
lights it for her.

                    MONICA
You think I love you?

                    SVEN
I think you drank too much.

                    MONICA
I don't love you.

                    SVEN
No?

                    MONICA
I never loved you.
                    (beat)
Get out.

Sven tries wrapping his arms around her. She shrugs him off, ashes her cigarette.

                    MONICA
          Just leave me. I won't wait for someone
          to fall in love with me. I won't wait for
          you to hurt me.

She walks out into the bedroom. He puts out cigarette in overflowing ashtray, follows her.

INT. APARTMENT, BEDROOM - CONTINUOUS

He watches her standing at the window, her back to him.

                    SVEN
          Can I bum another cigarette?

She throws the pack and the lighter on the bed.

His eyes on her, he grabs the pack and lighter. Lights up.

                    MONICA
          Why don't you love me?

                    SVEN
          I never said I didn't love you.

                    MONICA
          You never said you *did* love me.

Sven slips off his clothes and into the bed. He sits smoking a beat or two, looking at her back; she wraps her arms around herself, stands there smoking. He takes a long drag, turns off the light and then in the dark, puts out the cigarette.

This piece nicely shows how often in conversation, our words go right by the one we hope is listening. Even as their words indicate a need to connect, the words only show the distance between them. The whole scene makes the argument that just as we shouldn't drink and drive or drink and dial, we also should remember—don't drink and discuss deep stuff.

Multi-Tasking Dialogue

"It is not of so much consequence what you say, as how
you say it. Memorable sentences are memorable on
account of some single irradiating word."

Alexander Smith

When writing dialogue, always try to think of the multi-tasking power of words. Dialogue simultaneously conveys information, reveals character, moves plot forward and does all kinds of subtle things by way of subtext. While dialogue in a script imitates real speech, in truth it is much better than real speech. When you're out and about, listen to people talk—most of the stuff people say is a lot of blather. We exchange niceties; we talk about the weather; we complain about homework, jobs. We spend a lot of time rambling. As you go through your days, try to tune your ear to hearing, really hearing what people say. Often the conversation will lack much substance or insight, but often conversations can reveal worlds about a character or a relationship. At the end of the day, try to recall an interesting conversation you had or overheard. Maybe it was just a line that triggered an insight into the person speaking, or even better, an insight into some aspect of how we live in this world.

Before thinking about dialogue, recall some of your favorite, or maybe classic, lines from movies. The bits of dialogue may not be well-remembered for their wisdom, but rather for the way, with a little string of words, we see into the heart of a character or a situation. In other words, it's dramatic. And what do I mean by dramatic? Well, let's just say there's, tension, friction, a potential for movement there. A vase of perfectly arranged flowers at the center of a table in an empty room is static--maybe pretty, but static. Now put that vase on the edge of a kitchen counter with a bunch of rowdy, stoned teenagers looking for a snack while mom is at the neighbor's, and that vase, even just sitting there, holds potential drama.

Dramatic language suggests potential for action, and if not that, a character who is interesting enough to generate strong feelings which can then lead to action. Before we discuss how dialogue works like action—how it affects the listener—let's consider how dialogue reveals the speaker, how it can be a vital way of revealing his or her character. Look at these famous little lines and consider how they convey a sense of a character's agenda, class, education, and psychological proclivities. Bear in mind this insight on how dialogue can be heightened into something like poetry if you choose your words carefully. Sometimes a seemingly mundane line can suddenly resonate and take on meaning that transcends the particulars of the script.

"Keep your friends close but your enemies closer."

The Godfather

This line is great not only because it is clever and witty. It also suggests the kind of stealth of character that is necessary to be a successful, and long-living, mob boss. The idea of keeping enemies closer than friends surprises the viewer with a godfather's wily insight. He doesn't think the way most of us do, and we want to know more about his way of seeing the world. We might learn something useful from this ruthless man. The irradiating word here obviously is "closer." We don't expect this shrewd little ironic insight.

"Fasten your seatbelts; it's going to be a bumpy night."

All about Eve

Eve (Bette Davis) playfully draws on an airplane seatbelt metaphor to convey a kind of pleasure in the trouble ahead. The attitude of her words suggests that she is a woman who is rebellious and who doesn't mind a night of trouble one bit. "Bumpy night?" We know that's to be an understatement of the drama about to unfold.

"I love the smell of napalm in the morning."

Apocalypse Now

And any man who loves the smell of napalm has a wicked sense of irony, and also, perhaps, a wicked pleasure in war. Napalm is that "irradiating" word in this otherwise mundane sentence that shocks with reader with the character who speaks it and jolts us into the surreal normalcy of another day in a war.

"Toto, I've a feeling we're not in Kansas anymore."

The Wizard of Oz

Dorothy's understatement regarding the strange and newly colorful world of Oz has transcended its meaning in the film to become a cultural metaphor for anyone suddenly encountering a new and bizarre experience. The fact that she quietly addresses her dog about the situation and doesn't faint or scream that line we hear all too often as an exclamation over anything ("Oh my God!") says worlds about her resilience. Her cautious statement "I've a feeling" illustrates her unfamiliarity with accessing and declaring a situation. She is young, but smart, and being young, she feels the need to tone down her opinion. It's not an opening declarative statement; it's a feeling. And the irony is comic in that it's so clear to all that this brilliant place

214

is nowhere near the black-and-white world of Kansas. Dorothy, in spite of her youth, accepts the conditions, strange as they are, for what they are, and she goes bravely forward. She's a heroine any viewer wants to travel with, as she's calm and cautiously insightful.

"Life's too slippery for books, Clarice. Typhoid and swans come from the same God."
The Silence of the Lambs

Hannibal Lecter's line reveals his keen and brutal intelligence. You've got to have some respect and admiration for this serial cannibal.

Remember that you have two basic tools for telling your story on the screen: the images to be seen, and the voices to be heard. You want your dialogue to have vitality, just as you want your characters to have personality. And a key way we know characters is what they say and how they say it.

A mistake many new writers make is using dialogue to provide information. This is called expository dialogue—it just fills in the blanks of information and tends to fall flat. It just directly spills information in a puddle on the page, and no one wants to step in that. Expository dialogue is one-dimensional, and given that characters and the stories they enact are multi-dimensional, you don't want to use it. Expository dialogue does little to reveal character and offers no subtext to keep things interesting. You want your dialogue to do more than that. What you want to aim for is dramatic dialogue. Dramatic dialogue works double/triple time—it does much more to reveal various dimensions of character, and it moves plot forward in interesting ways, both internally and externally. The main point you want to remember is that DIALOGUE WORKS LIKE ACTION. There are verbs buried in the subtext of dialogue. Just as a character can, dialogue can bite, punch, caress, sneak, sting, soothe.

When you write dialogue, look at it for its subtext—what's underneath the language. Look for an underlying agenda, or perhaps something the speaker is revealing about himself that he doesn't intend to reveal. If you don't see an underlying action or agenda or personality beneath your dialogue, you might need to slow down, go back and rethink your character, rethink that character's operating "verb," what keeps him or her going. If the dialogue is just talk, with no underlying implied action or personality, it just isn't doing its job. Try to make your dialogue move your plot forward and reveal character as well as provide a bit of information about what's going on.

When you write your dialogue, you want to bear in mind that dialogue has to do many things simultaneously: reveal character, move plot forward, provide information about the context of the action, and perhaps reveal something about the theme of the dramatic piece overall.

Now that you've practiced showing a character by using external appearances and gestures to evoke the emotional and psychological inner workings of just who that character is and what he or she wants, let's get your characters talking. But before we get them talking, remember that dialogue on the page and screen is more potent, more complex than every day talk. If you were to record the regular conversations of yourself, your friends, strangers, you'd find it pretty dull. It pretty much just fills in blanks of information and is often loaded with more exposition (a statement or overview of facts) than it is with emotion, subtext, what I like to call "verb."

Remember you have a reader/a viewer who wants to be engaged by your dialogue. When we're on a bus or stuck in an elevator while a mundane conversation is going on, we can distract ourselves with our cell phones, an IPod, or a book. When someone is reading your script, the only distraction from flat dialogue is to put the manuscript down unfinished. And you don't want that. So bear this in mind.

Dialogue shouldn't subject the reader to an exchange of commonplace conversation of relevance only to the speakers. Such stuff pretty much runs like this:

> DEBBIE
> Hey, Donna, how's it going?

> DONNA
> Fine. Just too much homework. And that
> English teacher, still a jerk.

> DEBBIE
> Yeah. There's always too much homework.
> I'm glad my teacher's cool.

> DONNA
> You're lucky. So what you doing tonight,
> since you're not slammed with homework?

> DEBBIE
> Not much. I'm watching *Lost*, as usual.
> You know me and *Lost*.

> DONNA
> Yeah. We've all got our shows.

> DEBBIE

216

```
        You doing anything over the weekend?
```

Who cares?

There is nothing interesting about these girls, because their dialogue is so generic that most of us feel we could live the rest of our lives and never hear from these two again. Maybe they are more interesting on a better day, with something of interest going on in their lives. But who would want to read past this little exchange to find out? No one.

Writing well-crafted dialogue can be a powerful tool for bringing your characters alive and allowing us not only to hear them, but to see them by the way they talk. IF we were to read the above in a script, it would have to be in the context of far more interesting people speaking in more interesting ways. This little snippet then might be ironic with its flatness. These characters might make us laugh at just how dull they are.

Good dialogue isn't just words your characters say to one another across a room, across a car, or across a phone. Good dialogue gives more than facts. It gives us information about the characters as well as about their situation. Good dialogue reveals more about the character than she might intend to reveal when she speaks—this would be subtext, what lies between the lines of what a character is saying. Good dialogue also moves the plot forward in some way, by something as subtle as showing a little shift or change in a character's personality, or something big, like revealing a key piece of information that would change another character's state of being.

Let's have another go at the Debbie/Donna non-drama and make it a bit more interesting by adding a little tension, implying a bit of history, and, for starters, letting the reader know who initiated the conversation, who might want out of it. As I've said above on character development, one of the best ways to know a character is by having a look at what they want. What we want often defines us—and how we speak.

```
                    DEBBIE
        Hey, Donna, how's it going? I can't talk
        for long. I'm meeting Jimmy at
        the Latte Love Shop.


                    DONNA
```

Fine. Just too much homework. My English
teacher, she wants us to write a twenty-
page analysis of *Hamlet*. We have to cite
three different critical approaches.
You still have my *Hamlet* DVD? There's
some director's notes I could use.

                    DEBBIE
I thought I gave it back. I don't know
why they make every senior read that
stupid play. Should just be an Honors
English thing. You college types.

                    DONNA
Jimmy's doing honors.

                    DEBBIE
Yeah. But Jimmy's hot, and he got his
paper done last week. Look I've—

                    DONNA
So are you and Jimmy doing something
tonight, since you're not slammed with
homework?

                    DEBBIE
We're watching *Lost*. He's never seen
it, but you know me and *Lost*.

                    DONNA
Yeah. I know you and lost. Look, I've
got things to do. I've got to go.

So maybe these two aren't exactly folks you'd like to spend much time with, but here
they have a little depth—at least of one of them. And there is something going on
beneath, or in between the words they say. When we speak to someone else, we are
almost always a little preoccupied with something else. We might be thinking about
things like how we look if we are speaking to someone we like. We might be
thinking we're hungry, or we might be hoping a cold isn't coming on, or worrying
about money, or work, or anything.

Here, Debbie takes the upper hand at the get-go when she follows the "how's it
going" question with a statement that says she really can't be bothered—she has
better things to do--with a boy. Donna has work on her mind and wants her DVD
back. Debbie unwittingly reveals herself as not so smart with the indication that she
isn't in an honors class, and she dismisses those who are as "college types." She

obviously doesn't take college seriously. She just likes the honors student Jimmy because he's "hot." She also uses that casual idiom, "he got his paper done" instead of the more conventionally correct "he finished his paper." She's also a bit too engrossed in the television show *Lost.* I don't mean to insult you *Lost* fans, but hey, it isn't *Hamlet.* Donna gets her jab in at the end with the subtle "I know you and lost." I've chosen not to italicize the word here, as a way of indicating how the actor might intend the word lost—as in Debbie is a bit lost in the way of taking life seriously. Donna also gets the upper hand by leading the way out of the conversation before Debbie can brush her off.

So it isn't Shakespeare here, but it is a little bit of drama. We can hear character, and we can hear intentions in the way the characters speak. Dramatic language is much different from the language you hear every day—it's dramatic. That means it isn't passive or boring, but active. The speaker is DOING SOMETHING as he or she speaks.

It can be easy to lapse into expository or flat dialogue when you've got the assignment for homework, along with that history class chapter to read on the War of the Roses, and that Calculus test and oh yeah, the shift at the restaurant to work.

It's hard to write brilliantly with so many things pressing. Often we sit, type a name and see what the character says, let's say starting with the line "Where is it?" as in the dialogue exercise I offer below. I've taught this exercise for years, and often I receive a piece not much different from the non-drama exchange between Debbie and Donna. Bits of dialogue like that indicate that the writer hasn't sat and stared and thought long enough before typing. Before you set to typing, try to come up with a bit of history for your characters, a bit of who they are and what they want and what they feel about the person who is on the other side of the conversation.

Where Is It?

This is a simple exercise, but don't underestimate the challenge. You will start with the given line, "Where is it?" And then you provide the rest. You'll need to think about the characters in the works here. Who is in charge? Do you read that first line as a plea or a demand? Context is everything. The goal is to reveal character just through the way a character speaks. This isn't meant to be a riddle game—no need to be coy or mysterious about what the object is. We don't want to be distracted by wondering what the object is. We want to be intrigued, engaged by your characters.

Names and dialogue. That's it. Through dialogue alone, you want to convey the personality of your characters. You want to imply the space they are in. Are we in a house, on a roadside? Or are we in some surreal setting such as Beckett's world in *End Game*? Also, try to imply what happens. Write the scene toward some sort of conclusion, whether the object appears or not. Anything goes here. The object may be presented immediately, or may never appear. The object is just a device to get the characters talking.

Student Example of *Where Is It?*
by Vytas Nagisetty

> LES

Where is it?

> CALEB

Man, I've got some bad news.

> LES

What? You couldn't get it? Was he out?

> CALEB

No he was there. But I couldn't get
anything.

> LES

I mean was he out of it? What the fuck?
Tell me what happened!

> CALEB

It's kinda hard to explain, bro.

> LES

Okay, if you don't want to tell me, fine.
Just give me back my two hundred dollars
and we can forget about the whole thing.

> CALEB

Well that's the tough part-

> LES

I really appreciate you trying. I didn't
realize that scoring some dope was such a
pain in the ass-

> CALEB

I don't have it. He took the money.

(Beat.)

> LES

You're telling me that he just took the money
and then sent you along your merry way empty-
handed?

                          CALEB
Yep.

                          LES
How big a boy is he?

                          CALEB
He ain't that big.

                          LES
Really?

                          CALEB
But he's got a couple big dogs. Look man,
the dude is full ghetto. You don't want
to fuck with him. I know this. You'll get
your ass kicked.

                          LES
Well I wanna kick someone's ass.

                          CALEB
Man, I'm really sorry. If you want I can
try someone else. It just might not be as
good.

                          LES
As good as what? We ain't got anything!
Jesus fuckin' Christ!
                    (beat)
Are you going to front me the two hundred
bucks?

                          CALEB
Dude, I just got fired. I don't even
have money to get anything for myself.

                          LES
Maybe I should just get it on the street.

                          CALEB
You'll get ripped off.

                          LES
I just got ripped off.

                              CALEB
                    Look, bro, let me call another dude.
                    Lightning doesn't strike twice.

                              LES
                    Huh?

                              CALEB
                    Trust me.

                              LES
                    Okay.

I do hope you can see these guys through the way they talk. In the opening Les would seem to be in charge with the question. Caleb makes an attempt at a dodge by saying he's got some bad news. The line is an attempt to avoid responsibility, as if losing the money and not getting dope is something uncontrollable that happened, when the truth is Caleb blew it.

Les pushes and Caleb keeps trying to wiggle free of Les' grip by saying it's hard to explain, stalling. He doesn't give all the news at once. He admits to not having the dope, but delays revealing he lost the cash as well. While withholding the second part of the deal-gone-wrong, Caleb calls Les "bro." The "bro" word is an attempt at intimacy, an attempt to soothe Les' temper by reminding him, with that little word, that they are somehow in this mess together. But the "bro" doesn't prevent Les from demanding his money back. The line pushes Caleb into a corner; he is forced to admit he's got no dope and no money.

And backed into that corner, Caleb comes out swinging, instantly placing all the blame on the guy—and the two dogs. It's a good defense. But Les still pushes and tries to dominate the scene by declaring he'd like to kick someone's ass. Given he's not likely to kick the ass of the guy with a whole lot of nerve and two dogs, the subtext reads that he'd like to kick Caleb's ass. In response, Caleb cowers, says he's sorry, and offers to call someone else.

Les backs down from his pushing on Caleb when he realizes bullying will get him nothing. He opts to try to score on the street—a line that shows his weakness, his desperation, his need to be in charge of something. His weakness puts Caleb back on top of the game. Caleb is the authority now, with his warning that Les will get ripped off.

Les tries to take command again by pointing out that thanks to Caleb, he's already been ripped off. Caleb nicely ignores the jab and get's all nice with the "bro" word. He smoothly takes command of the situation by offering to call another guy, using the cliché that lightening doesn't strike twice. Oh yes it does. We all know this. When one guy tries to reassure another with a cliché, then says "trust me," the words don't bode good things to come.

But Les, again weakened by his desire to score, gives in to Caleb's "authority" on drug matters. The characters, however foolish, are quite alive. And we leave the scene with a bit of a smile at the incompetence, the folly, of both these young men out looking to score.

Remember when doing this exercise, as well as the following exercises, that your characters have a history. They have a relationship. And even if they are pretty much strangers, there is something at stake between them: the desired "it."

In your mind's eye, try to see these folks before they get to talking. Load them up with attitude. Does the object mean more to one than to the other? Be sure you know what the "it" is and what it means to each of your characters.

In order to know what the object means to your characters, you'll need to know a bit about them. In the above scene, we know Les is accustomed to being in charge—it was his money on the line. In the fictional world, just like in the real world, money is power. With money, he can urge his friend to take the risk of scoring. So it seems Les is the alpha dog. It only seems so. Caleb has the connections; Caleb also has the nerve to take risks. But not enough nerve to take on the guy with two dogs. As simple as this scene is, the characters are, after close study, complex. Each one has strengths and weaknesses, and it is this interplay of strengths and weaknesses that renders a power struggle interesting, and funny, to watch.

The writer of this scene didn't know where it would lead. And similarly, you don't need to know how your scene will end. If you load your characters and the situation sufficiently, the writing will unfold, and you'll get to have the pleasure of watching a drama, just a little bit out of your control, play out. That's when writing is at its best: the characters start saying and doing things you didn't plan. And it's good. You might find yourself marveling at the creatures that began as your creations but then went on to create themselves. You might finish a piece wondering just where those words came from. Every writer who has spent time with characters of his or her creation knows that our creation of a character is only the beginning. The completion and development of them most often hinges on a mystery.

> "Good stories do not resolve the mysteries of the human
> spirit, but rather describe and expand upon those mysteries."
>
> Tim O'Brien

Yes good stories often hinge on a mystery, but don't set out to explain the mystery of your characters or to resolve the mystery of life. Yes you'll profile your characters and do much work in getting to know them, but for them to be alive, to be as close to human as they can be, there should be a little something about them that's beyond you. A bit of mystery is something that keeps people, and characters, interesting.

I know sometimes, it's tough to sit and dream up characters with enough personality to move across a page, and it can be tougher still to make them sound clever, interesting, anything worth watching. We all have our blocks, even the most experienced of us. The wonderfully comic voiceover in the opening of the film *Adaptation* illustrates the mundane and rambling thoughts of a writer who is blocked. He has a book he's assigned to adapt; he's an experienced writer, and he can't think of a thing worth writing. His mind drifts from how he has no ideas, to how he could get girls, to things like what kind of muffin he'd like to eat as a treat for writing. His mind goes everywhere except to the task at hand. We've all been there.

Often when I'm stuck, I follow the advice of a friend Ed Falco, who is a very fine writer and excellent teacher. He says, when stuck, write to your lowest standard. I like that, and I often do that: Just get something on the page. If you have something on the page, you have something to rewrite, and that, my friend, is a whole lot better than nothing.

So let's say you have your scrawled-out dialogue scene on the page. Now look at it, first with gratitude, I suppose, then critically. There are a few things dialogue should not do:

Dialogue shouldn't provide a list of facts as background about the characters as a way of loading up the scene. This is called EXPOSITORY dialogue. It gets dull real fast, as in:

```
                FRUSTRATED GUY
        I don't know why you won't have faith in
        me trying to make a change. I'm not
        happy working in a factory. I'd like to
        take some online classes and try
        something new in life before I get too
```

225

```
old. Just because you were married twice
to guys whose plans didn't work out, I
don't know why you don't try to give a
little more support to me.
```

Someone put this guy out of his misery. This is plain awful dialogue, and I wrote it. I will say, however, you can make a person on a rant a little more interesting, if you take the time to put in some details to make the character unique, and maybe even ironically funny. I'm still not too fond of this frustrated guy, but I decided to have a little more fun with him by making his situation and his complaint a little more colorful. See below:

```
                   FRUSTRATED GUY
Just because you've been married twice,
once to that door-to-door brush salesman
with nothing in his pocket but dreams, and
then to that used car salesman who had no
qualms about dumping pure-grade alcohol in
a transmission to seal the leaks and
sawdust in the rear differential to smooth
out the whining noise of gears going to
hell, yeah you knew his tricks all along
too. I don't know why you have to be so
suspicious when I say I want to quit my
god-awful job at the factory, cash in my
early retirement to take some on-line
classes and try to make something of myself
and be a day trader on the stock market
when all you do is teach second graders and
go take those real estate classes at night
so you can pick up extra money in the
summers. Why can't both of us have a little
ambition that will count for something?
```

Well, there are certainly the seeds of a drama here, maybe even a comedy, but you don't want all the goods spilled out in one bit. There's certainly promise for some scenes in all this second bit of ranting exposition, maybe even a whole plot. But a viewer would rather learn all this info a bit at a time, as the characters are shown chasing their dreams—whether the dreams are pipedreams or not.

Dialogue also shouldn't be used for extended philosophical brooding by a character, unless, of course, you are going for ironic humor. Don't expect your reader to take a brooding character too seriously.

```
                    Doloris
        I don't know why God made us if we're
        just here to die.  I mean,like, why make
        something just to kill it? I don't want
        to die. No one wants to die.  Why does
        God get to be the only thing eternal?
        And nobody knows for sure about heaven.
        You're dead, you're dead. I mean it only
        makes sense.  We want our cars to last
        forever.  We don't make them to die. I
        know they all die in time, but that's
        because they're made by humans. But
        God isn't human. He's God. He can do
        anything he wants. So why would he want
        us to die after going to all the trouble
        to make us?
```

Okay, if you're not laughing, you're groaning. Doloris isn't asking any kind of original question, and any insight she offers is only, well, comic—comic for her lack of original insight.

I realize that Hamlet has his "To be or not to be" soliloquy. It is not dialogue. It is not even a dramatic monologue. Hamlet is addressing no one but himself. And the content of his soliloquy is far more complex and far-reaching than just a should-I-live-or-should-I-die speech. It also happens to be a beautiful piece of writing. And, well, it's Shakespeare, and there aren't many Shakespeares among us. If you want your characters to brood, don't take them too seriously. Your readers certainly won't.

Now let's hone in on how dialogue needs to work.

Don't forget that your dialogue is being spoken in a real world by living people. So use them. Incorporate action and gestures with the dialogue to avoid talking-head syndrome.

Don't forget that good dialogue contains a verb. We've all at sometime felt smacked by someone's words—even if they weren't yelling. We all certainly, at some time, have been seduced or conned with words. Dialogue can push, pull, trick, humiliate, coax, inspire. So when reading or writing dialogue, don't forget to look for what the characters are doing to each other.

Remember, dialogue is sound. And like a song, it has rhythms, repetitions, and it makes use of the pause. We don't think non-stop, unless we're using some drug to supercharge the brain—not a good idea. And we don't talk non-stop—unless we're somewhat neurotic or drugged. Use pauses. Write in those little beats to break things up, to let a spoken phrase sit out there a bit so that it can be absorbed.

And to keep things interesting, and real, remember that dialogue is not always grammatically correct. We often speak in fragments. And some people do speak in the kind of clichés your English teacher would mark in red on a composition paper. If you are writing about an uneducated character, she wouldn't speak as a college grad. Some folks are comfortable saying "I ain't got no more cookies for my milk." A character who speaks like this probably didn't go to Harvard, but she'd be welcome in any diner or home where I come from.

Here in Ohio, I discovered the common usage of ending a question with "at." The line troubled my ears in a way the above double negative statement didn't trouble me a bit. I know better than to judge an idiomatic way of speaking. Some folks would be insulted if you corrected them when they said, "Do you know where the nearest grocery store is at?" We all understand the question, and maybe we'll find the store. In dialogue, make use of idioms where appropriate for your characters, but don't go too far. Sometimes too much use of misspelled and poorly articulated words can be a distraction for the reader. Use the idiomatic word or two to indicate the way a speaker speaks, suggest the personality of the speaker. Don't beat the readers over the head with idiomatic expressions, or they will run away. You don't want that.

And finally, remember that no matter how personal a conversation might be between two characters, your reader/viewer is a participant, an invisible but very important third party. Don't forget the reader. I once heard Toni Morrison say that when writing stories, she always leaves room for her reader in the work. At first I didn't quite understand, then after consideration I remembered one of the many reasons I enjoy reading. I enjoy the way my own feelings rise to the page, the way my own perceptions can inhabit the lines. Reading is not passive; it's participatory. In the lovely film *Amèlie* that I will discuss in depth later, the protagonist admits that she likes to go to movies and turn to watch the faces of the audience in the darkness. The film then pans to show the softly illuminated faces looking up at the screen with pleasure, thought, intrigue. They are participating with the screen.

Don't use dialogue to feed information to your reader. Use dialogue for what it is: a VERBAL expression of the speakers. Let them act upon each other with words. And allow us the experience of really watching something happen when characters speak.

But for now, consider the following scene from *Blood Sisters*. The script tells the story of Grace Hanes, who struggles against her racist Southern culture of 1917 when she discovers her daddy has lynched a man, and in an inadvertent way, Grace is complicit in the murder. Her journey toward her redemption, punishment of her father, and justice for the victim begins when Violet, the daughter of the lynched man, confronts Grace with the truth of what her daddy has done.

Think of this Grace/Violet scene as a continuous scene of struggle. Violet wants to provoke Grace into facing the awful act her daddy has done; Grace wants to dodge a truth she suspects. You will note the scene is broken up with a brief cut to a scene where a reporter, Jonathan Jackson, comes to town. The reporter scene serves two functions: it introduces another force, Jonathan, who will prompt Grace to expose her father. The brief scene also serves to break up a rather long scene between Violet and Grace.

When you write your script, try not to let a single scene exceed four pages—that's four minutes. The average viewer out there, it seems, gets a little bored watching the same scene for more than four minutes. If you watch a mainstream movie with a watch in hand, you'll notice the four-minute limit on a scene seems to be the rule. Now consider this scene that illustrates dialogue functioning as action.


```
EXT. HANES' FRONT YARD - DAY

Grace kneels in her yard, lifts a SNAKE from a box, puts it
in the grass, toys at it with a stick.

Violet walks up the road, pauses to look at Grace, Grace's
house, back to Grace.

Grace says nothing, looks back toward her porch.

                    GRACE
          My daddy says I ain't supposed to talk
          to you.
                    (beat)
          But they ain't home.

                    VIOLET
          You do everything your daddy says?

                    GRACE
          No.  Sometimes I say I'm going to
```

prayer meeting, but I don't.

Grace glances up to Violet.

                    GRACE
          You like church?

                    VIOLET
          Somebody killed my daddy. They shoved
          a rock in his mouth so he couldn't
          scream. My daddy.

                    GRACE
          I'm sorry.

Grace puts the snake back in the box. Puts the lid down.

                    VIOLET
          They came and drug him out of my
          house. You know what it's like to see
          your daddy dead?

Violet wipes at tears, sucks in a breath, stands firm.

                    GRACE
          You can cry if you want.

                    VIOLET
          Ain't time to cry yet.

Grace stands, moves toward her house.

                    GRACE
          I cry sometimes. My daddy, he can be so
          mean, then he can be so nice. I don't
          know what to do sometimes.

She goes to porch. Carries a larger box to edge of the yard.

Violet observes the sick puppy staring up.

                    GRACE
          Daddy says I can keep this puppy.
          Momma fusses, but he says I can have
          whatever I want.

                              VIOLET
                    Your daddy. I seen him. You know the
                    things your daddy can do.

Grace backs toward the house.

                              GRACE
                    My daddy wouldn't hurt nobody. My daddy
                    wouldn't kill nobody. If--

                              VIOLET
                    Truth comes out in time.

                              GRACE
                    Frankie, he could kill somebody. You
                    know Frankie?

                              VIOLET
                    That ugly man. I seen him with your
                    daddy.

                              GRACE
                    Frankie. He'd do anything mean.

                              VIOLET
                    Took more than one man to kill my daddy.

                                                       CUT TO:

EXT. MAIN STREET - DAY

JONATHAN JACKSON, a late twenties, handsome reporter gets
out of a taxi in front of hotel. Pays DRIVER.

LOCALS on the porch of the country store stare as he
unloads.

He lifts out small suitcase, typewriter, a camera.

Frankie throws cigarette down, hurries in the store.

Jonathan nods in the direction of his audience. They look
away. He carries his gear to the hotel.

                                                       CUT TO:

EXT. HANES' FRONT YARD - DAY

                         GRACE
          Your daddy must've done something to
          somebody. He gamble? He drink? Momma
          says men always getting killed like that.
          You don't kill somebody less they do
          something wrong.

                         VIOLET
          You such a white, white girl.

Grace backs closer to her house.

                         VIOLET
          Meanness. My daddy say it's like a
          sickness. Sometimes folks want people
          on the outside hurt like they do on the
          inside.

                         GRACE
          Momma says it's the devil makes people
          mean. But my daddy--

                         VIOLET
          Everybody got a little seed of meanness
          inside.

Grace watches Violet pet the puppy.

                         GRACE
          You an orphan now. My daddy was an orphan.
          Made him real sad. He acts mad about it, but
          I seen the sadness in his eyes.
                         (beat)
          But Daddy says you coloreds ain't like
          white folks, more like some kinda tribe.

                         VIOLET
          They shoved a rock in his mouth to stop
          his talking. Wonder it didn't break his
          teeth. But I saw him when they brung him
          back this morning. His teeth, they pretty
          like always. He come to me in a dream this
          morning. He come and he say--

MEMORY HIT - Violet's dream

Benjamin still bound, gag hanging at his neck, speaks.

                    BENJAMIN
          Spit that rock, Violet. It will go flying
          like some pretty gray dove. That rock take
          wings. Spit the rock out, girl, and you can
          run free.

BACK TO SCENE

Grace backs up, grips banister on her porch.

                    VIOLET
          My daddy say, this world is always
          putting rocks in our mouths. Make it
          hard to talk. Got to spit them rocks out
          you want to speak.

A SOFT RUMBLING SOUND, THE SOUND OF ELEPHANT RUMBLING RISES,
MERGES INTO THE SOUND OF THUNDER.

                    GRACE
          You hear that?

                    VIOLET
          What?

                    GRACE
          Sounds like thunder, but it ain't.

                    VIOLET
          Might be storm coming.

Grace stands, moves toward her front door.

Violet walks away, points back to the snake box.

                    VIOLET
          My auntie says snake's got power. Bad luck
          to keep a wild thing.

Grace starts to go in, pauses, looks back at Violet.

                    GRACE
          I'm real sorry 'bout your daddy. My momma's

```
                  gonna be home soon.  I ain't supposed to be talking
                  to you.

                                    VIOLET
                  So why you always talking to me?

         Violet turns, walks away.  Grace watches her go.

         Grace hurries to the yard, lets the snake loose, watches it
         wriggle free in the grass.
```

Although these girls never touch, in the subtext of the dialogue there is much pushing and pulling going on. In just about any conversation there is a power dynamic in the works, and there is certainly a power struggle here between the privileged white girl and the African-American girl who is disadvantaged but driven for justice. Let's look closely at the scene for how the power play works out.

To begin, without a word Violet takes charge with her physical presence, in close proximity to Grace, who is occupying herself with a snake she keeps like a pet in a box. Grace quits playing with the snake when she becomes aware of Violet—when a character allows another to interrupt their activity, a bit of power is handed over. Grace resists this acquiescent movement by trying to take charge and put Violet in her place: she points out that she isn't supposed to speak to Violet. But by speaking, she simultaneously displays her weakness in wanting to speak to Violet, and also her strength in rebelling against her parents' rules. She CHOOSES to speak to Violet even though she isn't supposed to.

Violet will not be daunted by the racist implications of Grace's line. She punches back with the question of whether Grace always follows the rules. This question has Grace explaining herself when she says that sometimes she lies to her parents about going to church. The fact that she lies to her parents would seem to empower her. But in answering Violet's question, Grace is explaining herself to Violet. When a person is pushed into answering questions and explaining behavior, the person asking the questions is in charge. Grace makes an attempt to get hold of the conversation by asking a frivolous question about church.

Violet will not be swayed. She is on a mission to talk about the fact of her murdered father. She provides very graphic images that she knows will disturb the girl. And Grace, who is well aware of her father's racism and capacity for violence, struggles to bond a bit with the accuser by taking a sympathetic role and by trying to distract Violet with the sick puppy she hopes to keep. The puppy is her weak attempt to show her daddy's potential kindness—he'll let her keep a puppy. It also suggests that Grace is a nurturing sort of person. We know this nurturing aspect she tries to display is not quite the true Grace, as in the opening pages of the script we saw Grace being manipulative and cruel with Violet's daddy—she set the event of the lynching in motion by starting up the domineering exchange with Violet's daddy. Grace knows she's very likely involved, however indirectly, with the lynching, and in this exchange she does what she can to seem innocent. Violet is clearly in charge.

This bit of dialogue is something of a verbal arm-wrestling game, with Grace rallying now and then under the superior strength of Violet. Violet wants to bring out a secret, while Grace wants to keep one. In any exchange, a character who is lying or trying to hide something lacks the strength of the more proactive character aiming to bring truth out. With every little twist and turn Grace makes, Violet gets only stronger, and her line that Grace is such a white, white girl is nothing short of a slap to the face. At that line Grace goes silent and moves closer to her house—her bit of safety. She could always run inside. But she doesn't.

We know from earlier in the play that Grace feels tightly controlled by her parents. She wants to rebel. And here is this African-American girl defiant enough to openly insult Grace for her whiteness. It's a punch, but we know from earlier that Grace has the strength to take it. But still she scrambles and tries to say the devil causes all the meanness in the world, a stand she doesn't believe in herself. When Violet counters with the statement that we all have the capacity for meanness, this hits a little too close to the truth for Grace, so she scrambles to her racist stance that Black people aren't like Whites.

Violet then takes a tactic to ignore this comment and push on with the brutal details of what happened to her father. Remember, dialogue is a great place for a power struggle. If you follow the lead of someone else's conversation, you give them the power. If you ignore them and plow ahead with your own verbal agenda, you are in charge.

The force of Violet's words, along with the memory hit of her murdered father, loads the scene with a grisly truth that is palpable enough to throw Grace so off balance, she hears a thundering sound, sensing the metaphorical storm that is about to hit her house. Violet's presence and her announcement are the preceding thunder. But still, Grace doesn't want to turn away from Violet. She wants to keep the conversation going, as Violet possesses the kind of courage Grace would like for herself.

Sensing she is fully in charge of this nervous white girl, Violet goes even further and advises Grace that she ought to let her captive snake free. Grace, not to be bullied, ignores Violet's comment and makes for the house. But it's a failed attempt to take control. With the subtext of guilt, she says she's sorry for what happened to Violet's daddy. She doesn't admit to how she and her father might in any way be responsible, but she does show a bit of compassion. And it's this bit of compassion that will grow until she engages in the ultimate act of rebellion and reveals her father's guilt. Violet is the primary influence who empowers Grace to defy her parents and her racist culture, and by the end of this script they are "blood sisters," united not only by the childish ritual of cutting their fingers to bond in blood. They are blood sisters in that their friendship is conceived as a consequence of bloodshed.

And while I have your attention with this scene, I want to point out how characters can be nicely refined and developed through the use of props. I go into this in greater detail in the chapter on visual language, but I'll just point out here that Grace keeps animals for her entertainment—the snake and the puppy—things she doesn't need to keep because the snake is wild and the puppy dying. Her association with "pets" implies her loneliness and her need to control things. In the script Violet is associated with rocks. She will repeatedly throw rocks through the windows of Grace's house. The rock connotes her strength, her rebellion, and her power when it comes to shattering structures that need to be brought down so truth—and justice—can prevail.

Now that you've seen how dialogue can work as a verb, try a few exercises for practice.

Think of this exercise as something like practicing scales on your piano before you launch into playing your classical piece.

I've Got a Secret

Write a dialogue scene where both characters have a secret. Do not reveal the secret, but make the reader/viewer intuit it. For example, the dialogue might be between a father who has just lost his job and his daughter, who has decided she doesn't want to go to college because she plans to move to some exotic/or awful place to join a religious cult.

Remember, good dialogue always has a subtext—a something we can sense/suspect between the lines. And good dialogue says something about the speaker. In this exercise you might be tempted to play coy and deliberately withhold information from the reader/viewer and leave us feeling duped—that's not a good feeling. Remember, you are writing for the screen. We need to SEE what's on the screen as well as what is being said. We need to be engaged by what is said, and intrigued by both what is said and what isn't.

Now, draft below. The scene heading, a quick sketch of characters, and what the secrets are to be. Don't be too surprised if one of the secrets changes in the writing. Sometimes as we write, and especially if we have fully developed characters, they start saying and doing things we didn't foresee in the original plan. Remember, sometimes your characters can write a better story than you.

Distracted Dialogue

We've discussed how dialogue serves as action. Now try giving dimension to your characters by showing them distracted while doing something. This can allow for rich play with subtext. In movies, people tend to be doing things. Even if the point is that they lead bored and listless lives, they do get around to doing things. And they are often talking while they act. Sometimes their actions can show they have little interest in the conversation. And sometimes the action can provide a bond, a connection that will give ease to open honest conversation. Pick one of the following. Work up some characters, action, and write a scene.

A man repairing his car while talking to a boy—a classic but can be made fresh

A pedicure in process—lots of options here for characters and talk

Some guys around a poker game

Two women at a shoe sale

A man getting in or out of drag

Guys roofing a house

A photographer/painter with the subject

Two guys working the back of a garbage truck

The Dramatic Monologue

Now that you've practiced dialogue, consider the monologue. It is often used quite dramatically to illustrate how one character can walk into a room and take it over, just with the power of his words. I can't think of a monologue that does this more powerfully than that classic monologue by Karl Childers (Billy Bob Thorton) in *Sling Blade.* Originally the short film, *Some Folks Call it a Sling Blade*, grew from this monologue. Thorton conceived the monologue long before he wrote the feature length script at a time he was very depressed about his acting career. He left the shooting set of a film, where he was playing a small part they he didn't like, and went off into a room to make faces in a mirror and try out voices. Amazing, where stories can come from. Thorton says that finding that monologue began with the facial expression we've all come to know as the face of that gentle, yet deadly, giant, Karl, and then the grunting noises came, and then came the story of Karl's childhood and how he came to kill his mother and her young lover. The short film was a stunning success and quickly brought the backers to make the feature length film that was written and directed by Thorton—it also won an academy award.

Now let's look at what makes this monologue dramatic. Karl has an audience. A young reporter has come to the mental asylum to interview Karl about his being released after twenty-eight years—he was institutionalized when he was twelve. As she walks down the hall toward her meeting with Karl, she complains to her friend about the idea of Karl being released. She strongly feels that he should never be released because he is a murderer who is a danger to the world. She's all cynicism and judgment. Then in a darkened classroom, with the hospital director present, she meets Karl. He sits, grunts, wrings his hands a bit, blinks his eyes slowly as if he's going deep inside to summon language. And he very candidly starts the monologue with, "I reckon you want to know what I'm doing here," and he goes on to say it's "'cause I killed somebody. I reckon you want to know why." He simply, calmly, takes complete charge of the interview and goes on to tell the horror story of his childhood of being forced to live in a shed in the back yard of his parent's house. Being mentally handicapped, he was obviously revolting to his parents, and they told him he was God's punishment for them having sex. He tells of how he didn't go to school; the boys in town liked to "make sport of him." He has no self-pity in his story; he just matter-of-factly tells of how he dug out a hole to sleep in, and how a few times a week he'd be fed biscuits and mustard.

What grips us—and the reporter—is the speaker as much as the story. Karl grips and rubs his own hands as if holding himself is a comfort, as if he has to work to contain himself and stay in his body. He closes his eyes as if it's hard to see, and hard to summon, the story he is telling. He repeatedly grunts, sometimes as if it's a struggle to get the words out, and sometimes the grunts seem to be some kind of secondary affirmation of the words he speaks. Thorton has said that it actually hurt to speak in that voice we've all come to know as Karl. He said playing the role of Karl required a lot of Chloraseptic. The pain is fitting to the role in that Karl carries a life of pain inside. Of course speaking would hurt.

The camera cuts to the reporter shortly after Karl starts speaking, and we see she is softened, open to Karl. There is no judgment or fear. Dramatic monologues are dramatic because they do more than provide information; they affect the listener. Karl's words, awful as they are, deeply touch the reporter and cause a change in her attitude. The words also reveal more about Karl than he realizes. Karl, in spite of being a brutal murderer, is one of the most innocent characters we've come to know on film. He hasn't learned guile. He knows only how to be what he is: A man who sees much more into people than they might guess, a man who is much wiser than he knows.

He goes on to explain the events of the murder, how he was in the shed and heard a ruckus from inside the house, and he picked up at sling blade. He pauses here and points out how some folks call it a Kaiser blade, but he calls it a sling blade. He goes on to describe it to be long-handled and has a blade "kind of like a bananer." The way he pauses to elaborate on the brutal weapon serves to heighten his innocence. His words personalize him, and render him as still a boy somehow and not a killer. He goes on to tell of how he went to the house and saw his momma on the floor with the local bully "having his way with her." In response Karl lashed out and "pretty near cut the boy's head off." And when Karl's mother started yelling, and Karl could see she liked what the boy was doing, Karl was so swept by fury he killed her too. When Karl says he killed his mother, there is no fury on his face, none. There is nothing but exhausted pain there. We see the reporter, still soft, no horror. She just pulls back a little as if the words cause her pain; she seems to have empathized with Karl instead of being revolted by his actions. This is quite a change.

The story concludes, and, ever-polite, Karl asks if there's any more the reporter would like to know. She gently but boldly asks if he will kill again. Here is a long close-up on Karl, and he thinks really hard about this. He's not looking for a lie; he's looking for an answer. He finally says, "I don't reckon I got no reason to kill nobody." A truth. And a statement that leave the plot open to the possibility that he might one day find a reason to kill someone. He does not say he would never kill again. He simply says he doesn't have a reason. And while that line brings closure to the interview and the monologue, it opens the door to the plot that will unfold. On leaving the hospital the girl is so changed by meeting Karl that she says thank you and offers to shake his hand, a touch he's incapable of accepting. In any case the scene shows this girl quite transformed by the seven-minute monologue from the man she previously saw as a murderer. Now she sees him as a sorrowful man, and she's been made somewhat a better person as the result of meeting him.

Another fine example of dramatic monologue can be seen in the film *Glengarry Glen Ross*, a film based on the play by David Mamet. Set in the context of a real estate company that sells suspicious investment properties, the story reveals the cannibalistic impulses that can drive the need for profit. In the opening minutes of the film we learn that four salesmen are in a slump, not for lack of talent, but due to a lack of good leads on customers. It seems big management has assigned this particular office a pool of potential customers least likely to buy developmental property. Given their low sales records, the salesmen are required to attend a "sales conference" set up by the invisible forces of downtown management. The "motivational speaker," played by Alec Baldwin, takes possession of the office immediately as he gives his speech on the need to increase sales.

But this speech is no pep talk. It's an assault. He controls the actions and the emotions of the men. He tells one man he can't have the very cup of coffee he is holding in his hand, the way a father might tell a child to put down a toy. He tells another not to speak. He then proceeds to insult the men for their lack of power and wealth. He pummels them with insults, then knocks them flat with the statement that they are all fired and will have to compete to have their jobs back, but that the two salesmen with the lowest number of sales will remain fired. Then, being a smart strategist, he gives the men a flicker of hope. He offers bait: a golden stack of good leads. And the good leads will only go to those who can close deals on the bad leads.

The speech illustrates brilliant psychological torture: punish your victim, and then offer a slim chance at reward. At ten minutes into the film, the "sales conference" is the catalyst that sets the plot rolling. The more Baldwin's character yells about the men's shoddy sales records, the more he reveals that he is an arrogant, brutal man who personifies the worst aspects of capitalism. While pitched as a tough management speech, the monologue has the effect of revolting the salesmen themselves with its savage slant on Darwin's notion of survival of the fittest. Baldwin's character, who arrives in an eighty thousand dollar Beamer and a thousand dollar suit, and a hundred dollar hair cut, looks civilized, even refined, but his speech reveals him to be a beast.

Dramatically, his primary purpose is to corner the men into improving sales; his secondary purpose is to humiliate the men by gloating over his own fortune and suggesting that he is a more valuable human being because he is rich. But the monologue does something more than reveal character and provide the triggering event that moves the plot forward. The monologue also reveals the author's thematic concerns; it provides a scathing critique of corporate greed and a dark look at the trap door underneath the path to the American dream.

Whether writing monologue or dialogue, you want to try to have a sense of a "verb" underlying the speaker's words. Maybe in the monologue he is trying to manipulate the reader. Maybe in the monologue he is trying to make the listener know him, like him, and that's fine for awhile. But have you ever had a stranger sit next to you on a plane or subway or in a bar and proceed to tell you all about himself, assuming you are interested? How do you react? Even if you find that person attractive, after awhile you start to distance yourself, because we can only take so much of being a passive listener while the speaker blathers on. We can distance ourselves in a variety of ways: we nod along while our brain goes about planning the rest of our day, or the rest of our lives, while the stranger rambles on.

Or maybe—and if you're a writer you're likely to do this—we listen, and we start to observe the speaker's gestures, really listen to those words for a subtext as we read between the lines. We start noticing things the speaker is revealing about himself or herself that he or she doesn't realize. This effect is called dramatic irony: the speaker talks about himself and reveals something he doesn't realize. Irony means a contradiction. There is a contradiction between what the speaker intends to say and what is actually said, or revealed.

One of the classic illustrations of dramatic irony is in the poem "My Last Duchess" by Robert Browning. Written in 1842, the language and syntax can be intimidating to many students, but the story implied is the makings of a horror tale. The persona, or speaker of the poem, is a duke who is addressing a visitor who happens to be representing a wealthy count who has a daughter possibly to be "the next Duchess." In other words, the speaker of the poem has an agenda: to impress his listener. The speaker directs the visitor to study the portrait of the "last duchess." The duke refers to the portrait of the duchess as if she is just another impressive piece of art he has collected. The more he speaks about his "last duchess," the more he reveals that he is a jealous, controlling, proud and cruel man who resented his wife for her ability to love the world, not only him. The reader of the poem dramatically takes on the passive position of the visitor or audience, and we are not impressed. And as readers, we become engaged by the irony of seeing the flaws in a man who talks with great confidence that the listener is impressed.

One thing to bear in mind is that dramatic monologue, like dialogue, must do at least two things simultaneously. A dramatic monologue does more than provide exposition or background for the story unfolding. While revealing the personality of the speaker, a monologue has a "verb" operating in the subtext—it has a purpose. A monologue wants to convince, explain, argue, and justify something to the listener. Often a monologue is the crucial event that moves plot forward by triggering action or by triggering an emotional response in the intended audience of the monologue. My point is that a monologue is an active tool of drama, not a passive device for just providing information.

In order to write a dramatic monologue, you must know the complex motives stirring within your character, because in your monologue you are going to reveal both what the character knows and what he doesn't know about himself. A good strategy is to think of your character as having two motives—a larger, ongoing motive that shapes how he or she chooses to live or consistently feels about living in this world. And for the sake of the scene you need a smaller, more particular motive in regard to the listener.

You might try a dramatic monologue based on one of the prompts in the above Multi-Tasking with Dialogue Exercise, or perhaps you already have a character and scene in mind. For a monologue to succeed and not grow too tedious, be sure to break it up with a bit of action, in the way Alec Baldwin punctuates his speech with showing off his watch and pulling the brass balls from his briefcase. Or you can break it up with a showing a bit of response to the monologue, as in the Sling Blade monologue.

You can also dramatically enhance a monologue with memory hits, as I illustrated in the "What a Script Looks Like" chapter where, in a scene from *Blood Sisters*, Clifford recalls his father's abuse when Frankie asks about his sore mouth. In the following scene, I use memory hits to break up a monologue as Clifford tries to justify his impulse for random and racist violence. He speaks with full enthusiasm and pleasure, assuming his listener, Frankie, will understand. But we are listeners, too. And instead of identifying with his explanation of the pleasure in violence, we are appalled. Not only is Clifford revealing that he is a brutal man, he is revealing that he is completely amoral. He has no idea that what he does is absolutely wrong.

In this scene Frankie, who helped lynch Benjamin Woods, argues with Clifford, who kept a souvenir from the lynching: a finger cut from the dead man's hand. Frankie fears that a friend of theirs, Wilson, who witnessed the beginning events of the lynching then ran, might tell someone of what they did. Frankie wants to be rid of all evidence, while Clifford feels securely beyond the reach of conventional law in his racist little community.

In this scene, Frankie is rolling ivory dice cut and carved from the elephant that was recently hanged—he doesn't see anything gruesome in that, no more than Clifford sees anything wrong with keeping his own souvenirs. Frankie is worried about being caught while Clifford is driven by the need for power. Clifford will take risks to secure that feeling of power. He keeps a box of evidence from fights he has won: a clump of hair, a tooth, and now the finger of a dead man. Clifford's memory hit—in a sick way—explains his sociopathic urge.

The visual memory hits are written in here to make the monologue not only more dramatic but more visually interesting. It takes one superior actor to engage the viewer's attention while the camera holds on his face and he rants on. When I first wrote this monologue, I didn't use the memory hits, and it read flat: a talking head remembering something. When I broke up the monologue with visual action, the ugliness came jumping off the page. The scene is much improved. Perhaps this bit can guide you in writing your own *dramatic* dramatic monologue.

INT. LIVING ROOM, HANES' HOUSE - NIGHT

Clifford fingers a tooth, drops it in his cigar box. SIGHS.

                    FRANKIE
          Should have let me kill him, Clifford.
          He'll come back with the sheriff next.

                    CLIFFORD
          Sheriff won't give a damn.

                    FRANKIE
          That shit's evidence, Clifford.

                    CLIFFORD
          It's a sign of what I done. Like one
          of them medals they give in the war.

                    FRANKIE
          Supposed to get rid of evidence of a
          crime. Last I heard, killing a man,
          even a colored man, was against the law.

Frankie goes back to rolling his dice.

                    FRANKIE
          Wilson. Wilson, he—

                    CLIFFORD
          He don't' get it. I didn't get it
          either 'til I got me a handful of hair.

MEMORY HIT - RURAL FIELD - NIGHT

TEENAGED CLIFFORD holds TEENAGED BLACK BOY on the ground,
grips his head by the hair and PUNCHES his face while
CLIFFORD'S FRIENDS look on.

BACK TO SCENE
                    CLIFFORD
          We was out for fun. Drinking 'shine.
          Hollering,driving around. This boy,
          he's   crossing the road. Somebody said
          let's do him, I guess. So we did it. We
          jumped out of that truck and . . .

MEMORY HIT - DIRT ROAD

Clifford and friends bound out of the truck WHOOPING AND
HOLLERING, head for the young black man.

BACK TO SCENE

Clifford sips from the bottle.

                    CLIFFORD
          Couldn't even see what I was doing. I
          could hear him though. He wouldn't yell,
          just "Humph!"

MEMORY HIT - RURAL FIELD

Teenaged Clifford's fist SMACKS into young black man's
face. The young man PUNCHES him back. Clifford stumbles.
Regains balance, knocks the young man to the ground,
straddles him and PUNCHES him AGAIN and AGAIN in the face.

BACK TO SCENE

                    CLIFFORD
          He was tough. I'll give you that.
          Everybody grunting and punching 'til
          I got him down on the ground and kept
          punching, and punching. Just me
          hitting him. Me smacking that boy to
          the ground!

Clifford stands and stares, BREATHING HARD, anger twisting
his face.

Your dramatic monologues need not be so violent to be effective. The student example below is quite low-key and sensitive. It does nicely reveal the character's personality, as well as his not-so-closely listening friends.

So read the example, then write a simple dramatic monologue, and remember, this is for the screen. You are responsible not only for the dialogue, but for what is on the screen while the dialogue is going on. A talking head gets boring pretty fast. So work in a few pauses, interruptions, gestures, description, all meant to characterize your speaker, maybe to reveal something more about his or her motives

For example, you may choose to write a monologue where your character is in a coffee shop and is telling her friends how she's had it—she's done with men. And yet, when a man enters, she looks up and notices him, or better, she does some little shift in posture or adjustment to her hair, or maybe, distracted, she misses hearing some wise response or insight a friend has just stated. Or you may use the device of memory hits as I did above. But get your character talking, and let's see what is revealed. But before you write, have a look at the following scene.

Student Example of Dramaitic Monologue
by Vytas Nagisetty

EXT. TACQUERIA PATIO - NIGHT

The gig over, BAND MEMBERS sit around a table crowded with
empty beer bottles. SCAT, 50's, sports a Hawaiian shirt and
baseball cap. CHARLIE, 30's, wears a t-shirt and worn
jeans. BOB, 30's, an awkwardly big man, in an old suit.
CLYDE, 30's, in a freshly pressed linen shirt. Behind them,
restaurant WORKERS mop the floor.

> CLYDE
>
> Every place I lived had a particular
> smell to it. I swear, the brake pads
> they use on the Paris Metro must only
> be used there. It's not that it smells
> good. You just know you're in Paris
> when you smell that brake dust. The
> smell of the New York subway is totally
> different but equally recognizable.
> Paris is a bit more perfumy, but both
> are kind of putrid, like something's
> died up in there, at the source.

Scat and Bob LAUGH. Clyde remains serious. Charlie plays
with the ice in his glass, pretending not to listen.

> CLYDE
>
> I'm just trying to be objective. But I
> tell you, for me, when I smell either of
> those things, I get choked up. It
> brings back memories. I miss the smell.

The guys quiet down. Clyde takes a moment to think.

> CLYDE
>
> I remember one time in New York I was
> working for this songwriter up near the
> Brill building. That's where like
> Gershwin and Rogers, and so many other
> famous songwriters, worked.

                          BOB
Wow.

                          SCAT
The Dodgers?

                          CLYDE
Rodgers. Richard Rogers. Of Rogers and
Hammerstein, Rogers and Hart.

                          SCAT
Damn! You met him?
                    (beat)
Isn't he dead yet?

                          CLYDE
No. I didn't meet him. He's been dead
a while. Anyway, one time my boss and I
went down to get a slice. And we're
standing on the sidewalk eating our
slices. It's a hot day out, and we're
standing near some subway vents.
They're everywhere. We both get a big
whiff of the subway exhaust and he kinda
grimaces in disgust. He puts his pizza
away like he can't eat it anymore. I
tell him, you smell that smell? Only in
New York.
                    (New York City accent)
Only in New York baby!
                    (regular voice)
You might hate it, but that smell is a
constant reminder of where you are,
which is a constant reminder of why
you're here. Everyone comes here for a
reason. That smell is your reminder.
It's my reminder.

The guys think about it in SILENCE for a moment.

                          CLYDE
He laughed. But I tell you what, he got
his pizza back out and ate the whole
thing!

The guys LAUGH, except for Charlie, who's still acting like he doesn't care.

                         BOB
          You know what's weird? I don't have a
          sense of smell.

                         CLYDE
          Are you kidding me? I've never heard
          of that.

Charlie leans forward, suddenly interested.

                         CHARLIE
          That is weird. Has it always been like that?

Bob nods.

                         SCAT
                    (to himself)
          I can't believe he met Richard Rogers!

                         CLYDE
          No wonder you're always farting and
          acting like you didn't do it!

Everyone LAUGHS except for Scat, who shakes his head, muttering.

                         SCAT
          Damn. . . Richard Rogers.

This little scene provides a dramatic monologue that not only reveals Clyde to be a complex, introspective person, but it also uses dialogue to show that often, no matter how much we talk with our friends, how much we bare our tender thoughts and feelings, often we don't connect. As much as we talk, there is often little communication going on. We each tend to be so preoccupied with our own worlds that when others speak, we hear them vaguely through the ambient noise of our own talk with ourselves.

7. Setting—It's More Than Just a Place

A finely crafted story (whether on the page or screen not only tells a good story, but it draws on all its elements of character, action, setting and image patterns to accomplish its aims. Remember, as a writer you CHOOSE your setting, and you need to USE that setting. Your characters aren't acting just in any old place, but in a specific place, a place that functions almost like a character in itself, in that it reinforces a character's sentiments. Setting can be used to emphasize mood, conflicts, and desires. Setting can work as a metaphor for your character's interior landscape; it can also work as a character.

Setting can motivate or limit your character, just as one character can motivate or limit the actions of another. Consider that setting of the mini-van in the darkly comic road-trip adventure in *Little Miss Sunshine*. The barely running vehicle is the Hoover family's only opportunity to get little pudgy and charming Olive to a girls' talent pageant, an event so dear to her heart and her self-esteem that the family reluctantly decides to put her needs before their own.

The van as opportunity quickly turns to limitation when it breaks down and can't be shifted out of first gear—in a similar way, the family has trouble shifting out of first gear when they must overcome their inertia and indifference to get Olive to the pageant. This collection of quirky and largely irate characters comes under great pressure as they try to get along and stay somewhat upbeat during the trip. The van both confines the characters and, in that confinement, pushes the characters to grow past their grudges and frustrations in a selfless gesture to get the somewhat plump but ever-optimistic girl to a competition she is sure to lose. Thanks to that van, the plot centers on the family dynamics at work and at war in the in the beater of a vehicle that's temporarily a place like home. They are all changed for the better— even the old grandfather who dies—by this road trip. The van itself, with all its limits, discomforts and malfunctions, forces this dysfunctional family to function after all. Had the vehicle been a smooth-running Cadillac Expedition, the trip no doubt would have been a different journey, with probably less interesting results.

Another film that uses setting as a powerful element of plot is the classic *Casablanca*, set in the town which provides the last-resort airport where Europeans can flee World War II and aim for a new life in the United States. The tiny Moroccan town becomes a holding pen where people do desperate things in an effort to obtain visas while the Nazi regime bears down. Given the limits of the tightly monitored town, and given the fact that the airstrip is the only way out to safety, the drama is high and characters are pushed to do sometimes noble, sometimes sordid things to achieve their goals. One young woman who adores her husband is willing to sleep with the crooked police officer to obtain visas—limitations sometimes compromise our values. Meanwhile Rick (Humphrey Bogart), a man who repeatedly says he sticks his head out for nobody, finds himself taking noble, selfless actions, not only when he rigs the roulette table so the young couple can buy their visas with the winnings, but when he makes the ultimate sacrifice--when he risks his life to save his ex-girlfriend and her husband. Without the limits (and the opportunities) of the crooked little town of Casablanca, it's doubtful the characters would have grown in such   ways.

Other films that use setting as a plot device are all the *Alien* movies, with the claustrophobic settings invaded by a voracious aliens. There's also the quite original setting of the inner worlds of minds under experimentation in *Eternal Sunshine of the Spotless Mind.* *The Matrix* also provides an artificial setting that threatens and motivates those being consumed by the grand manufactured illusion. Others are *Platoon* and *Apocalypse Now,* where the jungles of Viet Nam challenge the minds and hearts as well as the bodies of the soldiers trying to survive the experience. The settings don't have to be exotic or computer-generated fantasies to warrant great stories. They can be as mundane a broken-down van or as exotic as a fantasy world of mind controllers, but I encourage you to think small, simple, to think of the particulars of a place and how it can affect someone.

It's your job as a writer to create a place that entices the reader, makes the reader want to inhabit it just to see what's at stake in terms of potential feelings and actions that could develop in that place on the page or screen. Your characters aren't just anywhere; they are somewhere of your making and design, so make that place count for something. If you don't create an atmosphere, a sense of when and where a story takes place, your reader will put down your script and go find something interesting. It doesn't have to be a dramatic place to be a place where dramatic things happen. Consider the success of *Clerks*, a movie basically set in a convenience store and made on the shoe-string budget of director Kevin Smith. With that one movie, Smith established a career with the award-winning story about two store clerks, Dante and Randall, who try to put as little as possible into their jobs, while sidekicks Jay and Silent Bob seem to try to put as little effort as possible into anything.

Fiction writers, playwrights, and screenwriters are most often advised to write scripts out of "pro-active" characters, that is, characters who initiate plots through their desires and actions. Who would have guessed an award-winning script could focus on guys who want to avoid action? On second thought, Dante does have a strong desire to play hockey during the work day. The witty dialogue and the accessibility of the characters are what make this unlikely story work.

All right, I'll confess—it's not my kind of movie, not in my top ten, but it does entertain. The writer opens the movie with the cliché I tell writing students to avoid: don't start a story with some character waking up to an alarm or a phone call. Well, Mr. Smith does this, and what oddly makes the scene work is Dante slowly tumbling out of his closet, and in a half-asleep state he blindly reaches for the phone half-buried in pile of laundry. He's coerced by his boss on the phone to go open the convenience store where he works—and you have to feel for Dante: he's just recovering from working the late night shift. He just wants to sleep in and play hockey later in the day.   But Dante is a good guy. He goes in and begrudgingly takes the minimal steps to open up the place.

Doesn't sound very interesting, but the director hones in on this unremarkable setting so comically that we are entertained and keep watching, and why? He gives a sense of atmosphere, a sense of a guy's life, a guy with not much ambition who still lives with his mom, a guy who wants to get through his day and keep his girlfriend from getting too angry with him, a guy most guys can understand and root for.

No, the store never gets robbed, and the girlfriend doesn't get pregnant. The challenges are mundane, but refreshingly comic. Not long after the store is open, a man shows up and wants to drink his coffee by the counter. No problem, it would seem. But immediately he starts harassing customers buying smokes. With some disgusting props, he convinces smokers to avoid the deadly habit and to buy gum instead. When Dante tries to defend their right to smoke—hey, he's just trying to keep the peace—they pelt him with cigarettes and vilify him. Who knows how ugly it could have gotten without the comic intervention of the girlfriend, who tames the mob with a fire extinguisher and reveals the gum zealot to be a gum company representative.

So it's not a movie for everyone, but it's a hit with a big population of viewers who can identify with the day-to-day life of these anything-but-heroic characters doing their best trying not to work too hard at their most likely minimum wage jobs.

No matter what your setting, you can give it tone, feeling, that something that will draw us in. Setting helps define the dimension of your story. A story's setting is not a static set. It defines and confines the possibilities of the story about to unfold.

Although your setting is a fictional creation, there are limits on what can happen there. Within any setting, no matter how imagined, only certain events are likely to happen. If your setting is a jail cell, we aren't likely to get the story of a housewife trying to pay for her daughter's braces by selling Avon door-to-door. Okay, maybe it's possible, but a stilly stretch. No matter where your script is set, setting can be used to emphasize mood, conflicts, and desires. Setting can work as a metaphor for your character's interior landscape; it can also work as a character. So think of your setting as a personality quietly at work in your story—and sometimes not so quietly.

As for your own project, I would suggest you think small for your setting. Unless you know the day-to-day life of a penthouse stockbroker, I suggest you don't try writing about Wall Street. Pick a street, a block, a place you know so that you can recreate it with veracity and without cliché. If you haven't been in jail, I suggest you don't write about it. That old rule about "write what you know" has its reasons. Often young writers venture into writing things they don't know, like the trials and tribulations of a brain surgeon—yes, I've had this attempted by a twenty-year-old English major whose parents worked in the local Jeep factory. It failed, and there was no redeeming it.

But you can choose to write about something you'd really like to know. In Robert McKee's classic book on screenwriting, *Story*, he notes that researching a story involves memory, research and fact. And I'd like to point out here that you need not do the research process in that order. Sometimes your story idea can be inspired by a memory, sometimes by something you discovered at the library, and sometimes it can be inspired by a fact you've seen or heard on the news. I've written a piece about a killer. And I did it for personal reasons and not for an ooh-I-can-sell-this-violent-drama urge. It was inspired by a fact: a friend's daughter was car-jacked and killed. I did extensive research on the facts of the case, and there was plenty of material, given the killer was caught and eventually killed while trying to escape prison. One of the things that intrigued me about the story, aside from why the killer did it, was the fact that the girl never made an attempt to fight him off or escape from the forty-five minute car ride that ended in her death.

So I had fact, research, then I dove into memory and imagination. I recalled times I've walked into risky situations thinking I could talk my way out of trouble. I recalled the motivations, the feelings of risking danger. I also know a little something about violence—I grew up in a violent home. I know something of violence and how violence can breed violence. So I drew on what I knew and felt about those who'll risk violence and those with the urge to inflict it. I did my research, and I imagined so long and hard I was plagued by nightmares while writing the scary stuff.

If you choose to write about a topic you don't know, but would like to know, it's quite possible *if* you'll commit to extensive research and a lot of good, solid time imagining—not daydreaming, but the kind of stretching, working imagining that makes you sweat.

And extensive research involves more that what you can Google up on-line. I've had many students write about girls obsessed with cutting themselves, or killing themselves. I don't get it, but I imagine that it's something like the frequency of film majors wanting to make a suicide movie. It's a plan that seems engaging, dramatic. My students who write about cutters do the research; they get all the textbook symptoms of a girl with the need to cut; they put the girl in the motions of cutting alone in her room. But they usually fall short of recreating the feeling of isolation, desperation until the cut releases anxiety like poison gas into the air—unless they've experienced this for themselves.

You can research your topic all day long, but unless you take time to sit back, imagine how a place or situation would feel, you won't write a piece that rings true. Let's get back to my plot inspired by the local Mother's Day brawl at the Golden Corral. I got the idea from the news. The factual story involved a young African-American woman with an unruly child. A middle-aged white woman referred to the child as an animal and said many other derogatory things before leaning close to the child and screaming, "Shut up!" The mother, on impulse, punched the woman in the face. Lines were instantly drawn in that crowded restaurant where lots of working-class families gather to eat all they can for a deal, and the fight was on. Several went to the hospital; several went to jail. It was a story I had to tell, but I hadn't experienced racism—and I had never even eaten a meal at the Golden Corral.

So I did my research. I went to the place and ate. I studied the routine of paying, getting the trays. I checked out the food options. I studied the kinds of folks there and how the tables were arranged. Then, being more interested in classism than racism, and knowing much more about being poor and judged for being poor, I imagined a woman on her last nerve and being judged for her less-than-middle-class appearance and her unruly kids. So when writing about someone you don't know, you can breathe real life into them by putting a piece of yourself into the character. I suspect there's a piece of me in every character I write, even the killers—a scary thought. But as I said in the chapter on characters, we've all got a little bit of everything in us. Our life is very much a consequence of what we CHOOSE to be. We create ourselves much in the same way we create characters—we put some stuff in, keep some stuff out. And we edit and revise continuously.

Setting works most potently as a dynamic force in disaster movies. The sinking *Titanic* greatly motivates the actions of the characters aboard. But bear in mind, even before the run-in with the iceberg, the setting of the ship contributes to character development. Jack feels it's the luckiest event of his life to win that trip in a card game. He's feeling confident and cocky enough the court the young woman who on land would be so far out of his league that they would never cross paths. And being stuck on the ship while being pushed into a marriage to a cruel man contributes to her feeling of confinement, coercion, making her perhaps more desperate to rebel and claim a little life/adventure for herself.

We see this strategy of chaotic setting affecting characters at work in many popular movies: airplanes in distress at 30,000 feet up, tornados, hurricanes, tidal waves threatening the lives of people in the path of immanent danger. Some have sat entranced as a fishing boat battles a perfect storm—even though we know everyone on that boat will die in the end, we watch, not to see if they'll live, but to see how they will develop, change in their struggle against the odds.

However, you don't have to work on such a grand—and melodramatic—scale to have your characters motivated into action by setting. You could go small-scale and tell the story of how characters develop while waiting in a safe place as a tornado passes over a town. It could be a small story; let's say a stranger manages to soothe someone through an anxiety attack and both are changed by the connection. It could even be a little love story where, temporarily trapped by real danger, someone afraid of intimacy could decide to open herself up to the offered affection of a friend.

On this note of characters being trapped by a setting, consider the numerous prison movies: *Cool Hand Luke*, *The Bird Man of Alcatraz*, and the mega hit *Shawshank Redemption*. In these movies, a relationship develops between the protagonist and his setting. The prison, in spite of being a static thing of walls and bars, is anything but static. Its rules, regulations, its limits and the people that enforce them are often as proactive as any character and stimulate, challenge our characters to respond, change. In *Shawshank Redemption,* Andy Dufresne (Tim Robbins) not only has to endure being wrongly sentenced for the murder of his wife, he has to figure out a way to "get on with the business of living" instead of the default path of dying, the path many take in a setting of no options, a place of despair.

The tagline for this blockbuster reads: "Fear can hold you prisoner. Hope can set you free." And the plot plays this bit of wisdom out in the lives of characters imprisoned under a ruthless warden and brutal guards. Setting is a powerful force in this script. It works very much as a kind of character that bears down constantly, controlling not only the bodies, but the hearts and minds of the prisoners. Andy and his buddy Red (Morgan Freeman) find a way to keep their personalities intact in an environment designed to strip them down to passive non-beings. The gripping plotline is based on a Stephen King novella, "Rita Hayworth and the Shawshank Redemption," and under the direction of Frank Darabont grew into a story that's become somewhat mythic in its powerful depiction of how good can survive and outgrow evil. The film was nominated for seven Oscars and went on to win eleven other awards. Again, I point out here that great projects can grow from small plans.

Maybe you aren't ready to write such a lengthy storyline with the complications of that plot, but you could consider how a character might change from one night in a drunk tank at the county jail. There's not much to do but sleep and talk to other drunks in such a place. But put in a nicely-developed character with potential to change, and that drunk tank could be something like an incubator all warmed up to hatch an egg or two. For new screenwriters it's a good idea to study the classic big-budget movies that use setting as a critical element of the storytelling. In addition you'd be wise to study the writing and the plotlines of movies that aren't mainstream, but are award-winning movies that can help you toward a writing smaller scale movie that might win you some awards as well as a loyal following.

Another classic use of setting is in *One Flew over the Cuckoo's Nest*, a film I mentioned above while discussing institutional conflict. The institution of the mental asylum isn't as massive a power as the prison in Shawshank Redemption, but it is a sinister force. It is a place where inmates have to struggle to maintain their humanity. While the antagonist to McMurphy is more precisely Nurse Fletcher than the institution itself, the hospital with its barred windows, locked doors and its threatening surgical instruments serves as a force that certainly limits the inmates. Given the smaller setting, the smaller cast, it would be a useful story to study in order to see how characters play out and develop against a setting that controls them.

You don't necessarily need a big drama to provide a rich story. If you haven't seen his films yet, have a look the work of Jim Jarmusch, a director known for his unconventional movies that often consider different cultures and how they interact in close settings; these interactions depict how those from different cultures both see and don't see one other. This theme is seen in his *Deadman*, *Ghostdog*, *Mystery Train* and *Night on Earth*. He frequently uses the vignette style of storytelling to portray how our stereotypes of others can blind us to what is there, but can also create bonds between unlikely strangers when curiosity pushes a character to know a little something about what is foreign and is therefore reduced to a stereotype.

Curiosity, I'd say, is the "verb" driving most of his plots. There's the wonderfully inventive *Stranger than Paradise,* where the curious Hungarian, Eva, comes to New York to meet her cousin, only to tag along with her cousin and friend to Cleveland, then Florida on a road trip that leads to transformative surprises. There's *Mystery Train,* where two young Japanese kids travel across the US by train to go to Memphis to satisfy their curiosity about 1950s America. She's obsessed with Elvis, while he emulates Carl Perkins. Their journey lands them in a seedy hotel, where the real story plays out when their lives intersect with strangers also residing in the limbo-land of a seedy hotel in a shady part of Memphis. In his more recent *Broken Flowers*, a middle-aged man's comfortable, albeit passionless, lifestyle is interrupted when a mysterious pink note appears under his door. The anonymous letter-writer claims to be an ex-girlfriend who is the mother of his 19-year old son.   The protagonist, Don Johnston (Bill Murray), at first wants to ignore this bit of news, but his neighbor, who loves a good mystery, sends him on a quest to visit his old girlfriends, a journey that serves more to reveal his lack of connection to others than to develop any new relationship.

Another, and I find more interesting, theme occurring in Jarmusch's films is the conflict between the need for intimacy and the urge toward indifference. His characters, even when on long road trips, or train rides, or jail sentences, or little cab rides, simultaneously push others away while pulling them close for an instant—just to push them away again. Such plots don't make for whopping dramas, but they do depict the little and very real drama of being human in a world of strange other humans—or should I say other humans who are strangers and, even after moments of intimacy, remain strangers.

Telling the quiet story of the push and pull of little human reactions invites the choice of a close and intimate setting where individuals who are strangers are forced together for a time. Under the close-up lens of time and space, we see the ways curiosity can spark a plot. When characters are in close quarters for a sustained period of time, their personalities, their desires, and their indifferences play out. Such settings allow for small stories to unfold, little opportunities for character growth to occur or not. The opportunity for a character to grow—or not—is all you really need as the basis for a plot to unfold.

 Jarmusch's *Night on Earth*, a film telling the stories of five different cabs rides all across the world on a single night, succinctly explores the lives of characters from many cultures, people who are prone to be stereotyped. The five inter-connected stories in the film dramatize how, as people, we approach strangers with a mix of curiosity and indifference. Jarmusch suggests that we like looking over the boundaries of our own lives to have a look at someone different. Opportunity might lie in the acquaintance of a stranger, but Jarmusch's characters most often retreat into their own insular lives, thinking maybe they have their lives all nicely figured out while the world flies by.

There's much to learn from any and all of Jarmusch's films, but for the purpose of discussing setting, I want to focus on the stories that play out—or refuse to play out in those five taxi rides. The reason? You can learn much about dialogue and character development and plot if you'll confine your story to a limited setting. The setting sets the parameters of where you can go with your story. Not much can happen in a taxi ride but conversation, two strangers choosing to connect or not.

257

The setting of the cab also allows you to employ that excellent plot device I call "enter a stranger."

Let's have a look at his five mini-stories. You could certainly see each one as a self-contained film that might serve as a model for one of your own shorts, but it's wise to look at the bigger picture of what these five stories spanning the world imply as to what the human critter is prone to be: curious, but driven more by self-interest than risky explorations.

In the opening, a shot of five clocks on a wall states the time across the world in major cities. This shot establishes the idea that we will see a little something of what will unfold, or not unfold, in these cities all in one night. We start in Los Angeles and end in Helsinki, and we meet very different characters in vastly divergent dramatic situations, but there is an underlying theme of our basic alienation from each other, even when some try to make a connection. The film can teach us much about how setting, even the simple setting of a cab, can be a powerful force that contributes to the plot of a story. I'll quickly break down the little plots for you just to illustrate how simple a story can be while conveying a powerful insight into human nature.

In Los Angeles, we meet Corky the cabbie (Wynona Ryder), a skinny, pale, chain-smoking, tough-as-pavement young woman. She rolls her eyes as she drops off a couple of stoned-out musicians to a screaming skinny woman, who seems to be their very angry agent, at the airport. Corky tucks their money in a cigar box along with a gun, and from this little glimpse of a prop, we know she's quite capable of holding her own, even though she has the face of an angel and looks about twelve. When she gets out of her cab to call her dispatcher on the pay phone to complain about the lousy state of the cab she's driving, she reveals that she's something of a mechanic who can take care of things when the slacker cab company can't.

Through match cuts of two women talking on phones we have the opportunity to meet the beautiful casting agent Victoria Snelling, who is about to get in Corky's cab. While Corky talks with her boss, Victoria answers her cell phone to speak with a picky producer about actors she's sent. The women are connected in that they both are using phones to reach out to a man with authority who can improve or inconvenience the daily business of their lives. Their scenes are intercut with the agent gathering fancy luggage, making her way toward Corky, who is tired but scrappy as she ends the useless conversation with her boss. They meet, clicking off the phones and announcing in unison: "Shit!" There a bond is made. They each have separate business, but they are joined in their frustration.

The women have a need that brings them together: the lady needs a ride; the cabbie needs a fare. And off go the unlikely pair to Beverly Hills. In the first few minutes of their being together, Corky continues to provide things Victoria needs: a light for her cigarette and a phone book. When, in conversation, Victoria reveals her problem (satisfying a producer who wants an actor who is eighteen, inexperienced, with the nerves of a paratrooper), we're pretty sure of a bond that could be developed on this little cab ride: an acting contract.

The casting agent getting into the cab of the shabby cabby provided the inciting incident for the story, but when Victoria states her need for a certain kind of actor, and we see that the unknowing Corky fills the bill, we have a plot in the works. When Corky, clearly smart, curious, and good at her job, overhears Victoria on the phone, specifically asking if there are any messages from a Mr. Kincaid, she asks a question that will open a door that previously separated their worlds. She asks if Mr. Kincaid is a boyfriend. He is. She then makes a joke about the frustrating necessity of men in women's lives. They share a laugh and bond. Plot, along with the characters, develops.

The plot is pushed now when Victoria takes an interest in Corky and opens a door to Corky's world by asking about her career goals. Corky announces in no uncertain terms that she wants to be a mechanic, to get married, have boys. But when she goes on to say she wants a man who is a good guy, who'll love her for who she is, Victoria nods thoughtfully, and they bond in a deeper sense.

The setting of the cab wending its way through the rundown, graffiti-marked streets of LA and on its way to Beverly Hills reinforces the theme of two worlds colliding. Corky knows the way through the trashed parts of town and knows the roads that lead to Beverly Hills. Victoria's eyes lock on Corky's all-attitude and lovely face. Each woman has a goal. They have crossed paths, and we watch to see the chemistry that will occur as these women keep opening doors to each other with their questions and with the answers that will articulate their goals.

You can learn much of how setting can frame a drama by watching and listening to what goes on in this cab, but remember to keep your eye on everything in the frame. Those run-down streets with fast food signs and used car lots look much like the real Hollywood, not the fantasy of Hollywood. Corky knows those streets. The unglamorous world of Los Angeles is her world, her home. When Victoria declares she is having a "brilliant streak" and offers Corky a chance to be a movie star, Corky doesn't give the option a thought. She instantly declines, saying she has her life all worked out and that she plans to be a mechanic. Here's where we see how different these two women are, given the worlds they come from. When Victoria declares that everyone wants to be a movie star, we know she believes in a dream that simply doesn't apply to Corky. Corky just shrugs and says that's not the life for her and that everything is going just right for her the way it is.

Victoria is a bit baffled—and impressed. How rare to meet someone happy in her world. Corky unloads the glamorous lady's luggage and drives away from a huge opportunity. Whether it is a wise choice or not is not the question to ask of this short story. Setting has limited the concerns of our plot: how will two strangers affect one another on a little cab ride? It could result in a big change, but it results in a small one.

Alone and lugging her fancy luggage inside, Victoria hears her cell phone ring in her briefcase. From the beginning of this short piece, we've seen that the phone is her basic prop. She needs it and lives her professional and romantic life through it. It rings, and she considers putting down her luggage and rushing to answer it as she has done previously. She looks toward the phone, says firmly, "Oh shut up." Aha, *she* is changed. Not the seemingly down-trodden cabby. Here we see Jarmusch doing what he so often does with stereotypes—he breaks them apart to show a quiet surprise inside. The life of our glamorous casting agent is expanded and improved by the cabbie—not the usual Hollywood story.

Now to the streets of New York, where Yo-Yo, an African-American man in a ridiculous furred aviator cap—and equally ridiculous had-to-cost-plenty white high tops—has no luck flagging down a taxi to take him to Brooklyn. Drivers see him, obviously see the stereotype, and drive on by.

Until along comes a stranger—an excellent plot device. This guy is a real stranger, some poor Eastern European refugee who can barely handle English, much less the clunking taxi he drives by lurching, squealing along as he alternately mashes gas, brake, gas, brake. He doesn't see our guy Yo-Yo as a stereotypical African-American who is potentially dangerous with his need to get to Brooklyn. This cabbie named Helmut simply sees a guy who needs a ride.   In seconds, Yo-Yo realizes that he'll have to drive the taxi himself if they are to get anywhere, and reluctantly, and naïvely, the cabbie lets him drive. And off we go on another little road trip where strangers proceed to open doors to one another. Given we are on a taxi ride to Brooklyn, the only doors that are going to open are the metaphorical doors to each other, doors that only questions can open.

This is a story where complete innocence and naïveté meet, fortunately, good will. Yo-Yo is astonished by the ignorance of the cabbie, but the only thing he ridicules is his name, which he pronounces as "helmet" instead of the correct pronunciation, which would be something like "Hel-mude." He teases that the cabbie has a ridiculous name, and might as well be called lampshade. Helmut, no fool, even though his only job experience is being a clown, counters by teasing that Yo-Yo's name is also silly. He also points out that they are wearing the same kind of hat. It's a bond, a comic, trivial one, but a bond nonetheless.

Through the props, the names, and the actions, we see a connection between strangers. Helmut trusts Yo-Yo to drive to Brooklyn. Yo-Yo likes Helmut enough to try to teach him how to drive a cab with advice like turning on the meter and putting the gear in "D" for drive in order to move forward.   Okay, it's time to suspend disbelief. It's quite unlikely that these two strangers would develop any kind of friendship on the road to Brooklyn. But it's New York—anything can happen.

The situation shifts with Yo-Yo driving and Helmut admiring the rundown streets, the tall, brightly-lit buildings, the store fronts and again, used car lots. He declares it all cool with a childish wonder in his eyes. They bond further as Yo-Yo teaches him some English slang. But we see just how far apart they are when Yo-Yo asks where Helmut is from. Helmut says he's from a little Czechoslovakian town near Prague. And Yo-Yo is so baffled by the words he's never heard, he doesn't bother to ask Helmut to explain.

Even though they share a cab, even though they fully trust one another, these two men couldn't be more foreign to one another. And their goals couldn't be more different. Yo-Yo has a clear goal. He knows where he wants to be: Brooklyn. Helmut, on the other hand, has no specific goal but to pick up some fares; he is happy driving around with no idea of where he is. He simply finds wherever he is, whomever he meets and talks to, interesting and potentially entertaining.

When Yo-Yo spots Angela, his hard-assed and lovely sister-in-law, walking the streets as if she has a strong intention to be somewhere in particular, he jumps out of the cab and man-handles her into it, with her all the while screaming insults but going along. Yo-Yo sees a willful sister-in-law who has to be reigned in, while Helmut can't quit staring at this new wonder and declares her beautiful. Helmut's innocent admiration eventually calms the rebellious Angela, and for a time they all ride along peacefully as old friends on a road trip.

Once in Brooklyn, Helmut, not knowing what he is seeing in the run-down neighborhood, declares Brooklyn "great" while Angela insists it's a "Shit hole" as she gets out of the taxi and dutifully heads back inside her apartment building. Helmut, remember, is a former clown. He sees even the most mundane things as something wonderful, and he shares this kind of innocent pleasure when he plays two piccolos at once in a little song to entertain Yo-Yo and Angela. They are amused, but only momentarily—they have the business of their lives, whatever that may be, to get back to.

Yo-Yo pays Helmut and gives him yet another lesson on counting the cash to make sure he isn't cheated. Helmut declares he's not that interested in money, that he's a clown and that yes, he needs money, but he's not that interested in it. This attitude toward money runs counter to Yo-Yo, who is mighty proud of those garish

261

expensive sneakers and that hat that appears to be exactly like Helmut's, but is different in that, as Yo-Yo insists, it is top-of-the-line and fresh.

The two from Brooklyn are very concerned with appearances—she's clearly put thought into her tough-girl chic look. Earlier, when Yo-Yo couldn't get a ride, he tried waving down a cab by flashing money, assuming that money will get a man what he needs. Obviously it didn't. It wasn't the money that got Helmut's attention. All he wanted was a customer to justify his position behind the wheel of a cab. His goal? To be a cabbie, not a clown.

Yo-Yo, being a nice guy, does take interest in Helmut making it back to the city. He gives what directions he can to assist him, but Helmut, more interested in the people he's just met than his own destination, gets the directions all wrong.

This unlikely encounter between strangers leaves them all unchanged. Yo-Yo and Angela go back to their pursuits of getting through a day and a night. And Helmut pops on his clown nose and goes back to being a clown, as he lurches once again down streets he doesn't know in some vague attempt to get back to the city, all the while murmuring to himself about the nice family he's just met. He hasn't seen them for who they are any more than they have seen him.

Curiosity provides only a thin connection between strangers. While this jovial but superficial encounter suggests that strangers can at least provide a temporary amusement for one another in this mortal world, the next one reveals how assumptions/stereotypical thinking can keep us alienated from one another just at a time when we could benefit from the kindness of a stranger.

Paris. A city known for its grouchy characters. And so we go there to play with that stereotype. At first glance we can see that the irritable cab driver is anything but content with his job. His sharply defined African features show a beautiful facial structure marred by anger, frustration, and flat-out weariness at the ramblings of the privileged business men who are his passengers. They are African but are clearly from a different country given they have very different features from the cab driver. They joke about how successfully they've ripped off someone in their white collar way. They are smug and proud. And within seconds of this story's start, they badger the cabbie as to where he is from, and they comment on his bad driving—he seems to have run a few red lights and in general doesn't seem to pay much attention to the road.

They speculate on which part of the "jungle" the driver is from, and guess Cameroon. Whereas in earlier cab rides personal questions were a kind of request to enter the "doorway" of a stranger, these business men use questions to barge their way into the cab driver's world. When, pinned, he admits that he's from the Ivory Coast; they insult him with the cryptic attacking remark: "That explains it." Perhaps the remark is meant to suggest that being from the Ivory Coast is the reason he's a bad driver, but whatever the precise intention, it's a big enough insult for the driver to throw them out of his cab. In his anger and haste, he forgets to collect his money, and that only infuriates him more as he heads out into the darkness looking for another fare.

Just ahead in the darkness he sees a blind woman with her cane and hailing a cab; muttering something about how at least this one won't give him trouble, he pulls over. He is immediately struck by the incongruity of her stunning beauty: a model's face with perfect cheekbones and a full, wide mouth, and cleavage nicely rising from her tight blouse. But then there is the awful sight of those blind eyes, with the whites rolling back, her head moving as if somehow getting her head in the right position could help her see. He stares until she yells at him to get going, and she, too, immediately sets to insulting his driving. There are indications so far that his bad driving is a result of the things he doesn't "see" very well, given he's so distracted by his thoughts. His intense, angry facial expressions, even when he is briefly alone in the cab, suggest that he's more preoccupied with his interior than his exterior world—interestingly, just like the blind girl. How perfect for him to meet a blind woman who could set him straight on a few things. First she gives him specific instructions on the route she wants him to take to her destination—he prefers another route, but seems to appease her.

As he drives forward, his gaze is on the rearview mirror. He's fascinated—and so are we—by the woman's ability to apply lip-liner perfectly to her beautiful, full lips. She then realizes that he is taking her through a tunnel—the route she did not want to take, as she hates tunnels. And we get a long, slow, claustrophobic shot of the road winding through the tunnel. The relationship is established as one of anger and frustration even though they don't know one another. He appeases her a bit by reaching back to light her cigarette, and he tries to open a proverbial door to her by asking a question on the order of "don't blind people usually wear glasses?" She slams the door on him by smarting off that she doesn't know, being she's never seen a blind person. After an apology for invading her privacy, he only goes "blindly" on to ask more intimate questions, such as what it's like to make love to a man she can't see.

Angry and insulted, she does answer his questions and explains how she sees with all her body and senses. She says she can do everything he can do, and to the viewer it seems she can do a few things better than the driver. She correctly guesses just from the sound of him and the sense of him that he is from the Ivory Coast. And when he tries to undercharge her out of some kind of sympathy, she guesses exactly what her fare should be and pays it. She will have none of his pity.

When he lets her out at her destination near a canal, he watches her. She keeps going, making good progress until she is walking right alongside the canal, and she seems to know the path as clearly as anyone who can see.

He drives on, but he is obviously distracted by her. We cut to the blind girl successfully, smoothly negotiating her walk on the path in the darkness, and we hear a car crash and the yelled insults at our driver, who didn't see the car he collided with. Our blind girl smiles at the blindness of the cabbie who can see but isn't very good at seeing what's just ahead of him. She walks on with a smile of something like success.

This little story features the strong current of indifference that keeps us isolated in our own worlds even when we have an encounter with someone so different he or she might teach us something. Both the driver and the blind girl are continuously caught up in a quiet anger and bitterness that keeps them from seeing or connecting with anyone. Just as he was content to leave those privileged men in the street after they presumed to invade his privacy, she is content to hear the sound of the cabbie in a car crash. Just as the businessmen rudely accosted him, the cabbie crudely attempted to invade her private world. He wrongly held assumptions about her because she was blind, just as the businessmen wrongfully held assumptions about a man from the Ivory Coast.

After their conversation, their angry brush with intimacy, they go off back into their own worlds of private bitterness unchanged.

The next cab ride, set in Rome and starring the award-winning actor/comedian Roberto Benigni, takes a completely different tone; our first shot is of the deserted streets of Rome and a couple having sex on a red Vespa and completely indifferent to the world passing by. Their sex life is all-consuming to them, and this narcissism foreshadows our cab driver's story. We meet him, happily driving in the night with his sunglasses on. He teases his dispatcher with sexual innuendo and sets out to pick up a fare. On the way, he amuses himself happily, somewhat manically, singing, indifferently going down streets in the wrong direction, doing whatever he wishes. Some might consider him comically self-sufficient; others might consider him manically self-absorbed.

His selfish nature takes over the plot when he picks up a weary-looking priest. He continues to call the priest a bishop in spite of the priest's repeated corrections. This oversight only foreshadows the larger, and deadly, oversight to play out. During the ride we see the priest grow uncomfortable with symptoms of a heart attack while the cabbie goes on about the need to confess the sins of his weird sexual history. The priest tries to prevent the cabbie from "confessing." When the driver complains about how hard it is to see his way in the night, the priest points out that the cabbie is wearing his sunglasses. The cabbie takes them off and is greatly relieved with his new ability to see. But alas, like so many other characters in this series of stories, he is blind to the needs, interests, the simple being of others right there in the cab.

Again, I want to point out the use of setting in this group of stories. If one can't "see" another who is right there in the small, contained space of a cab over the length of time it takes to make a trip across town, we have to ask whether human critters are really, by nature, any good at seeing much at all. The film would suggest not.

As the priest wrestles with the pain in his chest and the need to breathe, the cabbie rattles on about his sexual exploits with pumpkins, then a sheep, and then his sister-in-law. His tone is anything but confessional. His rambling on is more like a masturbatory verbal entertainment. Meanwhile the priest struggles for his heart pills, drops them, and eventually dies quietly in the back seat.

When the cabbie finally notices that priest is dead, being the narcissist that he is, the cabbie claims he has killed the priest with his shocking stories. Remorse? Nope. He dumps the priest on a park bench and covers the man's dead, wide-open eyes with his sunglasses. The gesture might seem compassionate, in that he covers the ugly dead gaze, but the gesture also suggests the glasses can somehow prevent the priest from seeing the cabbie's complicity in his death. In any case, satisfied with the arrangement of the dead man on a park bench, the cabbie hurries back to his cab and drives on.

The final story takes us to Helsinki with establishing shots of a cold, desolate night. Mika, the cabbie, fights the overpowering urge to sleep as he circles and circles a monument to keep himself busy. Finally the dispatcher gives him a fare to pick up. He goes through the deserted streets to find three men standing outside a closed bar. They appear to be passed-out while standing up, with only the support of their bodies leaning into each other to keep them from toppling to the ground. It's a promising image: three men leaning into each other for support. When he arrives, two of the men move and the drunkest, unconscious one topples to the ground. His friends gather him up, and they all climb in the cab.

The cabbie, being experienced, not only asks the destination, but who will pay. The two conscious ones admit they have no money but that their unconscious friend will pay the fare with his severance pay. Instantly we see here the limits of friendship. We also see the limits of friendship when the "friends" start arguing furiously over who will be dropped off first. When the driver threatens to throw them out of the car for fighting, they go passive and admit that it hardly matters who goes first, as they all live on the same block. Once Mika gets going, he opens the door to the others with his question—he asks twice—if the unconscious one is all right. He seems to be the first compassionate person we've seen in these stories. With a concerned face he pushes to know the details of the man's problems: it turns out that not only has the guy been fired, but his teenaged daughter is pregnant, and his furious wife turned on him with a kitchen knife and demanded a divorce.

It's a pretty rough story, but the driver says things could have been worse. This observation bewilders our drunks, and they immediately open the door to his life by asking "How?"

And now the opportunity arrives for the driver to tell his story. He begins by saying he and his wife work hard. He points to her picture taped to his dashboard—he's the first cabbie who keeps something sentimental with him in his cab. He tells of how they worked hard to have a baby, and when they finally conceived, their daughter was very premature and unlikely to live. He speaks of the misery of waiting to see if the little girl, so tiny, "like a peanut," would live. Unable to bear the pain of loving what he might lose, he decides to kill the love—something many of the characters in this movie seem to do, finding greater comfort in indifference than connection. The baby doesn't improve. Finally, the wife implores him to love the baby, saying (superstitiously) that the baby needs their love to live. So Mika allows the floodwaters of love to move up and through him. He and the wife go to the hospital to give the baby all that love, and when they arrive, they find the baby has died. So much for love.

This sentimental story sets the drunks to weeping. The death of a child puts all other trouble in perspective. They turn on their passed-out friend and are for some reason angry at him for his lesser troubles. It seems they are capable of only small bits of compassion at once. They get out and head for their homes, leaving their friend passed-out and stuck with paying the fare. Mika jostles him awake, makes him pay, and watches as he gets out of the car. The drunk seems disoriented, looks around, then just crouches on the sidewalk as if waiting for something. Mika still seems concerned. He watches him a bit, and drives off. We are left with the image of the drunk with the ruined life crouching there, something more like a bird on the streets than a man. Other neighbors walk by, give him a glance and keep going, as if there is nothing unusual about a man crouching alone on the streets in the pre-dawn light.

The film begins at sunset in LA and ends just at the beginning of sunrise in Helsinki. In this one night on earth, we've seen five vignettes of people with opportunities to connect in the confined space and limited time of a cab ride. With all these opportunities, not much happens. Given the human critter's basic self-absorption, they have trouble seeing or feeling much that is beyond them. Even the casting agent who seemed to be giving Corky the chance of a lifetime was only out to get her job of pleasing a producer accomplished.

We leave the film with the feeling that a night on earth holds the stories of people all over the world with pressing needs, ranging from something as simple as a career as a mechanic to something as serious as medication, emergency treatment for a failing heart. There are many failing hearts in this series of stories—well, if not failing, certainly compromised, limited. It seems that even when we try to connect with others on this planet, there is a gauzy membrane that lies between us and keeps us limited in movement, growth. The characters remain much like that premature baby. Maybe a whopping amount of love and compassion will help it live. Maybe not.

Before you get to work on your own use of setting have a look at the student example below that employs a calculated use of setting. The scene very nicely uses setting as a dynamic force that challenges the comfort of a character. The law office itself confines and limits Will, in much the same way that his deceased grandmother's rules for an inheritance will confine and limit him. The second example employs setting with a different strategy, the use of setting as a way of depicting a character. We see the neglected bedroom of a young man whose life is as random and chaotic as the bedroom he sometimes forgets.

Student Example of Setting as a Dynamic Force
by Caitlyn Dean

```
INT. A NOT-SO-UP-SCALE LAWYER'S OFFICE - DAY

WILL, wearing an expensive suit, fiddles with his cell phone
while he sits in an old high-backed chair. ALLIE, wearing
scrubs, sits next to him in an identical chair, fanning
herself with a magazine. Rain CLATTERS against the single
window.

Will tries pushing several buttons on the phone, waits, then
GROANS.


                         WILL
              There's no signal in this place. How's
              a man supposed to stay connected?


Will pockets the phone and tries to get comfortable. He
attempts to stretch out his legs, but the oversized desk
that dominates the room hinders movement. He GRUNTS in
annoyance, but tries to relax by rested his head on the
chair back. His eyes slide shut


                         ALLIE
              How can you sleep right now?


Allie begins to tear up and SNIFFLE.


                         ALLIE
I mean, at the end of this meeting we'll have nothing else
to do with your Grandma. She'll just be a picture on the
wall.


Will opens his eyes and rolls his head in time to catch
Allie reach up her shirt sleeve, pull out a tissue, and BLOW
HER NOSE. He stares at her for a moment, a look of baffled
confusion on his face.


                         WILL
Did you just pull that tissue out of your shirt sleeve?


Allie dabs at a tear with the unused corner of the tissue.
```

                         ALLIE
              Yeah, so?

                         WILL
              Aaand that's where you normally
              keep them?

Allie scowls at him.

                         ALLIE
              When I'm working, yes. Now can we please
              drop it. I'm not feeling well.

Will CHUCKLES LAZILY, leans back in his chair, closes his
eyes, can't get comfortable. He opens his eyes, GROANS, sits
up, pulls out cell phone, checks it, snaps it shut. He
reaches in inner jacket pocket, pulls out ear buds and Ipod,
plugs in.

Allie SIGHS in frustration and pulls at her shirt collar.

                         ALLIE
              It's so hot in here.

Behind them, the office door begins to open and a tall,
slim, mid-fifties IRVING STANLEY steps through the door.

                         IRVING
              Good morning, Mr. and Mrs. Lawrence.
              I'm sorry I kept you waiting.

Allie turns in her chair to acknowledge him.

                         ALLIE
                         (softly)
              Good morning, Mr. Stanley.

Irving takes the single step to Allie's chair.

                         IRVING
              Allie, how are you holding up?

Allie starts tearing up.

                         ALLIE
              I'm hanging in there. Thank you for

                            269

asking.

He smiles at her compassionately and pats her shoulder.

                    IRVING
          Good. Now, if you'll excuse me, my dear,
          I'll try to make it to my desk.

He slides between the chair and the wall to his desk. He
sits in the worn, leather chair.

                    IRVING
          Well, shall we start?

                    ALLIE
          That would be good. Don't you think,
          honey?

Allie looks to Will for a response, but he sits with his
eyes closed, and bobbing his head to music.

(Beat.)

Allie nudges his arm.
                    ALLIE
          Will.

Will sits forward, pulls out ear buds.

                    WILL
I'm sorry. What?

He looks over to Allie.

                    ALLIE
          Are you ready to go over your
          grandmother's will?

                    WILL
          Oh. Yeah...

Will SHIFTS in his chair and looks at Irving.

                    WILL
          You can proceed Mr....Mr...uh...

A look of embarrassment passes over Will's face. Allie hides her face in her hand.

Squinting his eyes a little, Irving reveals a slight annoyance with Will.

                    IRVING
          Stanley. Irving Stanley. We met a few
          days ago at the funeral.

                    WILL
          Oh, Right. Well, Irv...

Allie lifts her head up and looks at Will with a look of shock on her face.

                    WILL
          Let's get down to business.

Allie GROANS and drops her head back into her hand.

Irving takes a DEEP BREATH.

                    IRVING
          Well...

He CLEARS HIS THROAT and turns to a drawer. He pulls a manila folder, turns back towards Will and Allie, and sets the folder onto the desk.

                    IRVING
There isn't much to get down to.

He looks over the papers as if enjoying something.

                    IRVING
Your grandmother's last wishes were simply that all her remaining assets be liquidated into cash funds and given to you and your wife.

Will's eyes zero in on Irving, and he leans forward.

                    IRVING
          With the exception, of her Bible...

Allie lifts her head and watches Irving with interest.

                    IRVING
          Which is to go to Mrs. Lawrence.

Allie's chin begins quivering. She reaches for a new tissue
concealed in her sleeve and dabs at the tears in her eyes.

                    WILL
I'm sorry. Could you back up a second?

Will SCOOTS to the very edge of his chair, his knees BUMPING
into the desk.

                    WILL
          You said all her remaining assets. I didn't
          even know she had that many assets remaining.
          So...

Will fights a smile.

                    WILL
          How much are we talking here?

Allie snaps her head in Will's direction.

                    ALLIE
          Will!

Irving goes to answer, but hesitates when he notices the
angry tears rolling down Allie's cheeks.

                    WILL
          Irv? The money. How much?

Allie turns to look out the window, fanning herself angrily,
and taking STAGGERED BREATHS.

                    IRVING
          Well, sir...

Irving pulls his eyes from Allie and looks over the papers.
He looks up at Will.

                    IRVING
          In all, I'd say it's about a half
          million dollars.

The angry look on Allie's face changes to one of dazed confusion, and she turns to look at Irving.

Will closes his eyes for a moment and slightly pumps his fist, a smile playing at his lips.

> ALLIE
> Did you just say that Grandma Gerty left us half a million dollars?

Irving smiles when he sees Allie's touched look.

> IRVING
> Yes, Mrs. Lawrence, that's correct.

> WILL
> So when can we get our hands on it?

Allie drops her head in disappointment and the smile on Irving's face fades with a SIGH. He looks at Will.

> IRVING
> Well, Mr. Lawrence, it's going to take some time to process everything. Why don't we just stick to the task at hand?

Not hearing him, Will starts fishing in his pants pocket, pulls out his phone.

> WILL
> That sounds good, but would you excuse me for a minute...

Will starts to rise out of his seat.

> WILL
> I have to make a quick phone...

> IRVING
> Sit. Down. Mr. Lawrence.

Will, catching the tone of voice, slowly lowers himself back down into his chair.

                    IRVING
          Your excitement isn't doing anyone in
          this room any good.

Irving takes a quick glance at Allie, who is now hunched
over and holding her head with both of her hands.

                    IRVING
          So I'm going to ask you to try as hard
          as you can to remain silent as I continue.

(Beat.)

                    IRVING
          Now then.

Irving begins leafing through the papers.

                    IRVING
          Your grandmother, wonderful as she was,
          had some very specific stipulations tied
          to the acquisition of that money.

Will quietly GROANS.

Irving looks up and squints at Will threateningly.

(Beat.)

Irving goes back to the papers.

                    IRVING
          First, I would like to mention that you
          are required to follow these stipulations
          to the letter. Failure to do so results in
          all of the money going to various charities.
          Is that clear, Mr. Lawrence?

Irving looks up at him threateningly again.

Will nods once, an angry look on his face.

Irving smiles.

                    IRVING
          Very good.

Irving looks back down at the papers

                    IRVING
          Now then, it seems that your grandmother
          wanted you and your wife to spend some
          quality time together because she wants
          you both to go on a road trip.

Irving glances up, fights a smile, looks back to papers.

                    IRVING
          To Niagara Falls.

Will makes a CHOKING SOUND.

                    IRVING
          And may I remind you, Mr. Lawrence,
          your job is to stay silent now.

Will, mouth open, about to say something, closes his mouth
and sits back in his chair. His jaw flexes.

                    IRVING
          Secondly, on this trip you are not allowed
          to have any electronic devices. No computers,
          no GPS...

With a satisfied smile, he looks up at Will.

                    IRVING
          And no cell phones. You are also
          prohibited from bringing certain types
          of media: magazines, CDs, DVDs. To insure
          compliance, you and your wife will be
          monitored with surveillance equipment.

Will suddenly stands, and glares at Irving.

                    WILL
          Ok, I've had enough. Stop wasting my
          time and get to the real will.

Irving smiles a little, sits back in chair.

                    IRVING
          I assure you, Mr. Lawrence, everything

                    I'm telling you is right here in legal
                    print.

Will's face flushes, but he remains still.

                              IRVING
                    Would you like to read it for yourself.

Will sits.

Irving smiles.

                              IRVING
                    Shall we continue?

Allie weakly leans forward, very pale.

                              ALLIE
                    Um, I could use a break.

Will gets a determined look on his face, but his eyes never
leave Irving.

                              WILL
                    No we're going to finish this. Read on.

Will looks at Allie sympathetically.

                              IRVING
                    There isn't much left, Mrs. Lawrence

Irving looks at Will.

                              IRVING
                    The final requirement is that you take
                    the Bible. And you, Mr. Lawrence, along
                    with your wife are to memorize the provided
                    verses.

He raises a sheet of paper, offers it to Allie, who sits
stunned. He lays the paper on the desk, looks to Will.

                              IRVING
                    You will then have to recite them to me
                    on completion of your trip. Failure to
                    do so them completely by memory will

                              276

result in the entire sum being donated to
charities.

Will jumps up.

                    WILL
          This is ridiculous.

                    ALLIE
          Really, I need to take a break.

Will stands firmly, eyes never leaving Irving.

                    WILL
          I refuse to do it.

Irving looks at him matter-of-factly. Closes folder.

                    IRVING
          Then you'll lose the money.

Allie sits up in her chair, looking very flushed.

                    ALLIE
          I think I'm going to be sick...

INT. LAW OFFICE HALLWAY-CONTINUING

Will and Irving stand awkwardly in the hallway just outside
a woman's bathroom. VOMITTING can be heard within.

Will rubs the back of his neck.

                    WILL
          Look, I'm sorry about all that in there.
                    (beat)
          So you're telling me there is no way to
          get the money unless we do exactly as my
          grandmother wants.

                    IRVING
          That is correct.

Will looks away and clenches his jaw. A TOILET FLUSHES.

                              WILL
                  Then I guess we're going.

Irving fights a smile.

                              IRVING
                  Don't worry, Mr. Lawrence. You'll survive.
                  It's only a week, and all you have to do is
                  spend time with your wife and memorize a few
                  Bible verses. It might even be good for you.

Will glares at Irving, starts to speak. Allie, still looking
pale, comes out of the bathroom. She looks at the two,
shakes her head, BREATHES A SIGH OF DISGUST.

                              ALLIE
                  Work it out later. I need to go.

This scene serves as the inciting incident for a longer and comic plot to unfold. It's a
very successful use of the device of employing a place of transition to get a plot
going. The setting does much to contribute to the tension of the scene and, as I said
above, it nicely foreshadows the limits and restraints to be put on Will as his
grandmother's hand reaches from the great beyond to improve the life, and the
marriage, of her grandson.

8. Plotting and Scheming

> "Art is pleasing yourself. But you can please yourself
> and it won't be art. Art is having the mastery to take
> your experience, whether it is visual or mental, and
> make meaningful shapes that convey a reality to
> others."
>
> Gail Godwin

No doubt you have a reason for wanting to learn how to write stories to be
translated into film. By now you've been prompted by plenty of exercises to stir up
ideas, and you've written scenes that could be developed into longer films. I do
hope you've been inspired to write, and I do hope you've enjoyed the results. Now
let's think about committing to a complete story. At this point you should have a few
nicely developed characters worth a story. You've had an opportunity to get your
characters talking and doing things, and if they are talking and doing things, they're
on their way to helping you write your story.

The novelist E.M. Forster speaks at great length on the difference between plot and
story in his *Aspects of the Novel*:

> "Let us define plot. We have defined a story as a
> narrative of events arranged in their time-sequence. A
> plot is also a narrative of events, the emphasis falling on
> causality. "The king died and then the queen died" is a
> story. "The king died, and then the queen died of grief" is
> a plot. . . . The time-sequence is preserved, but the sense
> of causality overshadows it. If it is in a story, we say "and
> then?" If it is in a plot, we ask "why?" That is the
> fundamental difference."

So let's clarify what he is saying. He's using the word "story" to describe a series of events that keeps the reader asking "and then, and then, and then?" Many thrillers, such the as *Mission Impossible* series, run on this sort of story, much as in the old traditional murder mysteries where the operating, engaging question is "who dunnit?" Many of us have often sat through a movie and stayed seated because we were hooked by the "and then?" question.

After such entertainments we walk away, entertained maybe by the cool tricks and hot chicks and car chases and things blowing up, but some viewers want a little more substance to the storyline. They want something more sophisticated, complex, something that perhaps taps into the mysterious contradictions of being human, we want a plot that invites us to ask "WHY?" A narrative that addresses causality, a "why?" is the sort of narrative that results in a plot. And in exploring the answer to "why?" perhaps we as viewers will learn a little something about the human critter at work, learn a little something about ourselves.

Plot and story are terms that are often interchanged, and no one gets confused. But for the sake of writing bear in mind that there is a slight difference. Often when we walk away from a movie dissatisfied, it's because it was lacking in plot. Maybe it started with an intriguing idea. But ideas are like those proverbial castles in the air. You have to get out there and build foundations under them. Lots of people have ideas; there's a bazillion out there. But ideas are only seeds. They must be cultivated. And they must grow from inherent material. Once you have an idea, you have to test it. You have to ask why you are pondering it, why the character wants something or doesn't want something. Once you start seriously, or at least thoughtfully, exploring the why's of your story, you'll have a plot.

If you don't ask why and proceed with your idea with a "and then this happens, and then this happens," you'll have a pretty shallow story. And shallow stories are like shallow ponds—left out to the air and sun, they'll quickly turn to mud. And there you'll be, mired down in the muck, wondering how to get out of the thing gracefully. This sort of mess can be seen in the popular comedy *The Forty-Year-Old Virgin*. It began with a far-fetched and engaging premise, a guy is a forty-year-old virgin and his friends go on a mission to help get him laid. It's a nifty external storyline that gets a lot of laughs. But then there is the inner plot of a guy who would like a little bit of love along with getting laid. Here is where things get complicated. The script has played so lightly with the why's of his long-term virginity—comic mishaps rather than a serious fear of intimacy.

It's a comedy, so we don't need a serious reason as to how and why the man has managed to avoid having sex—please, no child molestation cliché. But if his character had been more fully developed, if his love interest were more fully developed, if the ups and downs of their growing intimacy were developed, then we might have a plot that would be endearing, memorable, maybe even enlightening. When such a light story tries to go deep with the kind of changes real love and intimacy require, it simply crashes into a wall of the ridiculous. And that's just how the movie ends.

Another far-fetched comedy, *True Lies*, does have a plot we like to hang onto, a story we like to see played out again and again. The story comically spins out the consequences when a bored housewife (Jamie Lee Curtis) tries to spice up her life by assisting a man she thinks is a secret agent and ends up caught in the serious— and funny—misadventures of her husband (Arnold Schwarzenegger), who is a real-deal secret agent who only posed as a geeky computer salesman. Yes, there is lots of slapstick humor and impossible chase-em-blow-em-up scenes, but the story of "and then, and then, and then" rides of a real plot of how and why marriages can weaken in spite of love. The plot point out that love isn't a static thing; it has to be nurtured. *True Lies* reveals that a family unraveling can be mended with attention, communication, a bit of honesty. Yeah, it's starting to sound like a sappy movie, but it isn't. It's a ridiculous plot, but it hinges on the desires of very real characters who change—and not by just getting laid. They change because they take risks; they let go of old patterns to grab onto something new, and they grow.

When considering your plot, bear in mind that a story is a playing field where dynamic energies erupt, evolve, and interact. The force generating your story can arise from internal motivation, as in *Shawshank Redemption,* where the plot grows from Andy's desire to survive and eventually escape the prison to which he has been wrongfully sentenced. While that internal motivation is what drives the story, many external events occur, like the friendship of Red, and a greedy warden who needs a smart man to keep the books; these events contribute to the plot by shaping, contributing to Andy's plan. And of course there are the setbacks. As I've said, you don't have a story without trouble. If Andy's desires moved forward without a hitch, there wouldn't be a story that would engage our attention, make us care about the outcome.

The Fall provides an excellent example of how interior worlds affect and are affected by external events. A paralyzed stuntman, Roy Walker, convalescing in a hospital, wants nothing but to die because not only has he lost his lady love, but he has also lost the use of the lower half of his body. In the opening minutes of the film, we see random clips of an early silent film being made. It's a cheesy western, and we see there's been an accident while a stunt was being played out. We come to learn that Roy is paralyzed from a bad fall from a bridge while he was attempting a dangerous and over-the-top stunt. The plot springs forward on the ever-popular inciting event I like to call "enter a stranger."

281

Enter Alexandria, a little girl recovering from a severely broken arm, who walks into Roy's hospital room. All she wants is a friend who will entertain her, someone to ease the boredom and loneliness of being the only child in a hospital of sick and dying older people. The girl has a box of little treasures, keepsakes from her life before she became a refugee migrant worker in California. When she asks Roy to tell her a story, he says he will tell her "an epic tale of love and revenge." Between his good storytelling and her powerful imagination, a story grows that so rivets her that she will do anything to hear another installment. They are both initially changed by each other's company, in that they are distracted a bit from suffering.

But Roy quickly sees an opportunity. He can manipulate the little girl into stealing morphine from the pharmacy so he can overdose and be out of his misery. Unaware of what morphine is, and wanting to hear more of the story, Alexandria steals the morphine, but it isn't nearly enough to cause death. So the storytelling goes on and tension builds as the girl realizes that it's up to Roy whether the "Black Bandit" in the story, or Roy himself, will survive in the end. They argue over the plotline. Roy, being depressed, keeps pushing his story toward a tragic ending, while Alexandria is desperate for a happy ending. Her motivation for a happy ending stems from the fact that she is a refugee who lost her father and mother when her former home was attacked and destroyed. This girl needs a happy ending as powerfully as Roy craves self-destruction. Alternately comforting and challenging one another, the two are changed. Their motivations are affected by their external encounters. The external events of the plot are charged by the nature of the imaginative story Roy tells as Alexandria's lush and fantastical interpretation of the story empowers her. She draws strength as well as happiness from the story playing out in her head, and with this strength she starts to insert her own demands and revisions into the story.

When Ray makes more storytelling conditional on Alexandria stealing more morphine, she tries to steal the bottle of pills, and she takes her own fall while climbing up to the shelf to reach the drug. She sustains a serious head injury, and that close brush with death jolts Roy into seeing the consequences of his selfishness. After much more argument over the story, as well as over Roy's death wish, the two characters grow into a friendship that ultimately brings the power of story-telling to the hospital when Roy, now healed of his paralysis, brings in movies to share with the patients and staff. At last, a happy ending for all.

Most plotlines interweave internal motivation with external events, and it's the interaction that yields the story. This strategy works because it so mirrors our own lives. Yes, we generally start our day with a motivation or intention, and yes, things happen to us, interact with us that might affect our motivation. Getting through a story, just like getting through a day, involves a pretty constant oscillation between internal and external worlds. But a story, unlike most of our days, results from thoughtful choices and structure. So you've gotta have a plan. You'll need to at least have an idea of where you're starting, what will happen and where it will go. Even people in the business of high finance say that you have to go into an investment plan with an exit strategy. So have an exit strategy for your story. You might change your ending when you get to the end of your script, but at the start have an idea of where you are going.

> "A film should have a beginning, a middle and end, but
> not necessarily in that order."
> > Jean Luc Godard

Plotting can often feel like trying to find the beginning of a circle. You will realize as you come to the end of your script that you are responsible for fulfilling expectations set up at the beginning. Bear in mind that when structuring a graceful story, you start writing the ending when you write your first word.

I don't care if it's a five minute story or a script of 120 pages that you plan to send to an agent; no matter what your story involves, it will need a beginning, a middle and an end. And this is where we discuss how to manage those sometimes unruly beginnings, middles and ends. You will notice that I spend a great deal of time discussing beginnings because much thought should go into where and how you set the terms of the story that will unfold.

Beginnings

Beginnings are doorways to worlds. And once you're out in that world and have taken some readers or viewers with you, you have a responsibility to be a good tour guide. You want to show the places and things worth seeing; you want the trip to be memorable, meaningful in some way; and you don't want to get lost.

Beginnings are fun in that you have the opportunity to start something, and starting something entails the kind of pleasure we take in striking a match, lighting a fire, whoosh. And like a fire, your story needs to be tended. It has to be fed so it won't go out. It has to be jostled a bit from time to time, limited in some ways so it doesn't grow out of control.

Enough of mixed metaphors. As you write your screenplay, I would hope you "see" it playing out on the screen. I also hope you "see" others watching that screen and that you'll be responsible to their interests, you'll take care not to bore or confuse them. Your first obligation is to catch the interest of your reader, because when you write a spec script, your reader is someone who may put in the time, effort and money to get your words and images up on a screen. If you plan on shooting your own film, you need to consider the labor and money that will go into the process, and you'll want the payoff of having an audience who will one day watch your movie and give you a nice round of applause.

How will you do that? You want to think hard about where your story is set, what is being said, and what people are doing. Your opening will need to do a lot at once, and it will need to do it well. To really appreciate openings, you'll need to study the opening scenes of your favorite movies. Get a watch and observe the first ten minutes; make notes of everything that occurs. I've already walked you through the opening of one of my all-time favorite movies, *Amèlie,* in the previous chapter on visual language. The opening of that movie sets the quirky tone; it establishes the protagonist as a lonely, but basically content and curious, woman. It establishes the idea of the far-reaching consequences of the tiniest of actions. It hints at the fleeting aspect of life, and the notion that before it all suddenly passes, we'd better get engaged in the world and enjoy it. It also provides the inciting incident that will drive the protagonist and the plot forward. Amèlie finds a box containing a boy's cherished, mundane things. And in that box are the seeds of the plot.

When you write the opening of your script, you may not know exactly where you are going by the end of your story, but you do need to know exactly where you are and what's at stake. You do need to know your central character and what you think you might have happen to him, or what he just might do.

Think of openings as first impressions. Think of them as hooks. How do you hook a fish? You get its attention by dangling some shiny thing, jiggling it, moving it, letting that fish know that there's something interesting and it's moving and the fish better move with it, for it, grab if it wants something good. I used to fish a lot. I know live minnows—even wounded minnows--make for better bait than dead ones. So you want your opening to offer a character who's lively in some way—even if he is depressed, he needs to have the potential to be interesting.

Your opening also needs to offer the potential for movement, change. Maybe it's something as simple as a road trip, as in *Thelma and Louise*—who knows what can happen when two good-looking women take off together? No, we don't expect them to go flying willfully off a cliff, but we do expect some kind of adventure. The potential for trouble is established with a strong-willed, no-nonsense woman driving the car and a passenger who is a repressed and wanting-to-be-reckless housewife. We see by her actions, like sneaking candy in her own home, that she is something of a naïve child in very womanly body. When naïveté sets off on an adventure, there's great potential for trouble. When a strong-willed woman sets off on a road trip, risky things can happen. When this combination of femininity takes off down the highway in a convertible with the top down, well, anything can happen.

Humans, I suppose all animals, are intrigued by movement. Maybe it's a primal thing. Movement could be a sign of an animal's next dinner, or it could be a sign that the animal is about to be someone else's dinner. Whatever the case, as humans, we like to watch movement; we are engaged by action—look at the audiences for spectator sports. We also like to watch the potential for change. We like sunrises, sunsets. We like to line up dominoes just to see them neatly fall.

When we are stuck someplace, bored, some of us go to sleep, and some of us, the more curious and perhaps artistic types, look for something to distract us, something that offers potential for change. Maybe we eavesdrop on a conversation to see where it leads. Will that couple at the next table in the restaurant get into a fight? Maybe you heard one line signaling tension, like "Where were you last night?" If you overhead that question, you'd probably lean and listen to find out the answer. Most likely you would listen in to see if things might move forward in a conflict or maybe in a happy discovery. There is great energy contained in a thing about to change.

Stories are like that. In your opening, be sure to let the reader know of an instability, a potential for change somewhere. There needs to be a silent or not-so-silent tension. Something in the setting, the dialogue, or the character's thoughts lets us know something needs to change or will change.

Lots of energy lies in instability—and readers like-crave-demand energy—even the quiet psychological kind. Let a stranger come to the scene—let's say a surprise visit from a friend. Let something odd be found on a kitchen table; offer some incongruency that cues readers that things will not be the same at the end of the story as at the beginning.

Middles

Oh, the middle of things. The middle of your story is all about choices. Whereas the beginning offers potential changes, the middle offers the action of choices being made as a result of the options and possibilities established in your opening. The middle can often be a bit of a muddle, as any one choice of any character can have a multitude of consequences. The middle of your story will depict the characters in the motion of change after having stepped into a new territory. Your main character will start changing, and as a result other characters will change. In the middle of your story, your characters take risks, and they often suffer a few set-backs and disappointments. In the middle of your story, some old things get lost or are left behind as your characters interact and change. You don't have to follow the three act story template made so popular by Hollywood, but do bear in mind that the middle of your story will require movement of some kind, and not just the eternal movement of action.

In the middle of your story you need to be keenly aware that a story involves the interweaving of an external plot and an internal one. You'll need to consider just how much the story is driven by internal motivation and how much by external circumstances. In *American Beauty*, Lester is strongly motivated to win the attentions of the young, hot Angela. This motivation has him working out and getting fit.

But there's also the external circumstance of the appearance of Ricky, who's just moved in next door. Ricky is an external circumstance who will change the motives of Jane as well as Lester. When Ricky introduces Lester to genetically engineered pot, Lester undergoes radical changes and takes huge risks that will greatly alter his life. He quits his job; he defies his wife, and he moves recklessly toward reliving his youth through smoking pot, listening to old rock, and pursuing a girl his daughter's age. In short, in the middle of your story is where characters get into that kind of trouble that can change their lives for the better, or the worse. If you are to tell an intriguing story, there will need to be a bit of conflict regarding the actions being taken. There will need to be a bit of trouble, and some setbacks.

The middle of your story will most likely contain lots of movement, ups and downs, at least a twist or turn for your protagonist. It's a bit like a rollercoaster ride at this point, and the middle should offer both something we suspect and a bit of a surprise. When writing the middle part of your story, it's a good idea to know where your story is going, and if you don't know, use your "middle" to figure things out.

We know at the beginning of *American Beauty* that Lester will soon be dead. You need not give away your ending at the start, but as a writer you need to know your

287

general direction.   Remember, every story is in some way about a little growth, or a little death. In *American Beauty* death ironically provides a kind of growth for Lester, as well as for his family.   Through his death they will be forced to grow into something new.   It's always a good idea to have a plan for where you are going; otherwise your middle can be quite a muddle of random actions and conversations. In early drafts that "muddle" can be just fine, as you can try out various pathways and options.   When lost in your story, don't forget that advice to write to your lowest standard just to keep things moving.   Then put the work aside. Let it rest. Then go back and revise. If you do become stuck in the middle of your story, have a look at the traditional feature-length plot template below for ideas on how to structure your story. You do not have to follow it closely, but it can offer some sound advice as to the internal movement of your protagonist. It might also help you come up with the kind of external event that needs to happen for change to occur.

Your ending will most certainly reveal consequences. And one would hope the consequences aren't entirely predictable. Your ending will address the issue set up at the beginning of your story, but will also shed a new light on the old situation. It doesn't have to be a hugely changed new situation. Remember that short film "Joe," where the ending simply shows Joe's happiness with his boots that were once black, and now are a bit snazzier, being white.   After the climax, or let's just say turning point, of your story, you will come to an ending that in a sense comments on the turning point. The ending will suggest whether that turning point was a good thing or a bad thing, a little growth for the protagonist, or a little death.   Try to work in a little something that the viewers, and the protagonist, don't expect. Everyone enjoys not being able to predict the ending; we love the fresh feeling of a writer who offers a bit of discovery, something we don't expect.   But your ending will have an obligation to grow from the seeds you planted at the start. You'll need to walk the line between delivering on some basic expectations and surprising us. Pulling this trick off will no doubt require much thought and several drafts.

Feature-Length Plotline Template

When I studied screenwriting for the first semester, we did nothing but plan, plot, map out the story that we would tell in a feature-length script. Not a scene heading was written, no action, no dialogue. We just wrote prose statements of what would happen in our potential scripts in incremental blocks of time. We planned our scripts by the Hollywood industry template of exactly how the plot would work, a template made famous in Syd Field's *Screenplay*—if you want a sure-fire plan for a feature-length script, consider this template.

According to this plan, a script is arranged in three acts, with Act I running from pages one to thirty; Act II is pages 30 to 90; Act III runs from page 90 to 120. The plan also has precise directions on when and how characters are developing by manipulating their interior and exterior worlds. This is the standard paradigm for Hollywood scripts; it was made into something like the one-and-only paradigm of feature-length film by renowned screenwriting coaches Syd Field and Robert McKcc. It's a plan that works. It's a plan that is so popular that you can pretty much watch any major movie with a clock in hand and predict exactly when and where certain plot developments will occur.

Every screenwriter should at least know that paradigm, if for no other reason than to mess with it. Frankly, when I set out to write my first screenplay with no experience whatsoever in screenwriting, it was a wonderful map. It helped me get the job complete the job, and it resulted in a successful script that won me some prizes and some money. Not bad.

Plotting, quite simply, is an arrangement of scenes where events unfold in some way as a consequence of actions. Most popular blockbuster movies are written in a straightforward, linear sequential narrative. Popular movies like *Jerry Mcquire*, *Thelma and Louise*, *Unforgiven*, *The Godfather*—you know those big hits. And they are big hits for numerous reasons, but primarily because the plotline begins with a problem or challenge or opportunity for the protagonist. We are engaged in the process of rooting for the protagonist, or just seeing what's going to happen given the adventure they're on. We want to know what will happen next and we've got a pretty good idea of the options: they'll find love or not; they'll get justice, or not; they'll pull off the heist, or not.

It's often hard to break down a plot, since the idea of a movie is to so thoroughly pull us into the fictive dream that we forget to step back and analyze the craft. But if you're going to be a screenwriter, you need to practice analysis. There are numerous ways to approach analysis, but I'm first going to offer you a simple tool. Watch a movie twice. The first time, just enjoy the story, noting whatever strikes you about the characters, dialogue, and plot.

Then watch it again and answer the following list of narrative analysis questions. I use these questions when I teach both feature-length and short films. They also work with analyzing short stories and novels. The questions guide you in seeing how the story is being told, the structure at work. With these questions answered, you'll be better able to understand the strategy of a film you enjoy, and you'll also become more adept at working through your own structure and strategy.

Analysis Questions for Narrative Films

1. Whose story is this? What are the primary motivations of the principle characters? Describe how the motivations are revealed. Are they believable? If the motivations aren't believable, are there any indications in the story that we should suspend disbelief? (For example in comedies, fantasies, or experimental films.)

2. How are the personalities of principle characters revealed? Appearance? Speech? Action?

3. Consider the action of the storyline, anything that moves the plot forward. Now consider how movement of the plot stems from internal or external sources. For example, does the protagonist's motivation develop as a result of some external event that occurred, or from a shift of will or emotion within? Identify moments of, and causes for, change.

4. In terms of internal change, what happens in this story?

5. What element of story primarily moves the plot forward? Dialogue? Action? A sequencing of scenes that comment on and build on one another? A surprise twist of situation?

6. Does the plot unfold chronologically? If flashbacks are used or if scenes are arranged non-chronologically, why? What is the dramatic or thematic effect?

7. What is the setting? How does setting play a dramatic role in the film?

8. Note that if an image frequently appears in a story, it is significant. Are there any images or objects that frequently appear in this story? How are such images important in terms of plot or theme?

9. Is the plot original? Predictable? Derivative?

10. What do you think the writer's/director's objectives were in this film? Just to tell a story? About what? Telling a simple, good story is a fine achievement, but now consider if there is any indication the writer indirectly (or directly) addresses a political, sociological or philosophical concern through the telling of the story.

11. What do you consider any weaknesses in the film? What are the film's strengths?

12. What did you learn from this film? About yourself? About the world? About writing?

Breaking Down a Plotline to Its Parts

"Every melodrama has at least three close calls."
Citizen Kane

You probably don't plan to write a melodrama, but any drama will have tension of some sort, close calls, ups and downs, movement. No matter what sort of movie you plan to write, it's a good idea to know the Syd Field-type Hollywood paradigm that shows you how to structure a plot with movement and well-placed development of the storyline. Not only will it help you break down the structure of mainstream feature-length movies, but it will also put a sense of structure in your mind to work with or depart from on your own. I offer this analysis basically because writing my first screenplay with these guidelines worked very well for me.

Have a look at the following standardized template for structuring a feature-length film. Bearing in mind a page of script basically is equivalent to a minute of film, watch a movie with the template and a watch in hand, and you'll see how so many movies do indeed follow this template.

Feature-Length Plotline Template

Pages 1-10 should establish who and what the story is about and should suggest tone, place, and time. They should subtly, or maybe not so subtly, give a clue as to the basic issue to be dramatized in the story.

Pages 11-30 should set up conflicts for the characters in main plot and subplot.

Pages 31-45 (Plot Point One): The protagonist moves into a new internal/external landscape. The world is shifting and offers the protagonist growth/change. This shift would be perceived as a kind of success for the protagonist. For the viewer, the shift could also suggest potential trouble.

Pages 46-60: Now the trouble should thicken up a bit for the protagonist, and for other characters as well. By page 60 the protagonist should cross that line known as the point of no return as the protagonist moves toward what he wants. The protagonist leaves behind an old self or situation by learning new skills, maybe meeting new people. He begins to commit to a new self or situation. He encounters a second conflict and wins again.

Pages 61-75: The protagonist can't keep winning. Having entered a new territory of self, the protagonist encounters a big problem not anticipated. Things become extremely difficult. The protagonist tackles the problem, but encounters a set back. Think of the roller coaster effect--lots of ups and downs. There is a big "down" here.

Pages 76-90: The protagonist experiences a real loss or setback that is the result of overcoming the first obstacle in the first 30 pages. The protagonist is scrambling for stability in this new territory. Protagonist discovers a key thing and has one choice: to do what must be done.

Pages 91-95 (Second Plot Point): The protagonist starts moving toward the final goal, which is the goal that he first sought, and it's now in reach. Subplots start wrapping while building to climax of the main plot. Restate the central issue of the story and the protagonist's commitment to a new life by revisiting issues of the first plot point.

Pages 96-113: Build to climax of main story. Confrontation erupts, and the protagonist wins or loses. Perhaps he gains something unexpected, more than expected.

Pages 114-115: Wrap up main story illustrating the ultimate and lasting growth of the character.

Note: Traditionally full-length screenplays are 120 pages. Mine was 121. But the trend is moving toward shorter scripts of 100-110 pages. So this template is not meant to be followed exactly. Just have it in mind to follow—or tamper with.

American Beauty Breakdown

Now let's consider a script and see how the movie unfolds in keeping with this template. *American Beauty* loosely follows the three-act paradigm, but with a non-linear twist. The plot follows conventions, but the beginning minutes, before the title comes up, throw us off course with a quick scene that we will see again later in the movie. Other than this opening clip, the unconventional story follows Hollywood convention. I've selected this movie not only because it won numerous awards, but because it illustrates that following a convention doesn't have to take the life, the freshness, or even the quirkiness out of a story. Let's have a look.

Pages 1-10: Establish who and what the story is about, and should suggest tone, place, and time. They should subtly, or maybe not so subtly, give a clue as to the basic issue to be dramatized in the story.

American Beauty opens with a disorienting little home video. We aren't quite sure what's going on in the grainy scene, where a teen-aged girl seems to be in her bedroom, and she complains about how she'd like a father who is a role model and not some geek who gets off on every high-school girlfriend she brings home. She goes on to talk about what a lame, useless geek he is and how someone should put him out of his misery. A male voice responds—it's the man behind the video camera—he asks if she would like for him to kill her father for her. She straightens, leans seductively close to the camera and says simply, "Yeah. Would you?" The scene suddenly ends and the film title comes up. And we have the question that the movie is asked to answer. Who's the guy who will kill her father? We're hooked.

But we aren't sure what kind of movie we are in for: Some teenaged kids quietly plan to murder a geek of a dad. It all seems like a game, but more of a flirting game than a murder plan. The connection between the girl and the unseen cameraman is intimate. The girl is titillating as she looks seductively into the camera, enjoying that she is the complete focus of the cameraman's gaze. The voices are soft, sincere; the lighting is shadowed and gray-toned, as if the scene were a dreamy confession of who the girl really is, what she really wants. Aside from the flip statement of wanting her dad to be put out of his misery, it's very clear she wants her male viewer's attention.

While this scene is doing the traditional, establishing the tone/theme of the movie, it's untraditional in that it's not linear and is quite confusing. We'll come to learn that the man behind the camera is the new neighbor, Ricky, whom she will come to meet in the first act of the film. The opening scene sets up the idea that the main plot will concern the girl's desire to have her father killed. But given the quietness, the sense that the main point of the scene is to establish the attraction between this girl and the guy behind the camera, we aren't convinced that this will be a psychopathic

295

patricide movie. The opening scene pulls us in with its tease of potential sex and death. We might be reading the tone/theme of the movie, but that opening gives little idea, really, of how the plot will unfold in a not-so-comedy of errors.

When the film title rolls up, the movie starts again with another opening that provides an establishing shot of suburbia, the point of view looking down from far overhead at the rows of homes, trees, lawns. Our protagonist introduces himself as 42-year-old Lester Burnham, and he calmly announces that in less than a year he'll be dead. He states that he doesn't yet know he's about to die. He's pretty calm about it, and explains that in a way he's already dead, with jerking off in the shower being the high point of his day.

In this second opening of the movie, we learn that the primary plotline is Lester's desire to get "it," a passionate connection with life. He wants to transform the conventional, unhappy man he has let himself become; he has no idea that his transformation will result in his death. There are so many other subplots established that will intertwine with Lester's goal to feel alive, that it's very hard to distinguish where the plotlines begin and end.

Remember that in the conventional paradigm, the first ten minutes need to establish tone and theme. This is what happens in the opening of the movie. We know Lester is unhappy, and we know he will die. We know the "who" and "what" of the plotline. What we don't know for sure is the "how" or "why." Surely the daughter and camera-carrying boyfriend won't do it. That opening scene was more about flirtation than death. And the voice of Lester from beyond—he's far too calm to have been murdered at the behest of his daughter.

During the long voice over that ultimately will frame the movie, we are never bored. Even though the soon-to-be-dead Lester sounds bored, he is not boring. Oh no, he's actually funny. We cut from the shot of him jerking off in the shower to the close-up of his wife Carolyn's pruning shears going "snip" at the stem of a rose. We are amused. Yes, the wife is an emasculating bitch, far more interested in cultivating her prize roses, along with cultivating a façade of a perfect family life, than she is in actually cultivating familial relationships. Lester points out that the fact that her gardening shears match her gardening clogs is no accident; we know she is a control freak married to a man who has long since given up on giving a damn about much of anything.

Next we meet the neighbors, handsome professional men who are gay lovers, who happen to be, so far, the only happy people in the story. Lester recalls that he and his wife were once happy. Then we meet the daughter, Jane, who sits at a computer researching breast implants. As she considers her reflection in a mirror, she looks sad and bored. In the voice over, Lester notes that she is angry and miserable. He says that he'd like to tell her that things will be better one day—but they won't.

The story doesn't promise to be a happy one, but we are amused by the mania of the wife and her pruning shears, the over-the-top happy gay couple. We're amused by Lester, who peers out the front window of his house as his wife, brittle with feigned cheer, tells the neighbor the secret of growing perfect roses. We are amused as the wife honks the horn of her SUV, hurrying her family out the door, the angry daughter who pretends that she doesn't care how she looks, the bumbling Lester spilling his briefcase on the sidewalk. Yes, our protagonist is inept; he's bored; he's miserable; and yet we want to see what happens. We want to know "how" and "why" such a non-character can be intriguing. And it's because of his own words at the end of this opening voice over. He says that he'd like not to feel sedated, and for all that weariness in the opening minutes, he states that it's never too late to get "it" back.

Now we're really intrigued. Will Lester get his love of life back before he dies? With so much against him, we wonder—why will he get enthusiasm back, and with that crazy wife and grumpy daughter, how?

The next scene is Lester at work in his cubical office. Bear in mind that at this point we are only five minutes into the film when Lester is called to his supervisor's desk and is told the company is trimming down and Lester will need to write up a report justifying his job. Lester responds with hostility, cueing us that it's highly unlikely he will keep his job. We doubt he'll even bother to write that justification—given his state of mind, he can hardly justify getting out of bed in the morning.

In the next scene, heading home with his wife, he whines about the job. She berates him, and getting out of the car they notice new neighbors—it's a great tactic to start a story with the device of "enter a stranger." These new neighbors, we'll soon find out, include the boy behind that video camera in the opening clip. These new neighbors will forever change Lester's life. While glancing at the furniture being moved in, Carolyn expresses relief, and also anger, that the property wasn't sold by her but by the "real estate king," another character who will come to play a key role in the plot.

I like to compare openings to a poker game; the dealer lays out the nature of this particular round, what the game is, what's wild, so we know what to make of the cards we are holding. In this opening, we know the game is about a dysfunctional family; we know there is a mystery guy involved who likes to frame the grumpy teenaged-girl with his camera. We know there are gay guys in this pristine conventional neighborhood. We know Lester is sexually frustrated, and that his wife is a fragile bottle of maniacal perfectionism.

We see more of this cold perfectionism at the family dinner table. The family, Lester, Carolyn, and Jane, are as arranged as a place setting. Jane sits center, her pretty and blank face poised above the carefully arranged cut roses as if she were an extension of the home décor—any all-American, good home needs meal-time, fresh flowers, and a child. We don't see food, just candles, dishware, and those perfect roses. Lester tries to connect with his daughter by complaining about his day. She promptly blows him off, asking why he's suddenly interested in her after not speaking to her for months. She splits. Then, after a few harsh words from his wife, Lester jabs her with the fact that she treats him like an employee. Her indignant response sends him heading to the kitchen, where again he tries to connect with his daughter. The attempt fails, and we cut to that grainy video format and know that spooky, voyeuristic camera guy is watching them, taping them through the kitchen window.

When we cut back to Lester, he seems to feel someone watching. He looks out of one of the framed sections of the window to darkness. The framed darkness is a counterpart to the camera-framed sad, domestic scene the camera guy sees though his lens. We see the voyeur's face, not creepy, but interested, compassionate. We know this stranger will intervene in the lives of the family next door.

And all this in the first ten minutes.

Pages 11-30: Set up conflicts for the characters in the plot and subplot.

The next "I will sell this house today" scene sets up Carolyn's conflict and shifts tone from spooky and sad to comic and crazy. More than anything, Carolyn wants to be a successful realtor. Her intention is more bent on selling houses than making a loving, relaxed home for her family. There's a bit of foreshadowing in this manic "I'll sell this house today" scene.

As she gets out of her SUV to prepare the house, she looks across the street and sees a sign for her competition: the "Real Estate King." We see his face on his real estate sign: handsome, a bit of a rascally gleam to his smile. He's been mentioned, and now we have a glimpse. We know there's more of him to come, and that her competition with him will build into a subplot.

Carolyn is depicted as a brittle, but pretty and well-groomed, cleaning machine as she tries to make a real dud of a house alluring. After supreme efforts and repeated failures to sell the house, she mechanically closely the blinds on the sliding glass doors. She stands rigidly and proceeds to cry, then slaps herself and reprimands herself, then cries again. It's a painful and scary glimpse of madness barely under control. She isn't evil. She's vulnerable and weak. Weak people can be dangerous

298

people. Carolyn is running on the volatile fuel of repressed sorrow and neurosis. If she doesn't get relief soon, she seems to have the potential of doing serious harm to someone. We wonder will she go after Lester? Or will she turn on herself?

In the next scene, Lester's conflict comes out smoking hot when he is dragged to see his daughter's dance performance at a high school basketball game. He's cranky. He'd rather be home watching James Bond re-runs than at his daughter's dance routine. But oh my, the distraction of lust rises when he spots his daughter's friend, the oh-so-Lolita-like Angela Hayes. Once he sees her, he can't take his eyes off the cutest, blondest, and the hottest girl in the line of dancers. His gaze zooms in on her so intently that he is no longer in the auditorium. He's lost in his fantasy of her exotic dancing for him, for him alone. She winks, she undulates those hips, offers her open thigh. She caresses her body, then unzips her sweater, again, again, again until suddenly she lets a metaphorical ejaculation of loose lush rose petals rush forth. The color and texture and movement of those soft bright petals spilling out is so vivid, we can feel it. We see Lester feel it. His face is transformed by wonder, longing, lust.

That night while lying awake next to his might-as-well-be-dead wife, he gazes up at the ceiling at a fantasy of the girl, nude, nymph-like, seemingly sprawled on a bed of rose petals, with some petals barely and strategically places to hide her nipples, that little alluring place between her legs. She gazes, stretches seductively, and gives a wave as rose petals waft down on blissful Lester who is completely intoxicated by his lustful fantasy.

This is a major plot development that sets up the serious conflict of craving the body of a teen-aged girl who seems quite willing, in his dreams, and perhaps in life to have him. We know from the beginning of the movie that Lester will be dead before the year is out—which implies that he'll be dead by the end of the movie. What intrigues us by the story isn't so much "what" will happen, but "how" and "why." Lester's desire for Angela will lead him down paths that will in the end lead to his death. For all we know at this point in the movie, Lester's wife could kill him in an indignant, jealous rage, maybe little flirty Angela's dad, or maybe that spooky camera guy who keeps mysteriously showing up.

Twenty minutes into the movie, camera guy reveals himself to Jane as she heads into her house after smoking with Angela. He flicks on his porch light and says nothing. He just continues to train his camera on her. She calls him an asshole and heads inside. But once the door is closed, we see her smile just a bit; she is intrigued by him, pleased. There's no creepiness to this guy, no embarrassment; he's very direct, ande has her attention—aha, another plotline in the works. Jane is ignored by her family, and is eclipsed by her hot girlfriend at school. Until camera guy decided to make her the star of his videos she was invisible. So here's another conflict, to move forward with this unusual fellow which is a risk, or to stay isolated, alienated, lonely, not such a happy place to remain, but it's familiar and controllable. What we have here is another subplot.

Okay, a lot of plotline conflicts are in the works; there's plenty of potential trouble to hold our attention. But let's stack another little conflict on the mess of unhappy characters: another dysfunctional family next door, the family of camera guy who's yet to have a name. This family is so unhappy, it hurts. Mom is borderline catatonic depressed. And the dad is a homophobic control freak who runs his home like marine boot camp. Our camera guy seems to float between them carefully as if touching one could break her and touching the other could set off an emotional hand grenade.

When the gay neighbors show up to give a housewarming gift to this pathetic family, the homophobic father, Frank, who is suspicious in all ways of all people, immediately distrusts them and their good cheer. They introduce themselves as partners who live in down the street and want to welcome the family. Homophobe at first can't comprehend a relationship—he assumes that they are partners in a business and are there to try to sell something. When they explain their very different professions, he reads between the lines and is so bewildered/disgusted that he can't speak of it.

Later in the car while driving his son to school, he rants about the faggots being shamelessly out there in your face—a bit of an overreaction that will violently play out later. He goads his son into taking the same hostile hard line, but we know the son's rant is simply the required placation needed to get through the morning. Nothing is to be wasted in a screenplay. While this little tangent of homophobia seems to be just another way of portraying a nutty family where the parents' problems are huge problems for the children, it's much more. The homophobic ranting of Ricky's father is loaded with a violent rage that will resurface as action by the end of the story, action that will change everyone's lives forever. Another subplot.

At school there is a brief encounter between Jane and Ricky when he interrupts a conversation between Angela and Jane. Angela is bragging that she has screwed a photographer and states that such behavior is just the nature of the modeling profession. Oh dear. She has deep delusions that she will be a model one day, and we know that while she's cute and hot, she certainly isn't model material.

Then comes Ricky who appears to be a geek. He approaches Jane and introduces himself. Given the peer pressure of her bitch friend, Jane plays the role of outraged bitch chick who doesn't need to be bothered by a psycho and his camera. He takes her smart-assed remarks with no shame, embarrassment, or apology. He just looks her straight in the face and says that he just really thinks she is interesting, that he's not obsessing, just curious. Powerful words for a girl ignored by her parents, a girl with low self-esteem. She's speechless. When he walks away, Jane remains stunned and says that he's so confident he can't be real. Angela is simply amazed that he didn't bother looking at her. She reveals that his parents once put him in a mental hospital. Okay another piece of info that intrigues us and draws us into wondering just how this strange young man might affect the lives of our characters.

All this intrigue and instability full of possibilities, and we are barely thirty minutes in yet.

The next scene adds more heat to this soon-to-be boiling plot. Lester is once again dragged along to an event that will surprisingly yield something of great interest. The unpromising realtors' party results in Lester meeting another stranger who will change his life. At the beginning Carolyn, ever eager to make good impressions and connections, urges her husband to try to act normal, and we can guess he'll do anything but that before the party is over. Carolyn immediately rushes over to Buddy the real estate king, a handsome man, that we know at first sight is a rogue. She pitifully, painfully strains to impress him. And Lester works to embarrass her.

As the party continues, Carolyn proceeds to get sloppy drunk while Buddy remains sober. Leaning unprofessionally close, she says she'd love an opportunity to "pick his brain." And when he tells her to call his secretary to arrange the lunch date, we know that something more than a mind will be revealed. More potential trouble is added to the plot. While she's busy with Buddy, Lester gets busy drinking his way to his own buzz where he meets Ricky who is working as catering staff. It's a fortuitous meeting that in a minute or two will start Lester down a path that will change his world.

Pages 31-45 (Plot Point One): Protagonist moves into a new internal/external landscape. The world is shifting and offers the protagonist growth/change. This shift would be perceived as a kind of success for the protagonist. For the viewer, the shift could also suggest potential trouble.

Here we are, right on time with the story structure template. , Within a minute of meeting Ricky, Lester is outside smoking premium dope with him. For the first time in the movie Lester is relaxed and having a good time. Much like his daughter, he is in awe of the independent nature of Ricky. When the boss man of the catering service comes outside and reprimands Ricky for not being at his job, Ricky calmly quits. The boy's self-possession is stunning. Now Lester has a role model, oddly the guy who at the beginning minutes of the movie offered to kill him. Now let's have a look at what happens in this fifteen-minute interval that will demonstrate the growth of Lester. To begin, when his wife steps outside to find him doing something suspicious with the strange guy, she's too drunk to be critical, and Lester is too stoned to get defensive. Once the wife leaves and says she'll wait in the car, Ricky lets Lester know more pot is available anytime. He's a dealer and just does odd jobs to give the illusion of making legitimate money to quell the suspicions of his dad.

Later at Lester's home, Angela moves toward stirring up a flirtation with Lester—she touches him when he offers her a root beer. It's a light but loaded touch, and it stirs up another fantasy where Lester is definitely more committed to pursuing sex with the girl—after a long hot fantasy kiss, Lester steps back and pulls one of those magical sensual rose petals from his tongue. Later in Jane's bedroom Angela teases Jane about how her dad would be hot if he worked out and built his chest and arms. Lester, listening through the door, stands entranced, and he is fully inspired when she says that she "would totally do him" if he worked out.

We know what's coming next for Lester. Meanwhile Ricky declares his intention to pursue Jane buy lighting up her name in the grass outside her house, and she is pleased even though her friend declares him psycho. And then, you guessed it, we cut to Lester in his garage frantically searching for and finding weights. He strips down to examine his sagging body in the reflection of the window and starts doing curls. Ricky who already has his eyes trained on the house, spots nude Lester and starts taping him declaring it one of American's weirdest home videos. This moment of watching Lester foreshadows bad things to come when Ricky's father steps in the room to get a urine sample to test for drugs. Ricky calmly says he'll do the test in the morning, and when the dad leaves, Ricky reaches in his personal refrigerator to take out a frozen urine sample to thaw by morning. Ricky is on top of his game.

Lester's fantasy of sex with the Angela becomes more physical when his lies in bed, imagining his hand reaching between the girl's legs while he whacks off. Carolyn wakes to find him busy with his hand, and appalled, she leaps out of bed. A fight follows where he, growing more aggressive, calls her bloodless and says he has changed and is a "new me" and that the "new me" whacks off. This sexual empowerment quickly turns to financial battle when Carolyn threatens divorce. He's smugly reminds her that he would be entitled to half her income. There's not much she can say to that—more growth for Lester.

Pages 46-60: Now the trouble should thicken up a bit for the protagonist, and for other characters as well. By page 60 the protagonist should cross that line known as the point of no return as the protagonist moves toward what he wants. The protagonist leaves behind an old self or situation by learning new skills, maybe meeting new people. He begins to commit to a new self or situation. He encounters a second conflict and wins again.

In the beginning of this section, Lester starts to get into trouble, but he is unaware of it. He decides to go running with the gay neighbors. They pass by Ricky's house where homophobic dad spots them and assumes Lester is another faggot. Completely unaware that he is a suspicious character to this man, Lester stops to chat with Ricky under the ruse that he'd like to borrow a movie when he really wants pot. Dad is not pleased when they head up to Ricky's room. We see trouble brewing; Lester doesn't.

In Ricky's room Lester crosses a line when he agrees to buy an ounce of genetically engineered pot for two grand. He's once again impressed by the entrepreneurial skills of Ricky. He admits that when he was Ricky's age he was content to flip burgers and get high—a bit of foreshadowing here. The next scene shows Lester lifting weights to Bob Dylan tunes and smoking dope. More change. When his wife confronts him, he responds like a hostile teenager. This behavior on one hand seems like childish rebellion, but for Lester who was previously too weak, passive, and depressed to argue with his wife, this regression is oddly a kind of growth.

His hostile adolescent behavior goes public when he turns in his job justification letter, and it's nothing but a litany of insults to management. Of course he is fired. This is definitely crossing a point of no return. But he wins here. He instantly, spontaneously demonstrates new skills when he goes on the offensive and blackmails management into giving him a hefty severance package.

And on another front more potential growth and trouble brews. Carolyn has lunch with the real estate king who quickly reveals that his wife is out of town and that they are on their way to divorce because his wife can't understand his commitment to his work. Fragile and so in need of flattery, Carolyn of course takes interest in their shared commitment to real estate, and she compliments his cool demeanor. In charge now, he states his philosophy that "to be successful one must always maintain an appearance of success." These words are like a drug to the woman who, as her husband previously said, makes her living selling images. She is smitten. We know what will come.

And now it's time for Jane to grow. At school she tells Ricky to stop filming her. He politely closes his camera. She grows bolder when she asks if he'd like a ride home. When judgmental Angela says no way will she let a psycho ride in her car, Jane goes further and declares that she'll just walk home—with Ricky. A new territory for her.

And now, just as we suspected, a motel sex scene fires up between Carolyn and the real estate king. It's a quick and wildly comic scene when all her carefully cultivated composure is gone, and we see nothing of her but her legs askew and sprawled in the air while the king pumps at her asking, "So you like getting nailed by the king?"

She slaps his back and cries, "Yes, your majesty! She is far, far away from being the woman we first met with that brittle face, tight smile and pruning shears. And yes, she's definitely crossed a line, has stepped into a territory of no return.

There's more development and new skills for Lester. Driving while smoking dope and with 70s rock blaring, he gets the munchies and pulls in for drive-through fast food. He spots a sign that they are hiring and he applies for a job. The boy-faced manager is reluctant to hire the middle-aged man, but Lester, with his newly acquired assertive skills, bullies the kid into hiring him.

Carolyn, now looking ten years younger from the great "royal treatment" gushes as to how she so needed that release from stress. It seems she has found her own intoxicant. The king tells her of an even better stress reliever: firing guns. The idea beckons to her the way young flesh calls to Lester. Danger signs are flaring up big and bright for the viewer. We've seen enough pent-up rage in her to know that a gun in her hand can only be trouble.

When this scene is followed by the sight of Jane and Ricky walking a street where a funeral procession streams by, we're pretty sure that death is coming soon for Lester, but we still aren't just sure why and how. The plot, as they say, thickens. At this point in the movie, all the major players feel they are "winning," growing, getting what they want. But a funeral passing bodes a loss to come. Ricky poetically rambles about death and how he once saw a dead homeless woman, and he says when he bent to look closely, he saw something like God looking back. He says he saw beauty there. Okay, maybe it's all that pot he smokes; maybe it's his sensitive nature, but this reflection is important and foreshadows how death will play out in this story. Lester will die, but we wonder just how that might be something like God communicating to us, how it could be beauty.

Pages 61-75: The protagonist can't keep winning. Having entered a new territory of self, the protagonist encounters a big problem not anticipated. Things become extremely difficult. Protagonist tackles the problem, but encounters a set back. Think of the roller coaster affect, lots of ups, and downs. There is a big "down" here.

On that note of death and a funeral, the trouble begins. We cut to Ricky's mom sitting alone in her perfectly sterile dining room. She is doing nothing but sitting in a kind of catatonic trance. She seems dead, and Ricky has to rouse her attention to introduce her to Jane. And when the mom speaks, she makes no sense, so the kids move on, but not to Ricky's bedroom, no to a more dangerous place, his father's gun room. There Ricky shows Jane one of his father's prized possessions: a plate that is a piece of the official state china collection of the Third Reich. And the on the back of the plate is the sinister little swastika. Okay, homophobic dad is even more weird

304

than we thought and much more potentially dangerous. When Ricky tells Jane his dad would kill him if he knew they were in that sanctum of deadly things, we take the statement more than metaphorically. The moment forebodes of how deadly his dad can be.

Next we have the scene that is a huge risk for the writer and director: the sentimental portrayal of a bag being tossed about, buffeted up, dropped, and buffeted up again by a swirling wind. Ricky sets Jane in front of the television and shows her this video clip, saying it's the most beautiful thing he's ever filmed. He says the bag seemed to be dancing, daring him like a child wanting to play. It's a scene that's much better seen than explained here, but essentially Ricky feels the bag being buffeted by the wind suggests that there is larger benevolent force behind all things of this world. The image seems to tell him not to be afraid. He admits to Jane that he needs to remember not to be afraid. And ultimately this will be the message of the movie: to remember not to be afraid. He goes on to say that sometimes he sees so much beauty in the world that he feels he can't take it, that he sometimes feels his heart will cave from all the beauty. The once surly teenaged girl is so moved by his confession of vulnerability, she reaches, takes his hand, a terrific act of growth on her part, but their growing intimacy will inadvertently lead to great trouble.

Jane returns home to a family dinner that is in complete opposition to the earlier repressed and cold-hearted dinner scene. Both her parents seem drunk and are recklessly tearing into each other. Jane tries to leave and her father yells "Sit down?" And she does. He's never yelled at her, only whined and begged. This is a new father running on rage rather than despair. Ultimately he throws a plate against the wall. The plate echoes the violence implied by that Nazi plate and is the first sign of violence in that once carefully controlled house. Things are emotionally and literally falling apart.

And it gets worse. Mom goes to Jane's room to blame her father for the family failure. She cries and chants to Jane something she's probably learned from Buddy the real estate king: "You can't count on anyone but yourself." She tries to bond with Jane, and when Jane snaps that her mom is the problem too, her mom slaps her and leaves. Nothing in this family is as it was. Jane looks out and sees Ricky is watching and taping the unraveling. She looks at him, lifts her shirt, removes her bra and stands offering her naked breasts. He calmly films her, a very significant beautiful thing in his world.

It's a lovely moment brutally interrupted when Ricky's dad tears into the room and beats the hell out of Ricky for going into his gun room. The beating is quick and fierce, and Ricky doesn't fight back. When Ricky gets the chance to say he only wanted to show the plate to his girlfriend, the dad backs down, but does not in any way apologize. He say's the beating was for Ricky's own good—in much the same way Jane's mom has just told her it was good for her to see the deterioration of her father so she would know to rely on herself. Ricky, backed into a corner on the floor, says everything needed to make his dad feel right. He grovels, and it hurts. The emotional suffering of everyone is coming out in such physical ways, we know there will be no turning back from destruction.

And to reinforce that feeling, the next scene is Carolyn at a gun range having an intoxicatingly good time being one hell-of-a-shot. She takes off from there driving and singing out loud in much the same way Lester was earlier, and she sings defiantly, fiercely that no one is going to "rain on her parade."

Her gun-buzz is immediately snuffed out when she pulls into the driveway to see the used red Firebird sitting there. Inside she tries to get the old upper hand and reprimands the cool and calm Lester. Unruffled he looks at her, sees the potent sexy woman she has become from her sex and gun therapy. He's a bit dazzled, dazzled enough to forget his anger, and he tells her she looks great. At first she's proud and tells him there's plenty about her he doesn't know, but he continues to complement her. They both soften. He moves over to her where she sits on the sofa. A slow lovely kiss seems just about to happen when she suddenly remarks that he is about to spill his beer on the couch. He leaps up, furious that she cares more for furniture than people. So much for making up. This family is going down.

Now we go back to that scene we saw at the very opening of the movie before the credits rolled up, and now it makes more sense. We know that this scene in Jane's bedroom is a progression of a tender relationship and not just a weird moment of planning a murder. This time the scene starts well before the talk of killing dad. It's a scene when Jane grows more assertive—she takes the camera and now puts it on naked Ricky, who is happy to oblige. She asks him about his parents putting him into a hospital. He explains with a sad but not crazy story. Caught for smoking pot, he was sent to military school, and that was a failure. Ricky's artistic and ultra-sensitive personality would never survive military school. One day another student made a smart remark about his hair cut, and Ricky snapped. Ricky confesses to Jane that he would have killed the kid if others hadn't pulled him off. That event resulted in him being drugged in a mental hospital for two years. She wonders why he doesn't hate his dad for putting him through all that pain. Ricky's personality runs on too much compassion to hate his dad.

With the camera back in Ricky's hand, we go back to the conversation we saw earlier where Jane talks about how her dad should be put out of his misery. We also see here where the conversation went after Ricky offered to kill her dad. He points out that it wouldn't be a very nice thing to do, and she teases that maybe she isn't a nice girl. But she is a nice girl. She looks Ricky in the eye and says, "You know I'm not serious, don't you." And the scene ends in tenderness. However, the reappearance of this conversation about the death of Lester serves to heighten our certainty that Lester will die.

Pages 76-90: The protagonist experiences a real loss or set back that is the result of overcoming the first obstacle in the first 30 pages. The protagonist is scrambling for stability in this new territory. Protagonist discovers a key thing and has one choice: to do what must be done.

Now the dark ending looms with Lester stepping out for a confident run, and his voice over suggesting that this day will be the last—not the first—day of the rest of his life. But before he dies, things have to get a bit uglier. Jane announces that her friend Angela will be staying over again, and she tells him to try to control himself, to try not to gawk and act stupidly drunk at the sight of the girl. He lashes out of control and says she's turning into a bitch like her mother. These words are the equivalent of a slap to the face, and he pretty much kills any hope of a relationship with his daughter.

In the next scene we see Lester getting into more trouble than he knows. Ricky's dad is growing more suspicious. When Ricky says he'll get a ride to school with Jane, his father carefully watches Ricky's moves as he heads for the neighbor's SUV. Before he climbs in the back seat, Lester, who's standing in the drive way, makes a secretive gesture to Ricky, who gives the nod. While we know it's a drug deal in the works, Mr. Homophobe, sees a sexual rendezvous in the works. He runs to search Ricky's room, and by chance looks out the window to see Lester, shirtless, doing curls in front of the garage window. To the suspicious father the sight of Lester seems some kind of proof that he's gay and is hot after Ricky.

Now things get worse yet again for Lester. Remember that his first obstacle was to overcome the control of his wife. He committed to a new way of life and that "win" involved moving into new territories of smoking pot, getting buff for the girl, and quitting his job. That "win" turns on him when Carolyn and Buddy show up at the fast food drive-through window and clearly looking fresh from sex. Lester sees Buddy kissing oh-so-willing Carolyn, and he responds with only hostility, no hurt. Still, we know he's hurt—anger is most often the desire to hurt for having been hurt. Carolyn tries to talk him into not overreacting, and he reverts to his hostile adolescent behavior. He yells to his wife, "You don't get to tell me what to do!" His marriage is over. Carolyn's earlier "win" of having an affair to boost her spirits also backfires. Right after they are "busted," Buddy says they'll have to stop seeing each other—his divorce is looking too expensive. She sits isolated in her car and screams with the kind of rage that will do anything.

Pages 91-95 (Second Plot Point): Protagonist starts moving toward the final goal which is the goal that he first sought, and it's now in reach. Subplots start wrapping while building to climax of the main plot Restate the central issue of the story and the protagonist's commitment to a new life by revisiting issues of the first plot point.

Lester is working out, looking more pumped and happy in all ways; he likes his new life very much.

Then we see Jane, strengthened by her new life with Ricky, stand up to Angela. She refuses to talk about her sex with Ricky. Angela is pissed that she can no longer dominate Jane.

Next we see Frank watching through the window as Ricky goes to Lester's garage to take him a new supply of pot. Given the angle of his view he sees what looks like Ricky giving Lester a blow job, when in truth Ricky is only leaning over a table to roll a joint. With the sudden arrival of Jane and Angela in the driveway, Ricky and Lester guiltily finish up their business, and homophobic Frank needs no more evidence that they are hiding a sexual relationship.

In the kitchen, the pissed off Angela flirts mightily with Lester admiring his new buff chest and arms. Yes, his goal is in reach. He flirts right back with an aggressive, "You like muscles, don't you?" And that sends her backing off. When he seems serious about sex, she runs for Jane. And this is some delicate foreshadowing that Angela isn't the lust-muffin she pretends to be.

Back home Ricky is confronted by his father in a very scary conversation. This will be their final confrontation, and given his father's violent temper, it feels deadly. At one point his father hugs him in a gesture that's more like a punch than an embrace and says, "I'd rather you be dead than be a faggot." Ricky doesn't grovel this time. He mocks his dad, claiming to have done all sorts of down and dirty sex acts with en. The scene ends with Ricky saying quietly: "What a sad old man you are." He goes downstairs and tells his mom that he is leaving, and we feel the story moving toward closure. And the death of Lester. The scenes move very quickly now gathering tension and speed.

In the next scene we see Carolyn driving, slowly melting down as she listens to a motivational tape encouraging her not to be a victim. She grabs a gun from the glove compartment, and we know where she is going.

Next Jane and Angela fight furiously when Jane demands that Angela not have sex with her dad. Angela, angrier than ever at Jane's defiance, says rather flippantly, "Why not?" This battle is interrupted by Ricky, who wants Jane to run off with him.

308

When Jane agrees to go, Angela goes on the attack about what stupid losers they are, and they counter with words that knock her down. Ricky says the worst thing Angela could hear, that she is ugly, boring and very ordinary. We've already heard Angela say there is nothing worse that being ordinary, so those words are a punch that sends her on the run to sit on the stairs and cry.

Pages 96-113: Build to climax of main story. Confrontation erupts, and the protagonist wins or loses. Perhaps he gains something unexpected, more than expected.

All the anger is boiling now. We know Carolyn is on her way home with a gun and a will to kill. And Frank goes to Lester's garage with what might also be a will to kill. He stands in the pouring rain and stares at Lester. We sense that he has murder on his mind, but we don't know everything. We do know Lester is in danger, and Lester doesn't have a clue. He invites Frank inside the garage, notes he is shivering and goes to comfort him, says they need to get him out of those clothes. Lester is referring to the cold wetness of the clothes, but Frank hears innuendo. He nods, crying. When Lester says his wife isn't home and that their marriage is a façade, Frank hears that the marriage is a cover for Lester's homosexuality. Here is only the beginning of where Lester will get something unexpected. Still aiming to comfort Frank, he softly says, "Tell me what you need." And Frank responds with an intimate touch, and he tries to kiss Lester. When Lester gently spurns Frank by saying that he has the wrong idea, Lester quietly leaves. But we know this battle can't be over. Frank is not the kind of man to back down easily.

Lester goes inside to find Angela in the living room, crying. They both admit to the strange events of the evening. It seems no one is getting what they expected. She tells him that she and Jane argued because Angela said Lester was sexy. This sounds like an invitation to spicy sex; he offers her a sip of beer. She takes it, touches him, and they kiss. It's no fantasy this time. Here we are with Lester at last getting what he's been wanting. When he asks what she wants, she says she doesn't know. So here is the girl who's been pretending to be so experienced, and with each second she seems to grow more into a little girl than a woman. When he tells her he wants her, she's trembling with a need, not for sex, but to be admired. She asks him to confirm that she's not ordinary. He showers her in complements, the right move as she is comforted and says for the second time in the movie that there is nothing worse than being ordinary. On the living room couch, she offers her body, as a reward for his admiration it seems, not because she craves him. In any case, she goes passive as he slips off her jeans.

We'll have to wait for the climatic moment, so to speak. We cut to Ricky and Jane lying on her bed planning their escape from this suburban nightmare.

Now back to Lester getting ready for action on the couch, and Angela tells him she is a virgin. He instantly backs off. Yep, he gets something he in no way expected. He covers her with a blanket and holds her as a father would hold a lost child, and he offers her a sandwich. This moment redeems him mightily.

Pages 114-115: Wrap up main story illustrating the ultimate and lasting growth of the character.

In the kitchen while feeding the troubled girl, Lester at last asks about his daughter. This moment continues to show his growth. Throughout the movie he was far more interested than Angela than his daughter, and now alone with his object of desire, he wants to know, to really know, how his daughter is. When Angela sincerely tells him that Jane is happy, that Jane is in love, for the first time we see genuine happiness on Lester's face; it's not happiness intoxicated by pot or lust. It's pure contentment that his little girl is happy, in love, at peace. Again more redemption of Lester's character.

When Angela grows out of her self-absorption to ask how Lester is, he says, as if it's a discovery, "I'm great." And he means it. We can see for the first time he isn't angry or troubled or off-balance in any way.

Angela goes to the bathroom, and Lester sits at the table, looking at a picture of his family in better days. He smiles, completely full of the happiness he has discovered in himself. And it is at this moment, the peak of his growth, that the barrel of a gun slips into the frame and points close range to the back of his head. And a blast splatters him on the kitchen wall.

We don't know just who was holding the gun, but we suspect it's the furious gun-wielding wife.

Lester's voice over kicks in as we look at his dead face lying on the floor, staring out as if he were watching something. And the voice over implies that he is. He calmly explains that when you die, your life does flash before you but not in an instant; it stretches out like the ocean before you. He goes on dreamily about how lovely it all is as we see Jane and Ricky head down the hall toward the kitchen. We see Angela in the bathroom and startled by the blast. We see Carolyn still furious and heading for the house with gun in hand when she hears the blast of a gunshot inside her house. We see blood-spattered and breathless Frank hiding in his gunroom. And finally in this sequence, we see Carolyn rush inside her bedroom where she slips her gun in her purse and throws it in the closet where she grabs Lester's clothes and falls down wailing with grief.

The world is in turmoil, and Lester continues to speak calmly about how he isn't angry about his death. He says it's hard to stay mad when there is so much beauty before you. His words recall the words of Ricky when he spoke earlier of the benevolent force behind all the things of this world. And like Ricky, Lester, the once cynical and despairing Lester, is overwhelmed by the beauty of things when he recalls boyhood memories, and happy memories of Carolyn and Jane. Much like Ricky he finds the beauty in the world too much to take in, but where Ricky felt that his heart would cave in from the beauty, Lester feels his heart will explode. And he tells himself to relax, his words reminiscent of Ricky's comment that experiencing so much beauty in the world reminds him not to be afraid.

In the final moments of this movie, Lester inhabits that place that Ricky imagines. His words confirm the somewhat whacky idea of Ricky that something benevolently moves beyond and within this mortal world. We see that Lester's body has died; his spirit has grown into something vast where beauty moves through him like rain. We recall the rain that poured down on Frank as he came first to embrace Lester, and then later to kill him. We recall the rain that poured down on Carolyn as she headed toward her house with the intention to kill him. We also recall the ironically deep words of the shallow Angela when she said that sometimes things happen exactly as they should. The story that began on quiet bitterness and ran on expressed rage, ends on peace, as it should, as we would like to think all life ends.

Yes, it's an ambitious story written by Alan Ball and directed by Sam Mendez. They took huge risks with sentiment while telling an ugly story that ends with a dead man, his face pooling in blood, and his mind reveling in beauty. A winner of five academy awards, including Best Picture, the movie took some outrageous twists, and all the while following that conventional Hollywood template.

Yes, following the template can lead to some very predictable plots, but it doesn't have to. So acknowledge the conventional template; it's conventional, but because it works. But following convention does not mean you have to write a predictable story.

Now to Your Plot

So let's say you have an idea, a story you'd like to see played out on the screen. I do suggest that you write out a quick synopsis of the beginning, middle, and end. Then you might list the events, or sequences, that are going to make up your story. A sequence is often more than a single scene. It is an important phase of the story development and uses only as many scenes or pages as it needs to complete that particular phase of the story. Since I'm not suggesting that you to write a feature-length film for your first script, I'll explain sequencing with an example of a story that takes little time, but is in no way a small story. Let get back to that story idea I took from the local news: the Mother's Day Brawl at the Golden Corral. I decided to depart from the news story and tell a different story about a recovering alcoholic with three kids and a boyfriend. In plotting this different take on the story, I decided it's was about luck and lack of luck, and titled it "Are We Lucky Yet?" Now I'll explain how I mapped out the sequences just so I could have an idea of what was going to happen and where.

I began with a young single mom, Vicki, with three kids at home: unruly twin four-year olds, and a toddler girl with an ear infection. Vicki settles a fight over cereal, gets the boys busy outside looking for a four-leaf clover to bring them luck, and she calms the baby with Tylenol. While her boyfriend sleeps in after a hard night of being a bouncer at the local strip club, our beleaguered protagonist takes a shower and gets dolled up to go out for her first time ever Mother's Day dinner out—her sweetheart of boyfriend is taking her out. Throughout this sequence, she says she wants things to be nice and goes to all effort to keep things nice.

Next sequence: outside the restaurant. There's a long, long line. The unruly boys, wrestling over the monster trucks, inadvertently nearly knock an old man down. The crowd turns to stare with great judgment at the skinny young mom who can't control her kids. They see a woman in too short skirt, a woman who smokes, a white woman with a tatted up Mexican—clearly not the father of her blond children. He asks how she kept the boys quiet so he could sleep, and she tells him about the search for the four-leaf clover game, and she reveals that her own mother used to send her outside to looking for a four-leaf clovers just to keep her out of the house. She admits that sometimes desperate to come inside, she would fake a four-leaf by squeezing two clovers together and tearing off a couple leaves. When she brought it in, her mom would throw the clovers in the trash and send her back out. Meanwhile the line to get inside the restaurant doesn't budge, and the kids remain restless. Tension grows.

Next sequence: inside the restaurant. Mom and boy friend get caught trying to pass off the four-year olds as three year olds to get the dollar meal. It's crowded. Christians at a near-by table pray over their food. Our weary mom wishes she could

312

join them and experience their peace and faith. There's an unspoken connection with the pastor. More kid chaos ensues with people give judging glances. Boys roam all over, grabbing food; a drink, of course, is spilled. A grumpy middle-aged woman and her dour old mother scowl, make comments. The baby grows more unruly, and the boys tease her until she wriggles free and stages a full-blown temper tantrum. The mom tries to control the baby, but looses her grip. The baby stumbles into the grumpy lady who swats her away. And so of course, the climatic moment: mom jumps up and punches the lady who then takes a swing at the mom, misses and falls into table. You can imagine the mayhem.

Next sequence: parking lot outside restaurant. The boyfriend is cuffed and questioned far from the wretched mom. She is surrounded by cops and questioned while she watches her boys who are being guarded by other cops. She hears her baby screaming from doorway of restaurant. One boy keeps trying to break loose from cops, and the mom tells him to look for a four-leaf clover in the grassy median that separates the restaurant parking lot from another lot. Meanwhile she argues her case with the cops. Things aren't looking good given her record for bar fights and DUIs.

Next sequence: the pastor comes out and speaks in defense of our unlucky mom to the cops. A detective comes out to say the mean lady who hit the baby will drop charges if our mom will drop the charges. All is looking good. Boy suddenly declares that he's found a four-leaf clover, rushes over with one faked by squeezing two together and plucking off a couple leaves. He asks if they are lucky yet. And unlike our mom's evil mom, Vicki embraces boy says they are lucky, and indeed they are.

Now believe me, before I mapped out the details of that series of sequences I gave a lot of thought to my characters. I gave them history, not a ton of history, just enough to load the characters sufficiently to carry off the story. I knew I needed three key scenes: before restaurant disaster, disaster, and an after restaurant disaster that would provide some sort of resolution.

9. Alternative Plotlines

Much of this text has been geared toward helping you write a character-driven plot that pretty much follows narrative conventions. It's good to know traditional structures if only to know how to tamper with them. No doubt, not all of you want to tell a traditional character-driven story. And I would be doing you a disservice if I didn't address alternative story lines.

But before we consider more contemporary movies that resist/defy/ignore the conventional Hollywood three-act plot line, we should consider the granddaddy of scripts that defy convention, Orson Welles' *Citizen Kane*. Made in 1939, a big year for Hollywood with additional releases of *The Wizard of Oz* and *Gone With the Wind*, *Citizen Kane* was nominated for eleven academy awards, but for political reasons received only one for the screenplay written by Herman Mankiewicz. In any case, to this day it is considered the best film of all time by The American Film Institute and The British Film Institute. Before we get to the discussion of the film, you need to recall that Orson Welles was the iconoclastic genius of radio who once terrorized New York City with a vivid and violent report that the Martians had invaded and were destroying the city. His mock news report was so convincing that when listeners heard it, they checked other radio stations for the same news story, and when the story wasn't heard on other stations, they simply believed that Orson Welles' station (CBS) was sharper than the others and had the lead on the story. Many of his listeners were sincerely preparing themselves for the end of the world.

To say Orson Welles was a maverick is an understatement. He was indeed a creative genius who went from radio to staging productions of Shakespeare like no one had ever seen. For example, he staged a *Macbeth* set in Haiti, a wildly successful production known as the "voodoo" *Macbeth*. And when he produced *Julius Caesar* in the context of the rise of the Third Reich, he created a mob scene that is considered to be the most powerful single moments to ever occur on a stage. No surprise that when he went to Hollywood at the age of twenty-four he was given free-reign and big bucks to make a movie. Being the kind of young man who couldn't resist his own versions of shock and awe, he opted to make a fictionalized chronicle of the life of multi-millionaire and newspaper baron, William Randolf Hearst. In what turns out to be a thinly-veiled and somewhat slanderous story of Hearst, Welles broke all conventions of Hollywood, not only in the structure of his film, but in his attack on the one man who had the power to make or break just about anyone in Hollywood.

Citizen Kane: The Granddaddy of Innovation

Citizen Kane traces the life of Charles Foster Kane, a man whose career in newspapers began with the mission to champion the underprivileged, a mission that became a ruthless pursuit of power. Narrated with framing voiceovers and flash backs that loop back again and again as the story of Kane's life moves forward, the story is revealed though the research of a reporter seeking to solve the mystery of the bitter and reclusive dying man's last word: "Rosebud."

Deliberately shot in black and white when color was making its grand debut in film, the film opens with the sinister images of chain-link fence, the shot slowly tracking up to a "No Trespassing" sign, then up to more and more fencing. The camera moves past gothic gates and the exotic statuary and landscaping of a seemingly abandoned estate. The camera then moves inside a palatial home and settles in the bedroom of a dying old man holding a snow globe. His dry lips utter the word, "Rosebud," as the snow globe crashes to the floor.

Then there is an abrupt cut to a scene where newsmen are reviewing a newsreel on the life and death of Kane. Here we have a quick overview. Kane was a very wealthy man who lived and died in the exotic estate called Xanadu. We learn he was poor as a child, and then was suddenly wealthy when gold was discovered in his family's mine. We learn that he went on to become a newspaper baron who made money from investments in many industries; he had two failed marriages; he was a man of conflicting principles in his pursuit for power, a power he only vaguely held before it disappeared. After the men watch the clip, they feel something is missing in the overview, and they want to find a way to personalize, maybe sensationalize the story. They opt to do what the news industry likes to do. They hire an investigative reporter to scrutinize the man's private life to try to find the meaning of his dying word. And there we have the inciting incident of the film. The quest is on.

And here is where the plot gets tricky, and it stays tricky. The plot is so intricate that it pretty much defies memory when you try to recall just how it unfolds. In the beginning we get the overview that will keep us grounded as the story moves back and forth through time. We know what happened in the most general way in Kane's life, but through a series of interviews we see flashback after flashback and gain more and more understanding of Mr. Kane. The intriguing element of these flashbacks is that they don't occur in any linear order. At first the reporter goes to Kane's ex-wife, now a drunk who'll say nothing. He then goes to the archive of the banker who was declared young Kane's guardian when the boy inherited wealth. Here we learn the sad story of the young boy being taken, un-willfully, from his mother to go live the life of a very wealthy and controlled young man who is to be heir to his biological father's fortune.

In this scene we see the first image of young Kane, a boy living in relative poverty in the mountains of Colorado, a boy who happily entertains himself with his sled, a very important sled, while his mother unsuccessfully deals with the representatives of the estate. Money wins over blood ties with mother, and the boy is whisked off to New York to live the life of a corporate prince.

This flashback gives us a bit of insight into a man who develops an obsession for collecting things as well as an obsession for power, a reaction no doubt to his powerlessness as a child. In later flashbacks, we will see a grown Kane state that he choked on that silver spoon forced in his mouth, and that he has a great disdain for the very wealth he holds. However he has no problems using and abusing his wealth and power to get what he wants.

In an interview with Kane's business manager, we learn that Kane once said "Rosebud" while holding that snow globe, but the reference is unclear. Other flashbacks reveal his cut-throat strategies at becoming the biggest newspaper man in the country, as well as his ruthless attempts to gain political power. He marries the niece of the president and devotes himself to exposing the worst of existing political powers while campaigning to become the governor of New York. He is well on his way to winning that office when his opponent reveals his affair with a local singer. This little scandal indeed parallels the affair Hearst had with a local actress. While Hearst never married his mistress, but did live with her until the end of his life, Kane does marry his mistress. And here is where the story gets sordid. In the film, Kane's young second wife becomes a screaming whining shrew who leaves Kane to his solitary old age. When she leaves, the furious Kane destroys her bedroom and leaves carrying that snow globe. The butler overhears him say "Rosebud," but still no one can make much meaning from the word.

The plot continues to shift back and forth from point to point in Kane's life, but the writing and directing never confuse. We only become more intrigued by the complex narrative of Kane's life, and that is because with every zig-zag back to a previously glimpsed moment of Kane's life, we learn a bit more. We come to see that the plotline is not at all chaotic, but a carefully orchestrated layering of facts. With every forward movement that makes us step back to the past, we learn a little more about something we've already seen. Yes, at the beginning of the story we see that Kane's second wife has become a hardened and bitter drunk, but as we step back and back again and again to see how her relationship with Kane started and developed, we see that she was at first a love object who then became a trophy wife, who then became a career project for Kane. He basically invented her career as an opera singer. Everyone, including her, knew her talent was a sham, but he pushed for her fame until she could only end his efforts by attempting suicide. In forcing her success he nearly killed her, and when that project failed, he sought to control her by keeping her in the way he kept all the exotic animals in his private zoo.

Through the series of flashbacks we come to see the broken woman who became the screeching bitch, who then became the hardened drunk. In a similar way of zig-zagging flashbacks we see how the powerful ambitious and wildly successful Kane became a lonely old man in the isolation of his fantasy land, Xanadu.

The reporter works on to find the mystery of "Rosebud" until in the end reporters gather to go over every item, junk and treasure of Kane's estate. As the reporter concludes in a voice over that "Rosebud" will forever remain an enigma, we see workers tossing an older sled into the furnace along with all the other useless things that are to be destroyed. The camera zooms in on the sled and we slowly realize that it is the same sled young Kane was playing with on the day the estate men came to whisk the boy away from his mother. Slowly we see the painted words "Rosebud," the name of the sled, start to blister and burn, and then a shot of black smoke rising from the chimney.

In this moment of irony, the viewer solves the mystery of "Rosebud;" it was the treasured item from his poor childhood, the only time he was happy and free from all the ambitions that sent him on a life of wanting and wanting things. After this plot twist that resolves the mystery, the film ends with another shot of that chain-link fence and the "No Trespassing" sign. It's an ironic closing image suggesting that on one hand Kane would never allow strangers to trespass into his private life, he also wouldn't allows visitors, not even his friends trespass into his private emotional world where the dearest thing to him was a sled. At another level we see that how in spite of the "No Trespassing" sign, through the art of the film itself we, the viewers, do get to trespass into the private world of Kane to discover the secret he held so dear.

The film was instantly considered a masterpiece that had accomplished something no one dared. Its innovation was on par with that never-done, never-dared radio broadcast featuring Martians in New York City. But the film brought something far more dangerous to the career and the life of Orson Welles. A declared genius at twenty-four, he was a has-been at twenty-five, and all because of the kind of hubris we saw in the character of Charles Kane. Welles chose not only to pull back the curtain on the ruthless ambition of William Randolf Hearst, he chose to ridicule his abuses of power. Worst of all, he harshly ridiculed and slandered the character of Hearst's mistress, the actress, Marion Davies who in truth was a much younger showgirl that Hearst took on as mistress, and then used his papers to overstate her acting talent. But Davies was never the shrill harpy-turned-drunk that Welles made her out to be in the movie. In later interviews, Wells admitted that what he did with her character in the film was a "dirty trick." Another "dirty trick" was the inside joke that "Rosebud" was Hearst's nickname for his mistress' private parts. When Hearst learned of the film, he did all he could to have the film destroyed, and when he couldn't do that, he set out to destroy the career of Orson Welles.

Running on the philosophy that a movie might make a man, but a newspaper could destroy him, Hearst proved correct. His papers were not allowed to run an ad or a review for the film. He exposed Welles' own illicit affairs. He suggested that Welles was a homosexual; he took on Hollywood itself and pointed out the vast number Jewish immigrants employed at studios, jobs that should go to solid "Americans." And then the killing blow: Hearst laid claims that Welles was a communist, and at time with a communist was equivalent to being a devil.

The battle over the film essentially stemmed from Hearst's need to defend the honor of his mistress who was so cruelly represented in the film. In truth his mistress was considered something of a comedienne, she was beloved by all who knew her—with the exception of Hearst's wife—and she stayed at Hearst's side even when he was bankrupted by the depression. She had accumulated much of her own wealth and possessions. She sold her vast quantity of jewels and gave them to Hearst. But none of this appeared in the film. Hearst went after Welles just as ruthlessly as Charles Kane went after his enemies, just as ruthlessly as Welles went after Hearst.

After *Citizen Kane*, in spite of the critical acclaim it received around the world, Orson Welles never gained control over any movie again, and the parts he did play were unflattering. He ended his career doing as his put it, "ninety per cent hustling, and ten percent making movies," and as he put it, "that is no way to live a live."

On one hand William Randolf Hearst won the battle over the consequences of the controversial film, but on the other hand, one might say that Welles won the war. In spite of Hearst's efforts to hush the film, his character as a man is better known through the representation of him in the film; Welles' myth of the man far outlived and out-reached the real life of the man. Orson Welles, even after death, is known as an unsurpassed genius, not only for his direction and acting, but for his daring to do what no one else had done before, or has done since.

Other Unconventional Plotlines

In the non-traditional plotline, often we don't know just what is going on, but we're willing to go with the confusion because there is something so intriguing about the character or the situation that we don't mind the confusion. The story looks something like a puzzle we'd to work out. The non-linear *Dead Again*, is a melodrama, but given the puzzling plot we can easily forget it's a melodrama. In the plot a Los Angeles detective (Kenneth Branagh) takes on the case of a woman (Emma Thompson) who suffers from amnesia. He soon learns that they are connected by reincarnation to a grisly 40-year old murder. In spite of the sensational and unlikely plot, we are drawn in and held by the circuitous plotline that always keeps us guessing as to the "how's" and "why's" of the story. It's a movie much like *Memento* (also a melodrama featuring murder if you're being honest) in that it only improves with multiple viewings.

In other movies which use unconventional plots such as *Adapation*, or any of David Lynch's works such as *Blue Velvet, Mullholland Drive* and *Lost Highway*, we connect with the intensity of the storyline and the oddly obsessed characters even when we don't quite know what's going on. If you are a fan of Lynch's work, you'll want to have a look at his short films; you can find them on a DVD, titled appropriately, *The Short Films of David Lynch*. It contains six shorts, and each one is preceded with an introduction by Mr. Lynch himself. Much to learn here.

Yes, many movie-goers prefer a conventional plot that doesn't require logical leaps and twists, but many film lovers enjoy the wild ride as the director uses a sleight of hand with the narrative tricks. We are engaged even when the logic feels not logical; a little confusion is okay with some of us. We often feel if we've watched a magic act, and we want to view it again and again to see just the trick play out. Such films require very clever plotting, and it's that cleverness that intrigues.

When writing an unconventional plotline you'll need to remember your audience and avoid that slippery slope of self-indulgence. You've got to give us a character worth following around a bit even when we're clueless as to where he is going. You've got to give us some kind of visual that enchants/ intrigues such as that ear found in the grass in *Blue Velvet* or the truly bizarre creatures imagined by the lonely little girls in *Pan's Labyrinth* and *The Fall*.

When it comes to writing engaging plots, never underestimate the power of surprise—like that ear on the ground in *Blue Velvet* or a portal into the head of John Malkovich. Everyone wants to see something they haven't seen before, or maybe to see an old familiar thing in such a new light that it's quite different. After seeing David Lynch's white picket fences and ultra green grass and flat-out weird looking robin with a worm in its beak, no one can see suburbia in the same innocent way.

Another more contemporary script that runs on an innovative plan is the groundbreaking *Pulp Fiction* that begins with the narrative ending and then loops back to tell the preceding stories that lead to the ending. And there's the backwards told tale of *Memento*. The plotline only works when told backwards; if you rearrange the script into a linear line, it simply doesn't hold interest. *The Machinist* also proceeds in a non-linear fashion that simultaneously confuses and intrigues. And there's the wildly unpredictable and imaginative *Being John Malkovich* with a plot that hinges on the discovery of a portal into John Malkovich.

There are many alternatives, and one of the most clever and entertaining departures from the Hollywood screenplay paradigm is the delightfully iconoclastic *Adaptation* by Charlie Kaufman which offers a kind of mobius strip of plotlines where a small personal story line runs head on with the conventional Hollywood movie paradigm; the introspective plotline of a troubled writer just trying to write an artistic script merges with an over-the-top action/thriller plot including the obligatory sex and drug and chance scenes. Kaufman offers quite a commentary on the Hollywood industry in this film that uses the Hollywood paradigm for screenplays while simultaneously turning it inside out.

If you're reading this book, you are probably planning on a smaller script, perhaps a script that you can make into a movie for a class project, for a graduate school application, or maybe just for the pleasure of posting it on youtube.com. If you are looking to write a small script that does not follow the conventional narrative plot line, you must see the classic French film *La Jettée*, a film that set the standard for futuristic stories and unconventional storytelling. The later futuristic nightmare movies such as *Brazil* and *Matrix* owe a debt to the innovative film made in 1962, *La Jettée* which can be found fittingly on The Short Series, Volume: *Dreams*

The futuristic plot of *La Jettée* loops from present to past to future and back again, and it questions conventional notions of a time/space continuum as it explores that shady area where we lose certainty of what is real and what is imagined. Directed by Chris Marker, it has been considered by many to be the most important work of science fiction since Fritz Lang's *Metropolis* which was made in 1927. The basic narrative is built around reflective layers that force us to feel the dis-ease that results when we have trouble distinguishing the differences between fact and fiction, reality and fantasy.

The film addresses issues of madness and dreaming as well as the idea of time travel as it depicts the story of a survivor of world apocalypse in Paris, France. He is the experimental subject of a group of scientists on a mission to use time travel to go to the past to gain insight into how this mass destruction could have been avoided, and to go to the future to gain clues on how humanity will survive. The short black and white film was the direct inspiration for the *Twelve Monkeys* and *Terminator*. Most of you no doubt would be surprised to know that such Hollywood mega-movies were conceived in response to a little twenty-nine minute black and white French film.

The writers of *Twelve Monkeys*, David and Jane Peoples, directly credit *La Jettée* for helping them to see how to construct a story they had been wanting to tell for years. Both had worked in mental hospitals, and they saw up close the suffering and confusion of severely mentally ill patients who didn't know where they were, who sometimes thought they were being constrained and tortured by mad scientists or hired inquisitors of a police state. The patients often also had a painfully hard time distinguishing between what they imagined from what was real. The story of a man in Paris being held captive for mind experiments in time travel inspired them with a way to tell their story.

La Jettée is a simple story, all told in voice over, as if the speaker is recalling a dark fairy tale. What's remarkable about the film is that it uses only still images. The narrative relies on a montage of images to tell the story of how past, present and future are all be interwoven in the imagination of one man who is the subject of the mind experiments. It lacks all the action, subplots and drama of *Twelve Monkeys*. But it offers something else in its reliance on grainy black and white still shots to tell the story of a world stripped of color, fluidity, life. It's a nightmare world, a very quiet nightmare, told in much the same way nightmare takes shape in our minds, slipping illogically from scene to scene to confuse and disturb us, returning us again and again to disturbing images we can't fully escape no matter how much we toss and turn in our beds.

The film opens with the roaring white noise of jets taking off as we study an establishing shot of Orly International Airport in Paris. And this Paris looks anything but adventurous or romantic. There is a ruined industrial quality to most everything we see in the movie, except of the face of the main character, the woman he seeks to connect with, the simple daily beautiful things he sees in his dreams.

A voice over narrates everything that occurs—a dangerous tactic that can easily go flat, but it doesn't. We are held by, and want to follow, the story of a man who is haunted by an image he saw in his childhood. He can't recall if he dreamed it or really saw it, but he keeps seeing and re-seeing the image of a man dying at the Orly Airport.

The narrator tells us the boy grew up to be a man, and we see shot after shot of the skyline of Paris gone to ruin, the repeated images of so much space so emptied out suggest the insignificance of one dead man in a world where so many have passed.

We see shots of the post-apocalyptical world of ruined Paris, survivors with mad empty gazes, and the cold faces of the scientists, men with hypodermic needles and probes and restraints. The narrator tells us that survivors went to live underground given that the above-ground world was a radioactive ruin. We come to learn that those cruel looking scientists are "head experimentors." Prisoners are subjected to time-travel experiments that either kill them or drive them mad. Then one day they select the man whose story we are being told because his mind has the ability to hold on to an image with great clarity and feeling. Given our man has such a powerful memory/imagination, the scientist theorize that he will survive these time travels and be able to provide the insights they need.

We see repeated and varied images of this man restrained in a hammock-like bed, in a place that seems more of a cave that a place of science. He has a mask wired with probes secured over his eyes while the doctors inject mysterious chemicals into his veins. We see his pain over and over: we hear the pounding of his heart as he grimaces with something that seems unbearable. Finally we are told that he starts to see peaceful things: fields, bedrooms, children, birds, cats. And then he sees a woman, "her," a very significant "her" at the Orly Airport.

The director keeps us engaged by alternating between the soft sweet images of a beautiful peaceful world of memories/dreams, and the ruined world of burned-out buildings, and burned, broken statures of beautiful female forms. After awhile our protagonist "meets" the girl of his dreams. He spends time with her and then gets so distracted by the textures and things of the peaceful world, she disappears.

The experimenters send him back again and again until, and he really comes to know the woman. He watches her sleep in the sun. They do all the tender, quiet things a man and woman might do when just getting to know one another: go for walks, visit a museum, mundane pleasures in a normal world. The man's powerful brain doesn't forget the nature of his time-travel mission; he knows that in order to be sent back to her, she must be dead.

A new series of experiments begins, giving him more time with the woman, but the lovely moments are steadily interrupted by images of the scientists doing their tortuous experiments. In the dream/memory sequences the couple is completely at ease, but we know this ease won't last since those scientists are ultimately in control of pleasure and pain. After an experience where the man feels he could actually stay in the past with the woman, those experiments are stopped.

The man is then sent to the future to see the humanity that survived. They are a frightening humanity who all appear to have been shot between the eyes, and yet they have placid faces, too placid. There is something undead about them rather than real, natural life.

Given that the man has sustained and survived the memory of twice-lived time, the scientists are finished experimenting with him, and he has the option to go forever forward or back. He wants the past, his childhood, and that woman back there. Going back, he thinks he will be the child he keeps dreaming of at the airport, but once there, he finds himself as a grown man, looking for the woman at the airport. He sees her at the end of a pier. He runs toward her, then spots one of the scientist's men who is there to kill him. Our protagonist dies, knowing now that the man he saw die when he was a child at the airport was himself. We are never quite sure what is "real" in the story, and what is imagined.

It's a grim science fiction fairy tale that tells a small story, but a very innovative one. And it paved the way for many other kinds of stories to be told, stories to be told in non-linear ways. La *Jettée*, does many things that are risky narrative strategies. The viewer is often confused. And the situation is implausible. But it works. We are engaged by a visceral reaction to the ugliness juxtaposed with such beauty and tenderness. We are also engaged by the logical need to work out the mobius strip of time travel; often just when we think we've rationally figured out the plotline, some new development throws us off again. There are leaps in the plotline that we have to make by way of emotion rather than logic. The convoluted plot remarkably does not distance the viewer. We are also drawn into the story of a boy who is haunted by the image of violence he saw as a child. We connect with his confusion, and we identify with his need to figure out the mystery.

The "how's" and "why's" of this plot are not smoothly, perfectly worked out. Just like the character, just like many mental patients, we are never quite certain of the logic of what we have seen. There's much to be learned from *Jettée*. The innovative Southern writer, Flannery O'Conner, was correct when she once said, "You can do anything you want in fiction—as long as you get away with it."

So Go Ahead and Tell Your Monster Story

There are some stories beginning students are just aching to tell, and while they may seem potent and fresh to the student, professors, I'm afraid, have seen the same story many a time. My friend and colleague in our film department, Tammy Kinsey has found that her beginning students often want to make a suicide movie. She struggled against this cliché plotline, but after awhile she gave in and said, "Okay, get it over with. Go ahead and make your suicide movie." Given free rein to make the cliché interesting, she did end up seeing some interesting little films.

In my experience as a teacher of writing, I've been overwhelmed with the girl gets pregnant story—the movie *Juno* did indeed to something fresh and delightful with that maudlin premise. But note that what saved the movie was the fresh twist on character. Juno is an audacious, clever, and passionate young woman who initiated unsafe sex with an unassuming and sweet young man—she was not the tragic victim of a do-her-wrong-and-run kind of guy. Juno got herself in her mess, and she uses all her smarts and heart and instincts to find a resolution to her problem and move on with her life. A clichéd premise was made into a delightfully moving story through smart plotting and inspired character development.

For many of my male students (and increasingly more of the women) there is a prevailing urge to write some sort of monster/zombie/vampire/slasher/ghost story. Okay, we've seen some fresh takes. Hannibal Lecter is somehow a man-eater we like to like. And there are lovable ghosts in *Ghost* and *Truly Madly Deeply*, where the ghost comes around only for the good of the loved one left behind. We folks can't seem to get enough of these things that go bump, and smash, and slash, and gnash in the night. So here's your permission to do it. You might try doing this with a small group and make it a collaboration—this strategy may help you avoid the self-indulgence that too often is intertwined with our fantasy or horror stories. No doubt you have the plot/situation in mind, but most likely you need to work at character. Remember good fantasy isn't just fantasy—that would ring of cartoon. A good fantasy or an excellent horror might have an unreal premise, but it grows out of REAL CHARACTERS in UNREAL SITUATIONS.

So first do a profile of your protagonist—it might be the potential victim, or the potential monster. Have a look at the building character exercise for hints. Note things like name, age, appearance, psychological tendencies, family relations, romantic situations, and basic on-going desires. For example is your protagonist the shy type? Vain? Power hungry? Computer geek? Rascal?

In creating your monster/slasher/scary whatever, use the same sorts of building blocks that you would for any character. You might want to work in a motive/background. Yes, even monsters have a history. Two of the most realistic disturbing fantasy bad guys are Golum in the *Lord of the Rings* trilogy and Penguin in the first *Batman*. Both of these bad guys' evil intentions stem form being victimized in some way at an earlier point in their lives. Like most malicious real people in the world, monsters are in a large part made by events—even Satan wasn't always a bad guy. So give your monster a history. The classic horror icons like Dracula, the Werewolf, and Frankenstein's monster all had a soft spot at some point. Consider that.

If you are inclined to write a monster story as so many are, I would urge you to first have a look at the short (fourteen-minute) film on youtube.com. It's titled, "I Love Sarah Jane," an unlikely title for a movie that concerns a world being taken over by zombies. The film was directed and co-written by a young Australian man Spencer Susser, who financed the whole thing with a credit card, staged it with some friends, shot it, made it and found an audience on youtube.com. As a result of his resourcefulness and his VERY FRESH take on a cliché, the director gained recognition and was given a two million dollar contract from Paramount. Getting the idea of starting small while thinking big? I suggest that you have a quick look at the movie for yourself before I break it down here. Now let's have a look at the narrative sequences to give you a sense of the pacing of the story.

I'd like to point out that Susser begins this movie quietly. We open with a tracking shot of a boy, whom we will come to know as Jimbo, on his bike pedaling along the trashed street of what would otherwise be a normal neighborhood. The more he rides, the more trash we see, and we gather from the lack of moving cars and people and the excess trash that something is wrong. No monsters, just signs of chaos, ruin, nothing really horrible, but nothing good. When we see an overturned, burned-out car and what appears to be some vague part of a corpse, we know we are in some sort of apocalyptic setting. And what's odd about this scene is that the boy moves along as if all is normal. But then there is that odd detail of the quiver of arrows strapped across his back and a serious looking hunting bow slung over his shoulder.

He stops in front of a graffiti-covered house and pauses to take a look at photo that he has taped to the handlebar of his bike. We see a sweet looking high-school photo of a girl that we guess to be Sarah Jane. He studies the photo for a beat—ah love—then goes to the house, knocks, a nice gesture of still being civilized in an uncivilized world.

Out comes tall, skinny, road-warrior type punk kid, also with a bow and arrows. He gives Jimbo a garbage bag of something liquid—we just hear the sound of it, and it bodes of something not good. He hurries Jimbo along to follow him to a destination across a burned-out field with smoke still rising in the distance

They arrive at a location on the edge of the field where teenaged boys are bullying a chained zombie, an emaciated cadaverous thing that is secured with chains so the boys can throw rocks at it, curse it, slap it and humiliate it the usual ways that violent boys bully. A trick to this movie is that the director has chosen to tell this horror fantasy in such normal language and with such basic human motivations, it seems very real. While one boy slaps at the zombie, the tall punk kids shoots it square in the chest with an arrow, a risky act that leads to a fight. Jimbo is not at all involved in the zombie abuse. He watches from a distance and heads into the house.

Inside we see Sarah Jane, sitting on the couch, nervously watching the news. Through voice over we hear that various governments are struggling to deal with this matter of the undead, how to dispose of them. The tone of the news anchor is much as the normal tone a news anchor might use while covering an environmental hazard or war story. No horrific dramatics, just news. Jimbo sits in a nearby chair and tries to make normal conversation with Sarah Jane, but she responds in the way any pissed-off and willful teenaged might. She wants nothing to do with him; she's preoccupied with the news, and she's just in a flat-out bad mood.

Next scene shows the boys rummaging in the kitchen for pots, pans, anything they can find. Punk kid looks for anything that could be used to hurt the zombie, and when he finds a weed-whacker, he leads the boys head back out to take the whacker to the zombie's' face.

We cut back inside to Jimbo, who is still trying to make conversation. He asks if Sarah Jane has ever wondered how a fish feels when it's caught and released back to the water. Is it angry? Grateful? Or does it just forget everything? Odd questions in a world of zombies. But Jimbo is a sensitive guy trying to make conversation, and he's willing to share his sweetly odd and compassionate imagination.

Sarah Jane has the zombie problem on her mind. Still pissed-off, she finally asks Jimbo why doesn't he go be with his own family. When he says that his family is all dead, he gains her undivided attention. She studies him closely as if to make sure of the truth; real pain flashes again and again across her face as she quietly cries and says she is sorry—a bit of character development here. He moves a little closer, and tries to lighten things a bit by saying sometimes he gets sad about the fish too. That line gets a bit of a smile from her, and it's a lovely quiet moment of more character development. Yes, you can have quiet character development in a zombie movie, because this is more than a zombie movie. It's a story about a boy in love with a girl in a world gone to hell all around them.

Outside, the punk kid, who looks more and more like a zombie as the film progresses, dumps plastic bags of fuel on and around the zombie. When we see this escalation of the violence that the boys enjoy, the line between zombie behavior and human behavior is blurred. Punk kid positions his arrow, tells his friend to "light this bitch up." The arrow is set on fire; punk kid lets it fly, and the zombie explodes into a column of flame.

Sarah Jane storms out—yes, she's fearless—and says something to the effect of what the hell are you doing. The boys, well, they're boys. No excuses. Punk kid just says he was putting the "mother fucker out of its fucking misery." She snaps that the "motherfucker" was her dad. There's plot development. Zombie wasn't always a zombie. He was her dad, and she's more heartsick than horrified. While they argue, the zombie manages to grab punk boy's leg and gnaw on it. Punk boy falls and instantly starts changing into a zombie.

With no hesitation, Sarah Jane grabs a shovel and proceeds to bash the guy's head in. We don't see this mess, just the repeated sight Sarah Jane raising and swinging that shovel to a thwacking sound again, and again, and again. Her face remains determined, calm. Once we hear the final thwacking/wet smacking sound, she stops. She looks down and sneers, "You out of your fucking misery yet?" That job complete, she moves on to the top half of the zombie that's still weakly alive and face-down, clawing at the ground. She fearlessly positions herself over him and uses the shovel to slice his skull in half. Job done, she throws the shovel down and heads back up the stairs to the house.

Jimbo watches her go, awe on his face, then he turns and smiles in the way only lovesick boys do. The movie fades to a kitschy 1950's love song. Somehow this zombie movie has a tender ending. That's because is really isn't a zombie movie, it's a love story, just as the title suggests. It's about very real characters in an unreal situation where zombies threaten the world while somehow tenderness continues to grow.

Lovely. That's a fresh take on a monster movie.

Many of my students have wanted to make a horror/monster movie. I would advise all to have a look that this little movie, not only because it's a fresh take on an old cliché. It's quite simply a good love story with all the ingredients of a good story: characters who are motivated by both internal and external forces.

10. Fade Out: Now Jump into Action

By now you know everything you need to know about writing a screenplay. While, yes, people like to say that there is power in knowledge, in truth there in only potential in knowledge. The real power comes with action informed by knowledge At this point you should feel confident in writing your script and given the practice with all the writing exercises and prompts, you should have the competence to write a script worth the love, money and labor of making it into a movie.

If you have completed a script that you'd like to see made at this point, take some time out and go celebrate yourself and your work. You deserve it. Put the script aside for a week or two while you get busy with something else. Then go back and look at it again with fresh eyes. No doubt you want to share it with everyone you know, but before you do that, register your script with the Writer's Guild.

The address is:

Writers Guild of America West, Inc.
7000 West Third Street
Los Angeles, CA 90048
www.writersguild.org

The registration fee is $20.00. Registering your script won't absolutely guarantee that it won't be plagiarized, but it will give you solid legal ground to argue for your work. Don't underestimate the potential power of your script. Bear in mind many very short movies led to very big careers for writers who did the work with all seriousness and passion. So protect your baby. It's worth twenty bucks.

That done, share your script with friends, with anyone with an interest in movies. Look at it with potential director's eyes, and not your overworked, and biased writer's eyes. Stage readings of your script, so you can sit back and hear the action, the description and the dialogue out loud. You'll be able to tell where lines ring flat, false, cliché, lines that sometimes are just hard to get out of an actor's mouth because of a clumsy arrangement of words. As you listen to your script being read, in your mind try to see what exactly is on the screen. If there is a long monologue where there is no action occurring, remember that the camera is on the speaker's face—that can go flat fast even with an enchantingly beautiful or handsome actor. Think as you listen, see in your mind what exactly is on the screen.

Revise it, polish it, until it sparkles. Now you can choose to rally up your friends and acquaintances with talent and start planning to shoot your script. You also have the option of sending your script and/or your movie out to competitions. There are numerous competitions for screenplays out there, for both feature-length and short scripts. The options keep changing with the ebb and flow of funding, so your best bet is to get on-line and do the research as to which competitions are right for your work. I searched under both short script and short film competitions and came up with these options, so you can start with these, but do have a look on-line for yourself.

Here are potential competitions for your short screenplays:

Short Screenplay Competition/ Slamdance Film Festival
http://archive.slamdance.com

Big Break Screenwriting Contest
http://finaldraft.com

"Picture This" Short Screenplay Competition
http://academiccsu.ohio.edu

American Gem Short Screenplay Competition
www.filmmakers.com

Gimme Credit Short Screenplay Competition
www.gimmecreditcompetition.com

Las Vegas Short Script Awards
http://shortscriptawards.com

Vail Film Festival Short Screenplay Competition
www.vailfilmfestival.org

MovieBytes Screenwriting Competition
www.moviebytes.com

Withoutabox Screenwriting Competition
www.withoutabox.com

First Glance Screenplay Competition
www.firstglancefilms.com

LA Shorts Fest Screenplay Competition
www.lashortsfest.com

Hypefest Short Screenplay Competition
http://digitalcontentproducer.com

IndieSpire Short Screenplay Competition
www.filmmakermg.com

And for you horror buffs:
Short Horror Screenplay Competition
www.myslateboard.com

And if you are interested in writing a script concerning AIDS:

Kaiser Family Foundation Screenwriting Competition
www.kff.org

There are numerous competitions for films. Just search on-line, but here are a few sights that are potential competitions for your short films:

The Indie Short Film Competition
www.IndieSHortFilms.net

Action/Cut Short Film Competition
www.actioncut.com

Short Film Competition
http://imaginecup.com

Tiger Awards Competition for Short Films
www.filmfestivalrotterdam.com

Guerilla Film and Video

I'll have to give my friend/former student, Vytas Nagisetty credit for this term for making your own film or video. You'll find yourself doing whatever it takes to get the mission accomplished. If you want to shoot your own video or movie, the first thing to do is call on all friends. We've heard that it takes a village to raise a child. Well it takes quite a posse to make your movie. You need actors, not hams. You need someone who knows something about a soundtrack. You need rehearsal time, space. And if film is your medium, you'll need money. Whether it's film or video, you'll need volunteers who are just about as excited, and serious, about your project as you are.

Before you start, you might want to keep in mind the old business model axiom on completing any project. Ideally we all want our work to be built well, built fast, and built cheap. In any project you can't have all three; you can have two out of the three qualities apply to your film, but not all three. You can try, but you can't cheat. So with that axiom in mind, be realistic about your goal and just how you plan to achieve it.

Outline just where and when and how you will shoot your movie. Get releases to use places and people BEFORE you start rolling that camera.

Set a schedule, and let your posse know you're serious about doing quality work and that you have a deadline.

Once in process, you should have an outline of when, where, how you'll shoot which scenes, but also be open to revision. Listen to your actors, friends, volunteers. Film making is much like staging a play in that it's a collaborative process. Be open to new ideas that might enrich your story, heighten its effect.

Once complete, show the movie to friends, classmates, teachers and welcome feedback. Always welcome feedback.

And always keep writing. There are no real tricks to success in this business. I'll assume you want to write screenplays because you love movies and because you love the pleasure in building things. Yes it can be a pain. Sometimes we build something and when putting on the final touch on it, we realize the foundation is cracked. There's nothing to do but knock it down and rebuild.

Remember to love the process and not just the end product. If you are honest and curious in doing this hard work of writing, it will be easier to remember that writing allows the luxury of play. Don't do this if it's just a goal of fame and fortune you are after. Do it because you love doing it and you love discovering things about yourself, your friends, loved ones, the world in the act of writing.

On a final note, I want to say that I'm of the believe that life is a continuous process of giving birth to ourselves, and we do this through the doors we open, the things we do each day, particularly in the creative work we do each day. So keep doing it. Be honest with yourself and your audience as you write. Remember every honest, sincere word we write allows us to lay a little more claim on who we are, what we think, what we believe. The writing isn't just about the script, it's about you. And the writing will lead you down your own yellow brick road to things you've never dreamed of and, as in Dorothy's journey, back to who you really are, what you really value, back to a humble appreciation of yourself.

Any comments on the text, and your discoveries, can always be sent to me at:

Janebradley101@gmail.com

Enjoy the journey.

Index